Avatars, Gods and Goddesses of Vedic Culture

Avatars, Gods and Goddesses of Vedic Culture

Understanding
the Characteristics, Powers
and Positions of the
Hindu Divinities

Stephen Knapp

Copyright © 2010, by Stephen Knapp

All rights reserved. No part of this book may be reproduced without written permission from the copyright owner and publisher, except for brief quotations for review or educational purposes.

COVER PHOTO:
A print of Lord Narayana (Vishnu) and Goddess Lakshmi (the Goddess of Fortune). Lord Vishnu, in His bluish complexion, holds His mace, disc or Sudarshan chakra, a conch shell, and a lotus. Lakshmi holds two lotus flowers and blessings. The *Om* is in the center. (This print is from the author's personal collection.)

Numerous color prints and photographs of the various Vedic Divinities can be seen, downloaded or printed for your perusal, meditation or use from the author's website at: www.stephen-knapp.com.

ISBN: 1453613765
EAN: 9781453613764

Other books by the author:

1. The Secret Teachings of the Vedas: The Eastern Answers to the Mysteries of Life
2. The Universal Path to Enlightenment
3. The Vedic Prophecies: A New Look into the Future
4. How the Universe was Created and Our Purpose In It
5. Toward World Peace: Seeing the Unity Between Us All
6. Facing Death: Welcoming the Afterlife
7. The Key to Real Happiness
8. Proof of Vedic Culture's Global Existence
9. The Heart of Hinduism: The Eastern Path to Freedom, Enlightenment and Illumination
10. The Power of the Dharma: An Introduction to Hinduism and Vedic Culture
11. Vedic Culture: The Difference it can Make in Your Life
12. Reincarnation & Karma: How They Really Affect Us
13. The Eleventh Commandment: The Next Step for Social Spiritual Development
14. Seeing Spiritual India: A Guide to Temples, Holy Sites, Festivals and Traditions
15. Crimes Against India: And the Need to Protect its Ancient Vedic Tradition
16. Destined for Infinity, a spiritual adventure in the Himalayas
17. Yoga and Meditation: Their Real Purpose and How to Get Started

You can find out more about
Stephen Knapp
and his books, free ebooks, research,
and numerous articles and photos,
along with many other spiritual resources at:
http://www.Stephen-Knapp.com

Contents

INTRODUCTION   1

CHAPTER ONE   2
WHY SO MANY GODS?
    Two Ways to View the Vedic Divinities

CHAPTER TWO   8
SRI KRISHNA
    Differences in Realization and Perception of the Supreme * Who is Sri Krishna * What Sri Krishna Says About Himself * The Mistake of Accepting Krishna As a Representation of Something Higher * Krishna is the Source of all Creation * Krishna is the Source of all Avatars of God * Why Lord Krishna Descends into this World * How Lord Krishna Took Birth in the Material World * Janmastami–Krishna's Birth Festival * Misunderstanding the Activities of Lord Krishna * The Beauty of Krishna * How to Understand God * The Result of Failing to Know Krishna * Krishna's Eternal Spiritual Abode

CHAPTER THREE   47
THE AVATARS OF LORD KRISHNA
    The Lord Appears in Each Universe * The Main Avatars of the Supreme Being * The Manu Avatars * The Yugavatars * The Shaktyavesha-Avatars * Conclusion

CHAPTER FOUR   61
LORD VISHNU
    Lord Vishnu is an Expansion of Lord Krishna * The Functions of Lord Vishnu

CHAPTER FIVE   78
LORD BRAHMA
    Brahma's Main Function * How Brahma is Manifested From Lord Vishnu * Brahma and the Dawn of Creation

CHAPTER SIX   89
THE IDENTITY OF LORD SHIVA AND GODDESS DURGA

Krishna Devotees are Dear to Shiva and Shiva is Dear to Them * Lord Shiva's Position * How Lord Shiva Appeared in this World * Shaivism * The Shivaratri Festival * The Shiva-Lingam * The Goddess Durga * The Identity of Durga and Difference Between Mahamaya and Yogamaya * The Two Energies of Material and Spiritual * The Shaktas and Tantrism * The Tantras * How Shiva and Durga are Considered the Mother and Father of the Universe * How Lord Shiva Assists in the Universal Destruction * Lord Shiva's Ultimate Spiritual Advice

CHAPTER SEVEN 138
THE GODDESSES
Lakshmi * Sarasvati * Meaning of Navaratri * Gayatri * Srimati Radharani

CHAPTER EIGHT 150
GANESH AND MURUGAN
Ganesh * Murugan * Ayyappan

CHAPTER NINE 160
THE REMAINING DEMIGODS
Adityas * Agni * Asvins * Indra * Kubera * Maruts * Soma * Varuna * Vasus * Vayu * Visvadevas * Yama * The Navagrahas * Surya * Hanuman

CONCLUSION 172

APPENDIX ONE 173
SRI CAITANYA MAHAPRABHU THE MOST RECENT AVATAR

APPENDIX TWO 180
THE SIGNIFICANCE OF DEITIES AND DEITY WORSHIP

APPENDIX THREE 183
DEITY WORSHIP FROM THOUSANDS OF YEARS AGO

REFERENCES 186

GLOSSARY 191

INDEX 200

Introduction

The reason why I decided to write this book was because of a series of incidents that happened to convince me of the need for such a book. First, I was approached more than once by people who wanted a book that explained all about the Divinities of Vedic culture. They asked if I knew of a good book that would answer all of their questions. Well, of course, I knew of some, but they were the books I had gotten while in India. Or there were a few others that were large photographic books, and a little out of the budget of most people. So, such books were not so readily available.

Then I gave a lecture and presentation to an interfaith group about how the Divine appears through Vedic art and in the deities in the temples, and explained the various personalities in the Vedic pantheon. These were people of all faiths, and many came up to me afterwards to expressed how much they liked the presentation, how they felt drawn to the various Vedic Divinities, and if I had anything more on that topic. Obviously, a book such as this one would have been most appropriate to further their knowledge about the topic I had spoken.

So, what to do? Obviously, a book should be written in a manner to make the information easily understood, and published in a way and priced so that it can be easily available. That is how I decided to present a book that focused on this topic.

Plus, it was to show that there are reasons for the various Divinities, and that it is not so complicated to understand when it is put into proper perspective. This is a complaint that is sometimes heard from those who are not familiar with Vedic culture: Why are there so many gods? They do not understand that actually there is only one God. And by understanding the Vedic Divinities appropriately, that becomes clear. This book will do that.

CHAPTER ONE

Why So Many Gods?

The four primary *Vedas*, namely the *Rig, Sama, Atharva* and *Yajur Vedas*, represent the accomplishment of a highly developed religious system. The primary function and goal of these four *Vedas* was to encourage satisfaction of material desires through worship of the demigods, or those Divinities called the Vedic gods. Therefore, the *Vedas* contain many directions for properly performing the necessary worship and particular sacrifices or rituals in worship to these *devas* (demigods) to get the blessings that would help increase one's power and position, or for reaching the heavens in one's future, or other goals.

The point is that the *devas* affect or assist in all levels of universal management and activities, including the weather, or who is bestowed with particular opulences such as riches, beautiful wife or husband, large family, good health, etc. For example, one could worship Agni for getting power, Durgadevi for good fortune, Indra for good sex life or plenty of rain, or the Vasus for getting money. Such instruction is in the *karma-kanda* section of the *Vedas* which many people considered to be the most important part of Vedic knowledge. But this is for helping people acquire the facilities for living a basic material existence.

There are, of course, various actions, or karmas, prompted by our desires to achieve certain results. This is the *karma-kanda* section of the *Vedas*. However, this is not the complete understanding of the *karma-kanda* segment, which is meant to supply the rituals for purifying our mind and actions while in the pursuit of our desires, and not to limit ourselves merely to live with the intent of acquiring all of one's material wants and necessities from the demigods. By having faith and steadiness in the performance of the ritual, one establishes purification in one's habits and thoughts. This provides a gradual process of acquiring one's needs and working out one's desires while simultaneously becoming purified and free of them. Such purification of our consciousness can then bring one to a higher level of spiritual activity. This was the higher purpose of the *karma-kanda* rituals. Without this understanding, one

Why So Many Gods?

misses the point and remains attached to rituals in the pursuit of material desires, which will drag one further into material existence.

Therefore, as different Vedic literature was compiled and presented, the goal of such texts changed from focusing on rituals and prayers and became more directed toward understanding one's spiritual identity and relationship with the Supreme. These included such texts as the *Upanishads*, and then on to the *Mahabharata* and *Bhagavad-gita*, and further to include the *Puranas* and other texts, to name a few. Thus, such Vedic *shastra* or spiritual books elaborated on the spiritual truths in the *Vedas* and also emphasized different Gods, such as Vishnu or Krishna, who were the Divinities who could bring one to a higher spiritual consciousness and help one attain *moksha* or complete liberation from material existence. The other demigods cannot provide for such liberation. Thus, the whole library of Vedic texts includes information on all levels of spiritual understanding, the heights of which direct a person to become free from the desires for material facilities, or the need to worship the demigods for such blessings, and for attaining entrance into the spiritual domain, which is the highest of all spiritual goals.

TWO WAYS TO VIEW THE VEDIC DIVINITIES

There are generally two ways that followers of the Vedic tradition view the Vedic Divinities. For some, who are swayed toward the impersonalist view, they feel that the Supreme is not a being but an impersonal force from which everything is created, like the great Brahman effulgence. They usually feel that all of the Vedic Divinities are but different forms or representations of the same Supreme or Absolute Truth. Thus, it does not matter whether a person worships Shiva, Krishna, Ganesh, Murugan, or any other of the Vedic gods or goddesses, because they all represent the same Absolute Truth or God in various forms. This is true with the *avatars* of Lord Krishna, but there are differences with the other *devas*, which will become clear as we go through this book.

On the other hand, there are those who feel that the Absolute Truth is, indeed, ultimately a personality. They hold the view that it does make a difference in which of the Vedic Divinities you worship, because they offer varying blessings and results from such worship. So, each one has a specific purpose.

This is the reason why some people ask why there seem to be so many gods within Hinduism or Vedic culture, and, such being the case, which one is best to worship? Yet, if we properly analyze the situation, we will understand that all of the Vedic Divinities have different purposes, and there is, indeed, but one Supreme Being who has many agents or demigods who assist in managing the various aspects of the cosmic creation and the natural forces within. And, like anyone else, if they are properly approached with prayer or worship, they may help facilitate the person by granting certain wishes that may be within the jurisdiction of that demigod. So, let us begin to explain.

First of all, in some places in the early portions of Vedic literature it is described that there are 33 Vedic gods, or even as many as thirty-three million. The 33 gods are calculated as being the eight Vasus, eleven Rudras (forms of Shiva), twelve Adityas, along with Indra and Prajapati (Brahma). Then there are also other positions that are considered major or minor *devas*. According to the *Vedas*, the *devas* are not imaginary or mythological beings, but are agents of the Supreme Will to administer different aspects of the universal affairs. They also represent and control various powers of nature. Thus, they manifest in the physical, subtle or psychic levels of our existence both from within and without. In this way, a transcendentalist sees that behind every aspect of nature is a personality.

The names of these gods are considered offices or positions, rather than the actual name of the demigod. For example, we may call the president of the country by his personal name, or simply Mr. President. It's the position itself that allows for him to have certain powers or areas of influence. In the case of the *devas*, it is only after accumulating much pious credit that a living being can earn the position of being a particular demigod. Then a person may become an Indra, or Vayu, or Brahma, or attain some other position to assume specific powers, or to control various aspects of material energy. Thus, such beings are not a God, but are demigods, they merely have a position within this material creation, as long as it remains in place, though some people may call them the Vedic gods for ease of conversation.

Another example is that when you walk into a big factory, you see so many workers and all that they are doing. You may initially think that these workers are the reason for whatever goes on in the factory. However, more important than the workers are the foremen, the managers, and then the executives who oversee and direct the activities and flow of work. Amongst these you will find people of varying degrees of authority. Someone will be in charge of designing the products. Another may be the Chief Financial Officer or main accountant. Another may be in charge of personnel, while someone else may be in charge of maintenance in the factory itself. Finally, a chief executive officer or president of the company is the most important of all. Without him there may not even be a company. You may not see the president right away, but his influence is everywhere since all the workers are engaging in projects according to his decisions. The managers and foremen act as his authorized agents to keep things moving accordingly. The numerous demigods act in the same way concerning the functions of nature, all of whom represent some aspect or power of the Supreme Will. That's why it is sometimes said there are 33 million different gods in Hinduism. It has also been referred that every living entity holds a form of God within them, as Supersoul. Right now there are over eight billion human beings that populate this planet, which means that just within the human species there are over eight billion gods that circulate through this world, if you look at it that way. Actually, there may be many forms, *avataras*, or aspects of God, but there is only one ultimate God, or one Absolute Truth. God means one, the predominate source from which everything else is created.

Another view of the Vedic *devas* or demigods is that they represent different aspects of understanding ourselves, especially through the path of yoga and meditation. For example, the god of wind is Vayu, and is related to the practice of yoga as the breath and its control in *pranayama*. Agni is the god of fire and relates to the fire of consciousness or awareness. Soma relates to the bliss in the *samadhi* of yoga practice. Many of the Vedic gods also represent particular powers of yoga and are related to the different *chakras* in the subtle body. It is accepted that as a person raises his or her consciousness through the *chakras*, he or she will attain the level of awareness and the power and assistance that is associated with the particular divine personality related to that *chakra*.

The reciprocation between the demigods and society is explained in *Bhagavad-gita* (3.10-12). It is stated that in the beginning the Lord of all beings created men and demigods along with the sacrifices to Lord Vishnu that were to be performed. The Lord blessed them saying that these sacrifices will enable men to prosper and attain all desirable things. By these sacrificial duties the demigods will be pleased and the demigods will also please you with all the necessities of life, and prosperity will spread to all. But, as explained, he who enjoys what is given by the demigods without offering them in return is a thief.

In this way, it was recommended that people could perform sacrificial rituals to obtain their desires. However, by the performance of such acts they should understand their dependent position, not only on the demigods, but ultimately on the Supreme Being.

As further explained in *Bhagavad-gita* (3.14-15), all living beings exist on food grains, which are produced from rain, which is produced by the performance of prescribed sacrifices or duties. These prescribed duties are described in the Vedic literature, which is manifest from the Supreme Being. Therefore, the Supreme is eternally established in acts of sacrifice.

Although the demigods may accept worship from the human beings and bless them with particular benedictions according to the sacrifices that are performed, they are still not on the level of the Supreme Lord Vishnu (who is an expansion of Lord Krishna). The *Rigveda* (1.22.20) explains: "The demigods are always looking to that supreme abode of Vishnu." *Bhagavad-gita* (17.23) also points out: "From the beginning of creation, the three syllables *om tat sat* have been used to indicate the Supreme Absolute Truth (Brahman). They were uttered by brahmanas while chanting the Vedic hymns and during sacrifices, for the satisfaction of the Supreme." In this way, by uttering *om tat sat*, which is stressed in Vedic texts, the performers of the rituals for worshiping the demigods were also offering obeisances to Lord Vishnu for its success. The four *Vedas* mainly deal with material elevation and since Lord Vishnu is the Lord of material liberation, most sacrifices were directed toward the demigods.

In *Bhagavad-gita*, however, Lord Krishna points out that men of small knowledge, who are attracted by worldly desires, take delight in the flowery words of the *Vedas* that prescribe rituals for attaining power, riches, or rebirth in heaven. With their goal of enjoyment they say there is nothing else than this. However, Krishna goes on to explain (in *Bhagavad-gita* 7.21-23) that when a person desires to worship a particular demigod for the temporary and limited fruits he or she may bestow, Krishna, as the Supersoul in everyone's heart, makes that person's faith in that demigod steady. But all the benefits given by any demigod actually are given by Krishna alone, for without whom no one has any power. Furthermore, Krishna explains that the worshipers of the demigods go to the planets of the demigods, but worshipers of Krishna reach Krishna's spiritual abode.

Thus, as one progresses in understanding, it is expected that they will gradually give up the pursuit for temporary material pleasures and then begin to endeavor for reaching the supreme goal of Vedic knowledge. For one who is situated in such knowledge and is self-realized, the prescribed duties in the *Vedas* for worshiping the demigods are unnecessary. As *Bhagavad-gita* (3.17-18) explains, for one who is fully self-realized, who is fully satiated in the self, delights only in the self, there is no duty or need to perform the prescribed duties found in the *Vedas*, because he has no purpose or material desires to fulfill.

CHAPTER TWO

Sri Krishna

DIFFERENCES IN REALIZATION AND PERCEPTION OF THE SUPREME

Out of all the Divinities of the Vedic culture, Lord Krishna is considered one of the most important, and even the pre-emanate of all the Divine personalties. He is considered the God of love, unconditional and ever-flowing love, which is freely given to His devotees. Yet, different people see Him in different ways, the reason for which is given as follows:

It is described that there are three aspects of the Supreme that must be understood in order to have a complete realization of the Absolute Person. These are the impersonal and all pervasive Brahman aspect, the localized expansion of the Lord known as the Supersoul or Paramatma, and then the Supreme Personality or Bhagavan aspect. Bhagavan means the Supreme Being who is the originator of all qualities and who possesses them to the fullest degree. He is especially full with the qualities of wealth, strength, beauty, knowledge, opulence, and renunciation to the maximum. All three of these aspects of Brahman, Paramatama and Bhagavan must be understood if one is to have a complete understanding and realization of God.

When one follows the basic process of yoga, a person will naturally attain the Brahman and then the Paramatma realizations sequentially. Of course, this depends on how thoroughly one follows the process. In essence, the Brahman realization involves perceiving the spiritual energy behind all aspects of the creation, opposite to the mundane world. Brahman is the passive aspect of the non-dual substance of the Absolute Truth. It is the realization of the Supreme Being without any of His potencies or qualities. If one goes no further, he will naturally conclude that realization of the Brahman is the ultimate perception and understanding of the Absolute.

The Paramatma realization is to perceive the Supersoul within all material forms, within all living entities and even all material elements.

Paramatma is the partial expansion of the Lord in the material world. Perceiving the Paramatma is one of the prime goals of most yoga systems. But to go further and attain the Bhagavan realization, one needs to attain a totally spiritual vision without any material conceptions or conditionings to perceive the completely transcendental form of the Supreme Lord, Bhagavan--as He is. The formless aspect of the Supreme Person is Brahman. But when that Supreme Brahman is endowed with His natural potencies and qualities, then the Brahman aspect is transformed into the more complete Bhagavan aspect. Therefore, Bhagavan is the original nature of the Absolute Truth with full qualities and potencies, while the Brahman is merely the impersonal, transcendental bodily effulgence.

Lord Narayana, Vishnu, is the opulent and potent manifestation of Bhagavan, husband of Lakshmi devi, the Goddess of fortune, while Sri Krishna is the naturally loving and sweet aspect of Bhagavan, Lord of Srimati Radharani, center of the spiritual worlds, and ultimate source of all other *avataras* of God.

WHO IS SRI KRISHNA?

It is the Vedic literature that most clearly reveals the nature and identity of the Absolute Truth or Supreme Personality. As with many of the Vedic texts, they begin to reveal this identity with hints that show how the Absolute is a person from which everything else originates. One such reference is the first and second verses of the *Vedanta Sutras*. The first verse states simply that "Now one should enquire into the Brahman." This means that now that you have attained a human body, you should use your intelligence to discover what is really spiritual and what is the Absolute Truth. Then the second verse begins to explain what is this Absolute Truth: "He from whom everything originates is the Absolute." Thus, as it refers to "He", the source of all that exists, the ultimate point of creation, is a person.

The *Katha Upanishad* (2.2.9) relates in like manner: "As with fire--the one original flame expands itself throughout the world by producing many more separate flames; similarly, the one Supreme Soul, who resides in every *jiva* [the individual spirit souls], enters this cosmos and expands Himself in replica images known as *pratibimba*, or the *jivas*." Thus, herein we have further confirmation that the Lord exists outside of the created universe. And expands Himself to enter into it.

10   Avatars, Gods and Goddesses of Vedic Culture

This is a typical deity of Sri Krishna, standing on one foot, holding and playing His flute, with peacock feather in His crown or hair, with His favorite animal, the cow, next to Him. Often He is standing next to Srimati Radharani. This deity is in a small temple located along a main street in Vrindavana, India.

Sri Krishna

So, who is this Being from whom all else is created? Much more information is supplied from numerous Vedic sources. For example, the early *Rig Veda* (1.22.20-21) relates that Lord Vishnu is that Supreme Being, the Absolute Truth whose lotus feet all the demigods are always eager to see. His most sublime region is only visible to those endowed with spiritual vision, accessed by ever-vigilant devotion.

The *Rig Veda* continues elsewhere (1.154.4-5): "Him whose three places are filled with sweetness and imperishable joy, who verily alone upholds the threefold, the earth, the heaven, and all living beings. May I attain to His well-loved mansion where men devoted to the Gods are happy. For there springs the well of honey [or Soma] in Vishnu's highest step."

The *Svetasvatara Upanishad* has a similar verse: "No one is superior to Him, nothing is smaller or larger than Him. He is the one Supreme Being (*purusha*), who has created everything complete. On His planet, He is situated like a steadfast tree, emanating great effulgence."

As explained in the *Caitanya-caritamrita* (Adi-lila 2.106), Lord Krishna is the original primeval Lord, the source of all other expansions. All the revealed scriptures accept Sri Krishna as the Supreme Lord. Furthermore (*Cc*.Adi 2.24-26), it goes on to relate that Lord Krishna Himself is the one undivided Absolute Truth and ultimate reality. He manifests in three features, namely the Brahman, Paramatma and Bhagavan (the Supreme Personality). The *Svetasvatara Upanishad* (5.4) also relates that the Supreme Being, Lord Krishna, is worshipable by everyone, the one adorable God, repository of all goodness, ruler of all creatures, born from the womb [in His pastime of Lord Krishna], for He is eternally present in all living beings [as Supersoul]. Furthermore, it states (3.8), "I have realized this transcendental Personality of Godhead who shines most brilliantly like the sun beyond all darkness. Only by realizing Him one goes beyond the cycle of birth and deaths. Absolutely there is no other means to get God-realization."

The *Svetasvatara Upanishad* (5.6) further elaborates that Lord Krishna is the topmost of all the gods. "He is the most esoteric aspect hidden in the *Upanishads* which form the essence of the *Vedas*. Brahma knows Him as the source of himself as well as the *Vedas*. The gods like Shiva and the seers of the ancient, like Vamadeva *rishi* realizing Him, ever became dovetailed in His service and therefore they naturally became immortal." And in (6.7) it continues: "Let us take our final resort at Him who is the Transcendent and the only adorable Lord of the universe, who is the highest Deity over all the deities, the Supreme Ruler of all rulers—Him let us know as the Paramount Divinity."

The *GopalaTapani Upanishad*, which is about Gopala or Krishna, is quite clear on this point, and naturally has numerous verses that explain the nature of the Absolute Truth and Lord Krishna. A few of such verses include the following: "Brahma with his full awareness emphatically said, 'Sri Krishna is the Supreme Divinity. (1.3) He who meditates on Sri Krishna, serves Him with unalloyed devotion and [makes His transcendental senses gratified by engaging one's own spiritual senses in] rendering service to Him–all of them become immortal and attain the summum bonum, or perfection of life. (1.10) Sri Krishna is that Supreme Divinity as the Paramount Eternal Reality among all other sentient beings and the Fountain-source of consciousness to all conscious beings. He is the only reality without a second but as a Supersoul dwelling in the cave of the hearts of all beings He rewards them in accordance with their respective actions in life. Those men of intuitive wisdom who serve Him with loving devotion surely attain the highest perfection of life. Whereas those who do not do so never gain this highest beatitude of their lives. (1.22) ... This Sri Krishna who is most dear to you all is the cause of all causes. He is the efficient cause of the creation of the universe as well as the superintending force for propelling the *jiva* souls. Therefore, although He is the enjoyer as well as the Lord of all sacrifices, He is ever *atmarama*, self-satisfied." (2.17)

So, summarily, as it is explained and concluded in a variety of Vedic texts, Lord Krishna is the Supreme Personality of Godhead. In other words, as it is said in Sanskrit, *krsnas tu bhagavan svayam* (*Bhagavata Purana* 1.3.28), Krishna is the source of all other *avataras*, incarnations, and forms of God. He is the ultimate and end of all Truth and philosophical enquiry, the goal or end result of Vedanta. He is the all-attractive personality and source of all pleasure for which we are always hankering. He is the origin from which everything else manifests. He is the unlimited source of all power, wealth, fame, beauty, wisdom, and renunciation. Thus, no one is greater than Him. Since Krishna is the source of all living beings, He is also considered the Supreme Father and source of all worlds. He is shown with a blue or blackish complexion. This is the color of absolute, pure consciousness, which also is unconditional love. Krishna is the embodiment of love. He is also *sat-chit-ananda vigraha*, which means the form of eternal knowledge and bliss.

The reason why the Lord is called "Krishna" is explained in a book known as the *Sri Caitanya Upanishad*, which is connected with the *Atharva Veda*. In verse twelve it is explained: "These three names of the Supreme Lord (Hari, Krishna and Rama) may be explained in the following way: (1) 'Hari' means 'He who unties [*harati*] the knot of material desire in the hearts of the living entities'; (2) 'Krishna' is divided into two syllables 'krish' and 'na'. 'Krish' means 'He who attracts the minds of all living entities', and 'na' means 'the supreme transcendental pleasure'. These two syllables combine to become the name 'Krishna'; and (3) 'Rama' means 'He who delights [*ramayati*] all living entities', and it also means 'He who is full of transcendental bliss'. The maha-mantra consists of the repetition of these names of the Supreme Lord." In this way, Krishna's names represent His character and qualities, which, in this case, means the greatest and all attractive transcendental pleasure.

So, as we further our investigation of the identity of Sri Krishna in the Vedic literature, especially the *Bhagavad-gita*, *Srimad-Bhagavatam*, *Vishnu Purana*, *Brahma-samhita*, and many others, we find that they are full of descriptions of Lord Krishna as the Supreme Being. These actually can help us understand the nature of God regardless of which religion we may affiliate ourselves with. So, let us find out more about God from these descriptions.

The *Brihadaranyaka Upanishad* says, *purnam idam purnat purnam udachyate*: "Although He expands in many ways, He keeps His original personality. His original spiritual body remains as it is." Thus, we can understand that God can expand His energies in many ways, but is not affected or diminished in His potency. And His original form and personality remain the same.

The invocation mantra of the *Sri Ishopanishad* says something similar:

> *Om purnam adah purnam idam*
> *purnat purnam udachyate*
> *purnasya purnam adaya*
> *purnam evavashishyate*

This means, in essence, that the Supreme Being is complete and perfect, and whatever is expanded from His energies is also complete and does not take away from His potencies in any way. He remains as He is, the complete whole and the complete balance.

The *Svetasvatara Upanishad* (6.6) also states: "The Supreme Personality of Godhead, the original person, has multifarious energies. He is the origin of material creation, and it is due to Him only that everything changes. He is the protector of religion and annihilator of all sinful activities. He is the master of all opulences." This verse specifically points out that only due to God's multi-potencies does the world continue to change and be maintained. He also protects religion, which could not be done if He were impersonal or without form. This is only logical since it takes a person to watch over, protect or maintain anything.

In the *Katha Upanishad* (2.2.13) there is the important verse; *nityo nityanam chetanas chetananam eko bahunam yo vidadhati kaman*: "He is the supreme eternally conscious person who maintains all other living entities." So, this Supreme Person is accepted by Vedic authority to be the Absolute Truth, as confirmed in the *Caitanya-caritamrita* (*Adi*.7.111): "According to direct understanding, the Absolute Truth is the Supreme Personality of Godhead, who has all spiritual opulences. No one can be equal to or greater than Him."

The *Svetasvatara Upanishad* (4.7-8) goes on to describe that, "The Supreme Lord is He who is referred to by the mantras of the *Rig Veda*, who resides in the topmost, eternal sky, and who elevates His saintly devotees to share that same position. One who has developed pure love for Him and realizes His uniqueness then appreciates His glories and is freed from sorrow. What further good can the *Rig* mantras bestow on one who knows that Supreme Lord? All who come to know Him achieve the supreme destination."

This is further corroborated in the *Katha Upanishad* (2.3.8-9) wherein it says: "Beyond the Brahmajyoti (*nirguna* or formless Brahman of the monist) there is the Great Purusha viz., Purushottama God who is all-pervading (as the Brahmajyoti) and without any empirical attributes, but having *sat-chit-ananda*--transcendental embodiment. He who realizes this Purushottama-tattva is finally liberated. Attaining a spiritual body he renders eternal service to the Purushottama [Supreme Being]. The Transcendental Personality of Godhead is beyond the purview of occult vision. But He can be apprehended through a pure transparent mind imbibed with intuitive wisdom born out of unalloyed devotional practices in the very core of one's own unstinted heart--those who have really got such a vision have gained final beatitude."

Additional references further describe how Lord Krishna exists beyond the impersonal Brahman. The *Svetasvatara Upanishad* (6.7-8) relates that, "The Supreme Lord is the controller of all other controllers, and He is the greatest of all the diverse planetary leaders. Everyone is under His control. All entities are delegated with particular power only by the Supreme Lord; they are not supreme themselves. He is also worshipable by all demigods and is the supreme director of all directors. Therefore, He is transcendental to all kinds of material leaders and controllers and is worshipable by all. There is no one greater than Him, and He is the supreme cause of all causes. He does not possess a bodily form like that of an ordinary living entity. There is no difference between His body and His soul. He is absolute [pure consciousness]. All His senses are transcendental. Any one of His senses can perform the action of any other sense. Therefore, no one is greater than Him or equal to Him. His potencies are multifarious, and thus His deeds are automatically performed as a natural sequence."

The *Chandogya Upanishad* (3.17.6-7) goes on to relate the need to become aware and focused on the Supreme Being, Sri Krishna. "Ghora Angihasa *rishi* advised his disciple that he should invoke Bhagavan Sri Krishna, the Son of Devakidevi [*devakiputra*], by repeating this triad thinking as if death is sitting upon his shoulder: 'Thou art the Indestructible; Thou art the Unchangeable; Thou art the very Substratum that enlivens the entire universe.' On culturing this he (the disciple) became free from desires. On this point there are two additional *Rig* verses. The light (Grace) that comes from the Primeval Fountain-Source dispels darkness of illusion like the morning sun dispelling the night darkness. [This is also found in *Rig Veda* 8.6.30] The Primeval Fountain-Source from Whom light (Grace) comes which dispels darkness viz., illusion of the soul like the morning sun dispels the darkness of the night and shines forth far beyond the universe. When we perceive that most Effulgent Highest Purusha (Supreme Person) dwelling in the world of Transcendent (*sarva loka urddham svah Bhagavat Lokam paripashantah*) and through unalloyed devotion when we attain Him, the most Effulgent One Who is the God of all gods. We in ecstatic joy proclaim, 'Yea, we have attained Him. Yea, we have attained the summum bonum of life--Yea, the final beatitude in life.'" [A similar point is also found in the *Rig Veda* 1.50.10, as well as at *Rig* 1.22.16-21.]

In the *Bhagavad-gita* (10.12-13), Arjuna also explains that Lord Krishna is the Supreme Brahman, the ultimate, the supreme abode and purifier, the Absolute Truth and the eternal divine person. He is the primal God, transcendental and original, the unborn and all-pervading beauty. All the great sages such as Narada, Asita, Devala, and Vyasa proclaim this.

He goes on to say that Krishna is the original Personality, the Godhead. He is the only sanctuary of the manifested material world. He knows everything and is all that is knowable. He is above the material modes. With limitless form, He pervades the whole cosmic manifestation. (*Bg*.11.38) Krishna is the father of the complete cosmic manifestation, the worshipable chief and spiritual master. No one is equal to Him, nor can anyone be one with Him. He is immeasurable. (*Bg*.11.43)

We can also glean the verses from the *Srimad-Bhagavatam* [*Bhagavata Purana*] to get a clearer view of who is Sri Krishna. The difference in the *Bhagavatam* is because other scriptures may also relate the nature of God, and even discuss Lord Krishna's pastimes, but do so with what could be said is a reporter's view, simply and impartially stating the facts. But the *Srimad-Bhagavatam* relates the pastimes and qualities of Lord Krishna from a participant's perspective. Thus, the nectar that can only come from the deep involvement of the associate and devotee is relayed within the vibrations of those verses. However, the receptivity of this nectar depends on two things: one is the qualities of the receiver and how open or faithful the person is to such high thoughts and vibrations, and the other is whether the ecstasies within the message of the *Bhagavatam* get perverted or spoiled from the misinterpretation of a disbeliever or speculator who improperly writes or speaks the message.

It is like a light bulb being properly wired to the powerhouse. Unless the light bulb is appropriately wired and works favorably, there will not be light. Similarly, unless the speaker and receiver of the message of the *Bhagavatam* are both properly connected with favorable and unalloyed consciousness, the purity of the message will not manifest.

So, as we get into the *Srimad-Bhagavatam*, we will present some of these verses as we move forward, such as the very first verse which summarizes Lord Krishna's position. "O my Lord, Sri Krishna, son of Vasudeva, O all-pervading Personality of Godhead, I offer my respectful obeisances unto You. I meditate on Lord Sri Krishna because He is the Absolute Truth and the primeval cause of all causes of the creation, sustenance and destruction of the manifested universes. He is directly and indirectly conscious of all manifestations, and He is independent because there is no other cause beyond Him. It is He only who first imparted the Vedic knowledge unto the heart of Brahmaji, the original living being. By Him even the great sages and demigods are placed into illusion... Only because of Him do the material universes, temporarily manifested by the reactions of the three modes of nature, appear factual, although they are unreal. I therefore meditate upon Him, Lord Sri Krishna, who is eternally existent in the transcendental abode, which is forever free from the illusory representations of the material world. I meditate upon Him, for He is the Absolute Truth."

Later, when Uddhava visits Vrindavana, he talks with Nanda Maharaja and explains things in a similar way: "Nothing can be said to exist independent of Lord Acyuta [Krishna]--nothing heard or seen, nothing in the past, present or future, nothing moving or unmoving, great or small. He indeed is everything, for He is the Supreme Soul." (*Bhag.*10.46.43)

These have been a few of the verses in the Vedic texts that explain the position of the Supreme Being, but what does Lord Krishna say about Himself?

WHAT SRI KRISHNA SAYS ABOUT HIMSELF

If we are expected to understand God, then who better to explain His qualities and characteristics than Himself? So in the *Bhagavad-gita*, Krishna provides the Self-revelatory truth about His position in His explanations to Arjuna. There are numerous verses in this regard, of which the following are but a few: "And when you have thus learned the truth, you will know that all living beings are but part of Me--and that they are in Me, and are Mine. (4.35) The sages, knowing Me to be the ultimate purpose of all sacrifices and austerities, the Supreme Lord of all planets and demigods, and the benefactor and well-wisher of all living entities, attain peace from the pangs of material miseries. (5.29) Of all that is material and all that is spiritual in this world, know for certain that I am both its origin and dissolution. (7.6) It is I who am the ritual, I the sacrifice, the offering to the ancestors, the healing herb, the transcendental chant... I am the father of this universe, the mother, the support, and the grandsire. I am the object of knowledge, the purifier and the syllable *om*. I am also the *Rig*, the *Sama*, and the *Yajur Vedas*. I am the goal, the sustainer, the master, the witness, the abode, the refuge and the most dear friend. I am the creation and the annihilation, the basis of everything, the resting place and the eternal seed. (9.16-18)

"I am the source of all spiritual and material worlds. Everything emanates from Me. The wise who perfectly know this engage in My devotional service and worship Me with all their hearts. (*Bg.*10:8)

"I am all devouring death, and I am the generator of all things yet to be. Among women I am fame, fortune, speech, memory, intelligence, faithfulness and patience. (*Bg.* 10.34) Because I am transcendental, beyond both the fallible and the infallible, and because I am the greatest, I am celebrated both in the world and in the *Vedas* as the Supreme Person." (*Bg.*15.18)

Going on to the *Srimad-Bhagavatam*, Lord Krishna specifically explains that before, during, and after the creation, there is always Himself that exists.

"Brahma it is I, the Personality of Godhead, who was existing before the creation, when there was nothing but Myself. Nor was there the material nature, the cause of this creation. That which you see now is also I, the Personality of Godhead, and after annihilation what remains will also be I, the Supreme Lord." (*Bhag*.2.9.33)

"Gold alone is present before its manufacture into gold products, the gold alone remains after the products' destruction, and the gold alone is the essential reality while it is being utilized under various designations. Similarly, I alone exist before the creation of this universe, after its destruction and during its maintenance." (*Bhag*.11.28.19)

"Before the creation of this cosmic manifestation, I alone existed with My specific spiritual potencies. Consciousness was then unmanifested, just as one's consciousness is unmanifested during the time of sleep. I am the reservoir of unlimited potency, and therefore I am known as unlimited or all-pervading. From My material energy the cosmic manifestation appeared within Me, and in this universal manifestation appeared the chief being, Lord Brahma, who is your source and is not born of a material mother." (*Bhag*.6.4.47-48)

"Fools deride Me when I descend in the human form. They do not know My transcendental nature and My supreme dominion over all that be." (Bg.9.11)

"Unintelligent men, who know Me not, think that I have assumed this form and personality. Due to their small knowledge, they do not know My higher nature, which is changeless and supreme. I am never manifest to the foolish and unintelligent. For them I am covered by My eternal creative potency [*yoga-maya*]; and so the deluded world knows Me not, who am unborn and infallible. O Arjuna, as the Supreme Personality of Godhead, I know everything that has happened in the past, all that is happening in the present, and all things that are yet to come. I also know all living entities; but Me no one knows." (Bg.7.24-26)

Lord Krishna also explains that he is the Supersoul of each and every living being, who exist only because of Him. He also establishes that He is the spiritual sound vibrations that can be chanted, as well as the forms of the deities that we can see. "All living beings, moving and nonmoving, are My expansions and are separate from Me. I am the Supersoul of all living beings, who exist because I manifest them. I am the form of the transcendental vibrations like *omkara* and Hare Krishna Hare Rama, and I am the Supreme Absolute Truth. These two forms of Mine--namely the transcendental sound and the eternally blissful spiritual form of the deity, are My eternal forms; they are not material." (*Bhag*.6.16.51)

"My dear Uddhava, I am the cause, protector and the Lord of all mystic perfections, of the yoga system, of analytical knowledge, of pure activity and of the community of learned Vedic teachers. Just as the same material elements exist within and outside of all material bodies, similarly, I cannot be covered by anything else. I exist within everything as the Supersoul and outside of everything in My all-pervading feature." (*Bhag.*11.15.35-36)

Lord Krishna goes on to explain how He is perceived by different people in different ways. "When there is agitation and interaction of the material modes of nature, the living entities then describe Me in various ways such as all-powerful time, the Self, Vedic knowledge, the universe, one's own nature, religious ceremonies and so on." (*Bhag.*11.10.34)

However, when a person reaches the vision of the Supreme by the process of Self-realization, which takes him or her above the influence of the material modes, the experience is one and the same, and on a higher level. Then there is no more confusion about what is or what is not the highest level of spiritual realization.

In conclusion Krishna explains, "Know that all opulent, beautiful and glorious creations spring from but a spark of My splendour. But what need is there, Arjuna, for all this detailed knowledge? With a single fragment of Myself I pervade and support this entire universe." (*Bg.*10:41-42)

THE MISTAKE OF ACCEPTING KRISHNA AS A REPRESENTATION OF SOMETHING HIGHER

Some people feel that Krishna is merely a representation of something higher, which is often mistaken for the impersonal Brahman. However, such texts as the *Taittiriya Upanishad* (2.1.2) explains, "One who realizes Brahman attains the summum bonum, highest goal of life. So who is Brahman? Who is to be known? What is the means to know Him? And what is the prospect? These are the four vital points in reference to which it has been declared: Brahman is eternally existent, source of all wisdom, and infinite or all-pervasive. One who realizes Brahman as such, he adores Him in the secret cavity of the heart which is converted into a transcendental plane, the replica of Vaikuntha, a resort of divine sports. Thereby he gets his objects fulfilled with the all-wisdom of Brahman i.e., he attains the summum bonum of life in rendering unalloyed devotion to Brahman, the Supreme Reality."

From this point, the above verse continues to explain how the various aspects of the material creation are manifested from the Brahman, directed by a Supreme Will. Yet, we can see in this verse that the Brahman is indicated to be a person whom we can render loving service, which is the means to reach the supreme goal of life. He is in the cavity of the heart as the localized expansion of the Supreme known as the Supersoul, Paramatma. Through this devotion the person will transform his heart and consciousness into the spiritual strata of Vaikuntha, the residence of the Supreme Being wherein spiritual activities are constantly taking place. Thus, the ultimate meaning of the Brahman is the Supreme Person from whom the Brahman emanates.

The *Brahma-samhita* (5.40) explains how the Brahman is but Sri Krishna's physical brilliance: "I worship Govinda, the primeval Lord who is endowed with great power. The glowing effulgence of His transcendental form is the impersonal Brahman, which is absolute, complete and unlimited, and which displays the varieties of countless planets with their different opulences in millions and millions of universes."

The *Isha Upanishad* (15) also confirms this: "O my Lord, sustainer of all that lives, Your real face is covered by Your dazzling effulgence. Kindly remove that covering and exhibit Yourself to Your pure devotee."

This Vedic evidence makes it clear that Krishna is not a mere representation for something higher or above Him, but He is the basis and foundation of the Brahman and all that is. The idea that the Supreme Personality or Bhagavan is merely a personified form or representational symbol for a higher abstract spiritual reality beyond Him is but the means to assign material attributes to what is inherently spiritual. It is a way of taking the Supreme and interpreting Him through our own limited understanding and misconceptions.

According to the Vaishnava understanding, Bhagavan is not merely a symbol of the Divine but is the essential nature of the Divine. A symbol would be like a national flag used as a representation of a nation, which is bigger and something different than the flag. So, to consider Krishna as a mere symbol created to make it easy for the mind to focus on what is spiritual is to say that Krishna Himself is but part of the material energy and only a representation of something else. This means that the Supreme Spiritual Reality must take assistance from *maya*, the material energy, in order to appear in this world, without which there is no possibility for it to have form. This is mayavada philosophy, along with the idea that any form of God, or His name, pastimes, or any demigod is but an equal symbol of what is a higher transcendent reality, like the Brahman. This means we are inflicting material qualities on what is essentially fully spiritual. But this is the wrong conclusion of those who do not understand the Absolute nature, energy, and power of the Supreme Person, Bhagavan. In this way, by forcing our own weaknesses and lack of depth on our attempt to understand what is beyond materialistic comprehension, the nature of the Supreme continues to escape us.

Therefore, we must understand from the Vedic evidence that is supplied herein, it is clear that Lord Krishna's name, form, pastimes, etc., exist eternally in the spiritual dimension and are never affected by even a tinge of the material energy. Thus, He can appear as often and whenever He likes as He is, or in any form He chooses within this material manifestation, and remains unaffected and no less spiritual. He is completely and totally spiritual for He is the Absolute Truth. As the *Vedanta Sutras* explain, the Absolute Truth is He from whom all else manifests. Thus, the Absolute Truth is the ultimate Person, as further explained.

KRISHNA IS THE SOURCE OF ALL CREATION

In the *Bhagavad-gita* (10.8) Krishna explains that He is the source of all spiritual and material worlds. "Everything emanates from Me. The wise who know this perfectly engage in My devotional service and worship Me with all their hearts."

Lord Krishna further relates that all other sages and creators also originate from Him: "The seven great sages and before them the four other great sages and the Manus [progenitors of mankind] are born out of My mind, and all creatures in these planets descend from them." (*Bg*.10.6)

Jambavan also says to Lord Krishna, "You are the ultimate creator of all creators of the universe, and of everything created, You are the underlying substance. You are the subduer of all subduers, the Supreme Lord and Supreme Soul of all souls." (*Bhag*.10.56.27)

When the demigods approached Lord Krishna to return to His abode and wind up His earthly pastimes, they also recognized that He was the supreme creator in their prayers: "You are the cause of the creation, maintenance and destruction of this universe. As time, You regulate the subtle and manifest states of material nature and control every living being. As the threefold wheel of time You diminish all things by Your imperceptible actions, and thus You are the Supreme Personality of Godhead... O Lord, You are the supreme creator of this universe and the ultimate controller of all moving and nonmoving living entities. You are Hrishikesha, the supreme controller of all sensory activity, and thus You never become contaminated or entangled in the course of Your supervision of the infinite sensory activities within the material creation. On the other hand, other living entities, even yogis and philosophers, are disturbed and frightened simply by remembering the material objects that they have supposedly renounced in their pursuit of enlightenment." (*Bhag*.11.6.15, 17)

Because Krishna is the source of everything, it is not possible for others to determine His origin, not even the demigods who have their source from Lord Krishna: "Neither the hosts of demigods nor the great sages know My origin, for, in every respect, I am the source of the demigods and sages." (*Bg*.10.2)

Arjuna also admits to this fact in the *Bhagavad-gita* after having understood Krishna's real characteristics: "O Krishna, I totally accept as truth all that You have told me. Neither the gods nor demons, O Lord, know Thy personality. Indeed, You alone know Yourself by Your own potencies, O origin of all, Lord of all beings, God of gods, O Supreme Person, Lord of the universe! (*Bg*.10.14-15) O great one, who stands above even Brahma, You are the original master. Why should they not offer their homage up to You, O limitless one? O refuge of the universe, You are the invincible source, the cause of all causes, transcendental to this material manifestation. (*Bg*.11.37) You are air, fire, water, and You are the moon! You are the supreme controller and the grandfather. Thus I offer my respectful obeisances unto You a thousand times, and again and yet again! Obeisances from the front, from behind and from all sides! O unbounded power, You are the master of limitless light! You are all-pervading, and thus You are everything! (*Bg*.11.39-40) You are the father of this complete cosmic manifestation, the worshipable chief, the spiritual master. No one is equal to You, nor can anyone be one with You. Within the three worlds, You are immeasurable." (*Bg*.11.43)

Even the immeasurable spiritual area called the Brahman is actually a tool that Krishna uses in which to create the cosmic manifestation. As He explains, "The total material substance, called Brahman, is the source of birth, and it is that Brahman that I impregnate, making possible the births of all living beings, O son of Bharata [Arjuna]. It should be understood that all species of life, O son of Kunti, are made possible by birth in this material nature, and that I am the seed-giving father. (*Bg*.14.3-4) Of all that is material and all that is spiritual in this world, know for certain that I am both its origin and dissolution. (*Bg*.7.6) I am the generating seed of all existences. There is no being--moving or unmoving--that can exist without Me. (*Bg*.10.39) Know that I am the original seed of all existences, the intelligence of the intelligent, and the prowess of all powerful men." (*Bg*.7.10)

In this way, Lord Krishna creates the material manifestation, and later absorbs it back into Himself. Then at His will, He again creates. "At the end of the millennium every material manifestation enters into My nature, and at the beginning of another millennium, by My potency I again create." (*Bg*.9.7)

"My dear Lord, the original *purusha-avatara*, Maha-Vishnu, acquires His creative potency from You. Thus with infallible energy He impregnates material nature, producing the *mahat-tattva*. Then the *mahat-tattva*, the amalgamated material energy, endowed with the potency of the Lord, produces from itself the primeval golden egg of the universe, which is covered by various layers of material elements." (*Bhag*.11.6.16)

Because Lord Krishna is the source of everything, there is obviously nothing that He personally needs from it, nor is He ever entangled in it. He is like the warden of a prison who can go in or out of it at any time he wants. Yet He is still overseeing it. "O son of Pritha, there is no work prescribed for Me within all the three planetary systems. Nor am I in want of anything, nor have I need to obtain anything--and yet I am engaged in work. (*Bg*.3.22) There is no work that affects Me; nor do I aspire for the fruits of action. One who understands this truth about Me also does not become entangled in the fruitive reactions of work." (*Bg*.4.14)

Akrura also admitted to Lord Krishna that, "You create, destroy and also maintain this universe with Your personal energies--the modes of passion, ignorance and goodness--yet You are never entangled by these modes or the activities they generate. Since You are the original source of all knowledge, what could ever cause You to be bound by illusion?" (*Bhag*.10.48.21)

The summary process of how Lord Krishna manifests and gives facility to the universe and the living entities within it is described in Vasudeva's prayer to Lord Krishna: "O transcendental Lord, from Yourself You created this entire variegated universe, and then You entered within it in Your personal form as the Supersoul. In this way, O unborn supreme Soul, as the life force and consciousness of everyone, You maintain the creation. Whatever potencies the life air and other elements of universal creation exhibit are actually all personal energies of the Supreme Lord, for both life and matter are subordinate to Him and dependent on Him, and also different from one another. Thus, everything active in the material world is set into motion by the Supreme Lord. The glow of the moon, the brilliance of fire, the radiance of the sun, the twinkling of the stars, the flash of lightning, the permanence of mountains and the aroma and sustaining power of the earth--all these are actually You. My Lord, You are water, and also its taste and its capacities to quench thirst and sustain life. You exhibit Your potencies through the manifestations of the air as bodily warmth, vitality, mental power, physical strength, endeavor and movement. You are the directions and their accommodating capacity, the all-pervading ether and the elemental sound residing within it. You are the primeval, unmanifested form of sound; the first syllable, *om*: and audible speech, by which sound, as words, acquires particular references. You are the power of the senses to reveal their objects, the senses' presiding demigods, and the sanction these demigods give for sensory activity. You are the capacity of the intelligence for decision-making, and the living being's ability to remember things accurately. You are false ego in the mode of ignorance, which is the source of physical elements; false ego in the mode of passion, which is the source of the bodily senses; false ego in the mode of goodness, which is the source of the demigods; and the unmanifest, total material energy, which underlies everything. You are the indestructible entity among all the destructible things of this world, like the underlying substance that is seen to remain unchanged while the things made from it undergo transformation." (*Bhag*.10.85.5-12)

"Thus, these created entities, transformations of material nature, do not exist except when material nature manifests them within You, at which time You also manifest within them. But aside from such periods of creation, You stand alone as the transcendental reality." (*Bhag*.10.85.14)

Being the source of everything, Lord Krishna explains how He is also the source of genuine religion. "The Supreme Personality of Godhead said: 'O brahmana, I am the speaker of religion, its performer and sanctifier. I observe religious principles to teach them to the world, My child, so do not be disturbed." (*Bhag*.10.69.40)

Lord Krishna goes on to say that the understanding of how He is the origination of everything is the knowledge which can free a person from sins: "He who knows Me as the unborn, as the beginningless, as the Supreme Lord of all the worlds--he, undeluded among men, is freed from all sins." (*Bg*.10.3) This is the special nature of this spiritual knowledge.

KRISHNA IS THE SOURCE OF ALL AVATARS OF GOD

Herein we can begin to see how numerous references establish Sri Krishna as the Absolute Truth, yet it is also established that He is not simply another *avatar* or incarnation of God, but He is the source of all other *avatars* of the Lord. This is verified in the *Bhagavatam* verse (1.3.28) where it explains: *ete chamsha-kalah pumsaha / krishnas tu bhagavan svayam / indrari-vyakulam lokam / mridayanti yuge yuge*, which means, "All of the (previously mentioned) *avatars* are either plenary portions or portions of plenary portions of the Lord, but Lord Sri Krishna is the original Personality of Godhead. All of them appear on planets whenever there is a disturbance created by the atheists. The Lord incarnates to protect the theists."

From this we can understand that Sri Krishna either descends directly, or it is one of His plenary portions who appears in order to perform the necessary activities. This is further explained in the following verses, which shows that even Maha-Vishnu, the Creator of the cosmic manifestation, and Garbhodakashayi Vishnu, the expansion in each universe, are plenary portions of Lord Krishna: "The Supreme original Personality of Godhead, Lord Sri Krishna, expanding His plenary portion as Maha-Vishnu, the first incarnation, creates this manifold cosmos, but He is unborn. The creation, however, takes place in Him, and the material substance and manifestations are all Himself. He maintains them for some time and absorbs them into Himself again." (*Bhag*.2.6.39)

"The Personality of Godhead is pure, being free from all contaminations of material tinges. He is the Absolute Truth and the embodiment of full and perfect knowledge. He is all-pervading, without beginning or end, and without rival. O Narada, O great sage, the great thinkers can know Him when completely freed from all material hankerings and when sheltered under undisturbed conditions of the senses. Otherwise, by untenable arguments, all is distorted, and the Lord disappears from our sight." (*Bhag*. 2.6.40-41)

"Karanarnavashayi Vishnu [Maha-Vishnu] is the first incarnation [*avatar*] of the Supreme Lord, and He is the master of eternal time, space, cause and effects, mind, the elements, the material ego, the modes of nature, the senses, the universal form of the Lord, Garbhodakashayi Vishnu, and the sum total of all living beings, both moving and nonmoving." (*Bhag*. 2.6.42) Here we can remember that Maha-Vishnu is the form of the Lord from whom all the universes are created, while Garbhodakashayi Vishnu is His expansion that enters each and every universe.

"I myself [Brahma], Lord Shiva, Lord Vishnu, great generators of living beings like Daksha and Prajapati, yourselves [Narada and the Kumaras], heavenly demigods like Indra and Chandra, the leaders of the Bhurloka planets, the leaders of the earthly planets, the leaders of the lower planets, the leaders of the Gandharva [angel-like beings] planets, the leaders of the Vidyadhara planets, the leaders of the Charanaloka planets, the leaders of the Yakshas, Rakshas and Uragas, the great sages, the great demons, the great atheists and the great spacemen, as well as the dead bodies, evil spirits, jinn, kushmandas, great aquatics, great beasts and great birds, etc.--in other words, anything and everything which is exceptionally possessed of power, opulence, mental and perceptual dexterity, strength, forgiveness, beauty, modesty, and breeding, whether in form or formless--may appear to be the specific truth and the form of the Lord, but actually they are not so. They are only a fragment of the transcendental potency of the Lord." (*Bhag*.2.6.43-45)

In Brahma's prayers to Lord Krishna, in a later portion of the *Bhagavatam*, He continues to explain, "Are You not the original Narayana, O supreme controller, since You are the Soul of every embodied being and the eternal witness of all created realms? Indeed, Lord Narayana [Maha-Vishnu] is your expansion, and He is called Narayana because He is the generating source of the primeval water of the universe. He is real, not a product of Your illusory Maya." (*Bhag*.10.14.14)

Once when Lord Krishna was beginning to prepare for leaving this world to return to His abode, all the demigods, sages, and celestial and subtle beings approached Him when He lived in Dvaraka. Then they offered prayers to the Lord which further reveals Lord Krishna's supremacy over all other incarnations and demigods. It is explained:

"The powerful Lord Indra, along with the Maruts, Adityas, Vasus, Ashvinis, Ribhus, Angiras, Rudras, Vishvadevas, Sadhyas, Gandharvas, Apsaras, Nagas, Siddhas, Charanas, Guhyakas, the great sages and forefathers, and the Vidyadharas and Kinnaras, arrived at the city of Dvaraka, hoping to see Lord Krishna. By His transcendental form, Krishna, the Supreme Lord, enchanted all human beings and spread His own fame throughout the worlds. The Lord's glories destroy all contamination within the universe." (*Bhag*.11.6.2-4)

Many Hindus and followers of the Vedic tradition show great respect to these Vedic demigods, and rightly so, but such demigods can also come under the influence of Lord Krishna's illusory energy. In this next verse, we see how Lord Krishna takes it upon Himself to relieve Lord Indra of his pride and ignorance. Lord Indra is the king of heaven who is known for his own mystical or magical abilities, which tend to be a source of pride for him, which encourages him to do inappropriate things. In one such incident, Lord Krishna explained, "By My mystic power I will completely counteract this disturbance caused by Indra. Demigods like Indra are proud of their opulence, and out of foolishness they falsely consider themselves the Lord of the universe. I will now destroy such ignorance." (*Bhag*.10.25.16)

In summarizing the contents of the *Srimad-Bhagavatam* as Suta Gosvami begins to close his talk near the end of this *Purana*, he states: "I bow down to that unborn and infinite Supreme Soul, whose personal energies effect the creation, maintenance and destruction of the material universe. Even Brahma, Indra, Shankara [Shiva] and the other lords of the heavenly planets cannot fathom the glories of that infallible Personality of Godhead." (*Bhag*.12.12.67)

Thus, from different angles of thought, it is established from these and other references in the Vedic texts that Lord Krishna is the Supreme Being and source of all other *avatars* or incarnations of God and demigods.

WHY LORD KRISHNA DESCENDS INTO THIS WORLD

Why the Lord descends into this world is for multiple purposes, but primarily for two reasons. One of which is that, since He originally enunciated the ancient religious path of the *Vedas* for the benefit of the whole universe, whenever that becomes obstructed by the demoniac or wicked atheists He descends in one of His forms, which is in the transcendental mode of goodness. Thus, He again establishes the righteous Vedic path. He is the same Supreme Person, and in His *avatara* as Krishna appeared in the home of Vasudeva with His plenary portion, Balarama. This was for the second reason, which is to relieve the earth of the burden of the demoniac. As Krishna, He came to kill the hundreds of armies led by the kings who were but expansions of the enemies of the demigods, and to spread the fame of the Yadu dynasty. (*Bhag*.10.48.23-24)

Sri Krishna Himself explains this in the *Bhagavad-gita*: "Although I am unborn and My transcendental body never deteriorates, and although I am the Lord of all sentient beings, I still appear in every millennium in My original transcendental form. Whenever and wherever there is a decline in religious practices, O son of Bharata, and a predominant rise of irreligion--at that time I descend Myself. In order to deliver the pious and to annihilate the miscreants, as well as to reestablish the principles of religion, I advent Myself millennium after millennium. One who knows the transcendental nature of My appearance and activities does not, upon leaving the body, take his birth again in this material world, but attains My eternal abode, O Arjuna." (*Bg.* 4.4-9)

Arjuna, after understanding the position of Lord Krishna, recognized His superior position and said, "Thus You descend as an incarnation to remove the burden of the world and to benefit Your friends, especially those who are Your exclusive devotees and are rapt in meditation upon You." (*Bhag.*1.7.25)

The sages at Kuruksetra, while addressing Lord Krishna, also summarized the reason for Lord Krishna's appearance in this world. They explained that at suitable times He assumes the mode of pure goodness to protect His devotees and punish the wicked. Thus, the Supreme Personality descends to maintain the eternal path of the *Vedas* by enjoying His pleasure pastimes. (*Bhag.*10.84.18)

It is also described that when the Lord assumes a humanlike body, it is to show His mercy to His devotees. Then He engages in the sort of pastimes that will attract those who hear about them. Then they may become dedicated to Him. (*Bhag.*10.33.36) These pastimes of the Lord are so powerful that they can remove the sins of the three planetary systems and deliver those who are trapped in the continuous cycle of birth and death. (*Bhag.*10.86.34) Those who desire to serve the Lord should hear of these activities. Hearing such narrations of these pastimes destroy the reactions to fruitive work [karma]. (*Bhag.*10.90.49)

It is through Lord Krishna's pastimes that He calls all the conditioned souls to Him through love. Thus, by His wondrous activities He attracts all beings to return to their natural, spiritual position by reawakening their dormant love and service to Him. This is the purpose of human life, which provides the best facility and intellect for understanding our spiritual identity and connection with the Lord. As Sukadeva Gosvami explained to Maharaja Pariksit, "He, the Personality of Godhead, as the maintainer of all in the universe, appears in different incarnations after establishing the creation, and thus He reclaims all kinds of conditioned souls amongst the humans, nonhumans and demigods." (*Bhag.*2.10.42)

"To show causeless mercy to the devotees who would take birth in the future of this age of Kali-yuga, the Supreme Personality of Godhead, Krishna, acted in such a way that simply by remembering Him one will be freed from all the lamentation and unhappiness of material existence." (*Bhag*.9.24.61) However, Lord Krishna also explains that when He descends in His human form, the fools who are ignorant of His spiritual nature and supreme dominion over everything deride and criticize Him. (*Bg*.9.11)

Nonetheless, Lord Krishna Himself further explains the reasons for His appearance in this world to King Muchukunda: "My dear friend, I have taken thousands of births, lived thousands of lives and accepted thousands of names. In fact, My births, activities and names are limitless, and thus even I cannot count them. After many lifetimes someone might count the dust particles on the earth, but no one can ever finish counting My qualities, activities, names, and births. O King, the greatest sages enumerate My births and activities, which take place throughout the three phases of time, but never do they reach the end of them. Nonetheless, O friend, I will tell you about My current birth, name and activities. Kindly hear. Some time ago, Lord Brahma requested Me to protect religious principles and destroy the demons who were burdening the earth. Thus, I descended in the Yadu dynasty, in the home of Anakadundubhi. Indeed, because I am the son of Vasudeva, people call Me Vasudeva." (*Bhag*.10.51.36-40)

HOW LORD KRISHNA TOOK BIRTH IN THE MATERIAL WORLD

The Supreme Being in His form as Sri Krishna appeared on this planet 5,000 years ago and performed His pastimes for 125 years before returning to His spiritual abode. The *Vishnu Purana* (Book Four, Chapter Twenty-four) establishes that the age of Kali-yuga began when Lord Krishna left this world in 3102 BCE. There are many stories in the Vedic literature which narrate how Krishna engages in loving activities with His friends and relatives when He appears in this world, and how He performs amazing feats which thrill and astonish everyone, both while on this planet and in His spiritual abode. However, He brings His spiritual domain and His numerous pure devotees with Him when He descends into this world. Descriptions of the many activities and pastimes which go on in the spiritual world are found in such texts as *Srimad-Bhagavatam*, *Vishnu Purana, Mahabharata, Caitanya-caritamrta*, and Sanatana Goswami's *Brihat Bhagavatamritam*, and others, which explain the many levels and unlimited nature of the spiritual realm. Indeed, the body of the Lord is described as full of eternal bliss, truth, knowledge, the most dazzling splendour, and is the source of all that exists.

It is described that when the Lord appeared on this planet in the nineteenth and twentieth *avatars*, He advented Himself as Lord Balarama and Lord Krishna in the family of Vrishni [the Yadu dynasty], and by so doing He removed the burden of the world. (*Bhag.*1.3.23)

The story of Lord Krishna's birth is a unique narrative, as told in the Tenth Canto of *Srimad-Bhagavatam*. About 5,000 years ago when the earth was overburdened by the military might of the demoniac who had taken the forms of rulers and kings, the spirit of mother earth took the shape of a cow and approached Lord Brahma to seek relief. Concerned with the situation on earth, Lord Brahma, Lord Shiva and other demigods went to the shore of the ocean of milk. Within that ocean is an island that is the residence of Lord Vishnu. After mentally offering prayers to Lord Vishnu, Brahma could understand the advice the Lord gave him. This was that He would soon appear on the surface of the earth in order to mitigate the burden of the demoniac kings. Therefore, the demigods and their wives should appear in the Yadu dynasty in order to serve as servants of Lord Krishna and increase the size of that dynasty.

Then one day Vasudeva, Krishna's father, and his wife, Devaki, were riding home from their wedding. Devaki's brother, the demoniac King Kamsa, was driving the chariot. Then a voice of warning came from the sky announcing that Kamsa would be killed by Devaki's eighth son. Kamsa was immediately ready to kill his sister, but Vasudeva instructed him and talked him out of the idea. Kamsa was still not satisfied, so Vasudeva said he would bring all of the children to Kamsa as they were born. Then Kamsa could kill them. As the children were born, at first Kamsa decided not to kill them. But later Kamsa learned from the sage Narada Muni that the demigods were taking birth and appearing in the Yadu and Vrishni dynasties and were conspiring to kill him. Kamsa then decided that all the children in these families should be killed, and that Vasudev and Devaki should be imprisoned in his jail in Mathura. Narada Muni had also told Kamsa that in his previous life he had been a demon named Kalanemi who was killed by Lord Vishnu. Thus, Kamsa became especially infuriated and a dedicated enemy of all the descendants of the Yadu dynasty.

Anantadeva (Balarama) first appeared in the womb of Devaki as her seventh pregnancy. It was Yogamaya, Krishna's internal potency, who made the arrangement to transfer Anantadeva from the womb of Devaki to that of Rohini, a wife of Nanda Maharaja in Gokul, from whom He appeared as Balarama. Then, with the prayers and meditations of Vasudeva, Lord Krishna appeared within his heart, and then within the heart of Devaki. So, Devaki's eighth pregnancy was Krishna Himself. Thereafter, she became increasingly effulgent, which drew the attention of Kamsa, who wanted to kill Krishna. Thus, he became absorbed in thoughts of Krishna. Devaki also drew the attention of the many demigods who came to offer prayers to her and the Lord in her womb.

When the Lord appeared, He first exhibited His four-armed Narayana form to show that He was the Supreme Lord. Vasudeva and Devaki were struck with wonder and offered many prayers. Yet, fearing Kamsa, Devaki prayed that Krishna withdraw His four-armed form and exhibit His two-armed form.

The Lord also told them of how He had appeared two other times as their son in His *avatar* forms of Prishnigarbha and Vamanadeva. This was the third time that He was appearing as their son to fulfill their desires. That night, during a rainstorm, Lord Krishna desired to leave the prison and be taken to Gokul. By the arrangement of Yogamaya, Krishna's illusory energy, the shackles and prison doors were opened and Vasudeva was able to leave the prison and take Krishna to Gokul, thus saving the child from the danger of Kamsa. At this time, Yogamaya herself had taken birth from Mother Yashoda as a baby girl. This baby girl was actually Krishna's energy, Yogamaya. When Vasudeva arrived at Nanda Maharaja's house, everyone was in deep sleep. Thus, he was able to place Lord Krishna in the hands of Yashoda, while taking her own newly born baby girl, Yogamaya, back with him. When he returned, he placed the baby girl on Devaki's bed, and prepared to accept his place in the prison again by putting the shackles back on. Later, when Yashoda awoke in Gokul, she could not remember whether she had given birth to a male or female child, and easily accepted Lord Krishna as her own.

When the baby girl, Yogamaya, began crying in the morning, it drew the attention of the doorkeepers of the prison, who then notified King Kamsa. Kamsa forcefully appeared in the prison to kill the child. Devaki pleaded with him to save the baby. Instead, he grabbed the little girl from her arms and tried to dash the baby against a rock. However, she slipped from his hands and rose above his head, floating in the air while exhibiting her true form as the eight-armed Durga, one of the forms of Yogamaya. Durga told Kamsa that the person for whom he was looking had already taken birth elsewhere. Thus, Kamsa became filled with wonder that Devaki's eighth child appeared to be a female, and the enemy he feared had taken birth elsewhere. Then he released Devaki and Vasudeva, being apologetic for all that he had done. Yet, after conferring with his ministers, they decided that they had best try to kill all the children that had been born in the past ten days in the attempt to try to find and kill Kamsa's enemy, Krishna. Thus started the atrocities of Kamsa and his ministers, which he would eventually pay for when Lord Krishna would kill him. Meanwhile, Lord Krishna started His pastimes with His devotees in Gokul and Vrindavana to display His unique characteristics, personality and beauty.

In this way, as Sri Uddhava explained to Vidura, "The Lord appeared in the mortal world by His external potency, *yogamaya*. He came in His eternal form, which is just suitable for His pastimes. These pastimes were wonderful for everyone, even for those proud of their own opulence, including the Lord Himself in His form as the Lord of Vaikuntha. Thus, His [Sri Krishna's] transcendental body is the ornament of all ornaments... The Personality of Godhead, the all-compassionate controller of both the material and spiritual creations, is unborn, but when there is friction between His peaceful devotees and persons who are in the material modes of nature, He takes His birth just like fire, accompanied by the *mahat-tattva*." (*Bhag*.3.2.12, 15)

JANMASTAMI--KRISHNA'S BIRTH FESTIVAL

The annual celebration day of Krishna's birth in this world is called Janmastami. It is one of the biggest of the Vedic festivals. It is held in the typical pattern of preparation, purification, realization, and then celebration. On the day of the festival, people will fast and spend the day focused on Krishna, meditating and chanting the Hare Krishna mantra and other prayers or songs devoted to Lord Krishna. Often times, there will also be plays and enactments of the birth and pastimes of the Lord. Thus, offering their obeisances and focusing their minds on Lord Krishna, the devotees hold themselves in such single-pointed concentration throughout the day. This, along with the fasting, indicates the overcoming of the false ego and the attachment to the body. After relieving ourselves of such hindrances, we engage in the worship of the Lord as the evening brings us closer to the occasion of His divine appearance. Therein, after a full day of purification, the Supreme appears and we realize our own connection with the Lord, who then manifests as the ultimate worshipable object of our purified consciousness. Then at the stroke of midnight Lord Krishna takes birth, which is commemorated by a midnight *arati* ceremony. Thus, this climax at night represents our overcoming the darkness of ignorance and reaching the state of purified spiritual knowledge and perception. Therein we overcome the influence of the mind and senses and enter the state of steady awareness wherein there is full spiritual awakening. If one can follow this process, then he or she can experience the real meaning of Krishna Janmastami.

MISUNDERSTANDING THE ACTIVITIES OF LORD KRISHNA

The activities and pastimes of Lord Krishna are full of meaning and purpose, all of which reveal the highest Truth. The level of perception depends on the person's depth of spiritual understanding. If a person has little depth in his or her spiritual realization and the life of Lord Krishna, then interpretations of such activities of the Lord can result in wrong or even absurd conclusions. This is the danger when those who are spiritually inexperienced wish to comment on something of which they have no real understanding, though they think they do.

For example, some people feel that if Lord Krishna encouraged Arjuna to fight in the war of Kuruksetra, as was instructed in the *Bhagavad-gita*, then this means that He was endorsing violence. However, we should point out that Lord Krishna never wanted war and exhibited much tolerance to the atrocities that the Kauravas displayed toward the Pandavas. But too much tolerance may also be seen as a sign of weakness and can make the abusers more egoistic and cruel, allowing them to think they can get away with whatever they want. When such a person is a ruler of a country, he must be removed. That is compassion for the rest of society. If such a ruler is allowed to continue, he will create more havoc that will affect everyone.

Lord Krishna wanted to protect *dharma*, the ways of truth, morality, balance, and Vedic culture, and asked the Kauravas, especially Duryodhana, to give up their evil ways. He even tried to negotiate for peace, but the Kauravas wanted no part of it. The Pandavas only wanted a small portion of land to live on, which was their rightful heritage. But the Kauravas said they would not give enough land to even push in a needle. So, they would not change. Thus, finally there was no alternative but war. However, even then Lord Krishna said He would only be Arjuna's chariot driver and not take up any weapon, even though He could have destroyed the whole world with a glance. So, He actually had no personal interest in fighting. The Lord acted in the appropriate manner to protect society and *dharma*. In this way, war may be utilized to protect *dharma* and the general welfare of society when necessary. To stand by and watch wickedness spread through the world without taking any action is a worse evil.

Even when Krishna killed His own uncle, Kamsa, He did so because Kamsa had completely given up all *dharma* and moral standards, and would not accept anyone's advice. He ruled in a cruel way and made so many plans and attempts to kill Krishna, thus terrorizing the whole society. So, finally there was a showdown when Kamsa invited Krishna and Balarama to a wrestling match that had been planned as another attempt to kill Them. Therein Krishna finally killed Kamsa. However, by this act of losing his body, Kamsa was delivered from his evil mentality and was transferred to a new situation after having been purified by the touch of the Lord. Thus, Kamsa lost his body, but his soul was lifted up and he achieved liberation.

Some people may also say that Lord Krishna consorted with women and the wives of other men, which shows devious standards. Yet, this idea again exhibits how ignorant such people are. First of all, He was only six or seven years old at the time He performed His *rasa* dance with the cowherd girls of Vrindavana, which holds much deep significance that few can fully understand. He is the Lord of everyone no matter what their position. He wanted to make everyone happy, and to awaken each soul to their relationship with the Supreme. To do this He wanted to break the limitations of pride and shame and whatever bonds keep us from an unbroken focus on God and our service to Him. Such bonds exist only within the mind, but we must become free from these unwanted conceptions. This was but one small purpose in bringing those select souls in the form of the girls of Vrindavana to the unlimited spiritual bliss of divine love with the Supreme Being. This is no common thing, most of which ordinary people cannot fathom or imagine. Therefore, one must look deep into Lord Krishna's activities. Otherwise, without proper insight, one may arrive at a wrong conclusion as to the purpose and meaning in the Lord's activities, or even what is the real identity of the Lord.

When Shiva went to see the Lord in His form as Vishnu, Shiva pointed out in his prayers how the Lord is perceived by different people in different ways, according to their level of understanding and consciousness. He said "Those who are known as the impersonalist Vedantists regard You as the Impersonal Brahman. Others, known as the Mimamsaka philosophers, regard You as religion. The Sankhya philosophers regard You as the transcendental person who is beyond *prakriti* [material nature] and *purusha* who is the controller of even the demigods. The followers of the codes of devotional service known as the *Pancharatras* regard You as being endowed with nine different potencies. And the Patanjala philosophers, the followers of Patanjali

Muni, regard you as the supreme independent Personality of Godhead, who has no equal or superior." (*Bhag*.8.12.9) In this way, though one's consciousness and ideas of what the Absolute is prevents one from arriving at a true understanding, the Supreme Being remains unaffected, waiting for us to purify and spiritualize our consciousness to perceive the ultimate reality as He is.

THE BEAUTY OF KRISHNA

Lord Krishna's beauty is described in numerous prayers, poems, and portions of the Vedic literature. So we could provide many verses that describe this aspect of Krishna. An example of this is found when Lord Brahma relates Lord Krishna's form in the many verses of his *Brahma-samhita*. He also explains the beauty of Lord Krishna in his prayers that he directly offered to the Lord in the *Bhagavatam*. He says that Lord Krishna's body is dark blue like a new cloud. His garments are like brilliant lightning, and the beauty of Krishna's face is enhanced by His earrings and the peacock feather He wears on His head. He stands beautifully while wearing garlands made from the forest flowers, carrying a herding stick, a buffalo horn, and a flute. (*Bhag*.10.14.1)

His personal form is so attractive that it is considered the reservoir of all beauty. In fact, all beautiful things emanate from Him. His form is so attractive that it directs one's attention away from all other objects. Those same objects then seem devoid of attractiveness after seeing Lord Krishna. Thus, He attracts the minds of all people. His words also captivated the minds of all who remembered them. Even seeing His footprints, people were attracted. Thus, Krishna spreads His glories which are sung everywhere throughout the universe in the most sublime and essential Vedic verses. Lord Krishna says that by hearing and chanting about His glorious pastimes, the conditioned souls within this world could cross the ocean of ignorance. (*Bhag*.11.1.7)

The attractive nature of God is further described in the *Caitanya-caritamrita* (Madhya-lila, 17.139-140): "The transcendental qualities of Sri Krishna are completely blissful and relishable. Consequently Lord Krishna's qualities attract even the minds of self-realized persons from the bliss of self-realization. Those who are self-satisfied and unattracted by external material desires are also attracted to the loving service of Sri Krishna, whose qualities are transcendental and whose activities are wonderful. Hari, the Personality of Godhead, is called Krishna because He has such transcendentally attractive features."

Many of the Gosvamis of Vrindavana who had personally realized the attractive features of the Supreme wrote many books about the transcendental personality of God. One of the greatest of these saints was Rupa Gosvami (1489-1564 CE) who wrote a list of Krishna's characteristics in his book, *Bhakti rasamrita-sindhu*. This list describes 64 different qualities of God that are mentioned in the Vedic literature. This again confirms that the Lord is not merely an impersonal force, but a person who interacts in every way with the creation and the living entities that are within the creation that manifests from Him.

The list includes the following qualities: 1) beautiful features of the entire body; 2) marked with all auspicious characteristics; 3) extremely pleasing; 4) effulgent; 5) strong; 6) ever youthful; 7) wonderful linguist; 8) truthful; 9) talks pleasingly; 10) fluent; 11) highly learned; 12) highly intelligent; 13) a genius; 14) artistic; 15) extremely clever; 16) expert; 17) grateful; 18) firmly determined; 19) an expert judge of time and circumstances; 20) sees and speaks on the authority of the scriptures--the *Veda*; 21) pure; 22) self-controlled; 23) steadfast; 24) forbearing; 25) forgiving; 26) grave; 27) self-satisfied; 28) possessing equilibrium; 29) magnanimous; 30) religious; 31) heroic; 32) compassionate; 33) respectful; 34) gentle; 35) liberal; 36) shy; 37) protector of surrendered souls; 38) happy; 39) well-wisher of devotees; 40) controlled by love; 41) all-auspicious; 42) most powerful; 43) all-famous; 44) popular; 45) partial to devotees; 46) very attractive to all women; 47) all-worshipable; 48) all-opulent; 49) all-honorable; and 50) the Supreme controller.

These fifty qualities, however, may also be found in varying degrees in some of the *jivas* or common living entities in this universe. But they are found in Lord Krishna to an unlimited degree. But besides these 50 qualities, there are five more which may also be manifested at times in the forms of Lord Brahma and Shiva. These are: 51) changeless; 52) all-cognizant; 53) ever-fresh; 54) *sat-cid-ananda-vigraha*--possessing a transcendental form of eternity, full of knowledge and absolute bliss; and 55) possessing all mystic perfection.

Beyond the above mentioned qualities, which may be seen in other forms of Divinity such as the demigods, Lord Krishna has the following exceptional qualities which are also manifested in the form of Narayana or Vishnu, which is His form as the Lord of the spiritual Vaikuntha planets. These are: 56) inconceivable potency; 57) uncountable universes are generated from His body; 58) the original source of all incarnations; 59) the giver of salvation to the enemies He kills; and 60) the attractor of liberated souls.

Besides the above-mentioned traits, Lord Krishna has four more qualities that are found only in Him, and not even in His forms of Vishnu, not to mention any of the demigods. These are: 61) the performer of wonderful pastimes (especially his childhood pastimes); 62) surrounded by devotees endowed with unsurpassed love of Godhead; 63) the attractor of all living entities in all universes through the expert playing of His flute; and 64) possessor of unexcelled beauty without rival. All of these qualities are those of someone who has a highly developed form and personality. Ultimately, these qualities are those of the form of the Supreme Being, Krishna, who can reciprocate in loving exchanges in a way that no other form of God or any of the demigods can manifest. You do not find such a loving reciprocation in the personality of Brahma or Shiva. This is why Sri Krishna is the God of love like none other.

Even the Bible verifies that God has a most beautiful form and is not formless, as is shown in the next few verses. As we read these, we can recognize their similarity to the Vedic description of God's form: "My beloved is white and ruddy, the chiefest among ten thousand. His head is as the most fine gold, his locks are bushy, and black as a raven. His eyes are as the eyes of doves by the rivers of waters, washed with milk, and fitly set. His cheeks are as a bed of spices, as sweet flowers; his lips like lilies, dropping sweet smelling myrrh. His hands are as gold rings set with the beryl; his belly is as bright ivory overlaid with sapphires. His legs are as pillars of marble, set upon sockets of fine gold; his countenance is as Lebanon, excellent as the cedars. His mouth is most sweet; yea, he is altogether lovely. This is my beloved, and this is my friend." (*Song of Solomon* 5.10-16)

Obviously, there is no more elevated truth or higher bliss than the personal form of the Supreme. As Sri Krishna says: "O conqueror of wealth [Arjuna], there is no truth superior to Me." (*Bg*.7.7) Many great transcendental scholars have accepted this fact, including Ramanujacharya, Madhvacharya, Vallabhacharya, Sri Chaitanya Mahaprabhu, Baladeva, as well as Lord Brahma, who, after performing many austerities for spiritual purification, became perfectly self-realized and, getting a glimpse of the Lord's spiritual nature, composed the *Brahma-samhita* many thousands of years ago and described what were his confidential realizations. One such verse is the following: "Krishna, who is known as Govinda, is the Supreme Personality of Godhead. He has an eternal blissful spiritual body. He is the origin and He is the prime cause of all causes." (*Brahma-samhita* 5.1)

HOW TO UNDERSTAND GOD

Sometimes people say that they want to see God, or that God is not perceivable. And this is confirmed in the Vedic scripture, but with additional points of instruction on how we can perceive the Supreme Being. The *Svetasvatara Upanishad* (4.20) explains, "His form of beauty is imperceptible to mundane senses. No one can see Him with material eyes. Only those who realize, through deep pure-hearted meditation, this Supreme Personality, who resides in everyone's heart, can attain liberation."

Krishna *lila* or His pastimes are eternally going on in the spiritual world, whereas they appear to be happening only at certain points in time within the material energy. However, one who has purified his or her consciousness can still witness these activities even while in the material body. This can especially happen at the holy places (*dhamas*) where the spiritual and material energies overlap, and where the spiritual world appears within this material domain. Such places include Vrindavana, Mathura, Jagannatha Puri, Dwaraka, etc. And when the Lord is pleased with your service, He can reveal Himself to you. In this way, many greatly elevated and pure devotees of Krishna have been able to have personal *darshan* of the Lord and witness His pastimes even while in the material body. Then they may leave instructions for the rest of us to follow so that we can do the same. This is verification that the process of devotion, bhakti-yoga, works.

The *Srimad-Bhagavatam* (10.14.29) continues with this point. "My Lord, if one is favored by even a slight trace of the mercy of Your lotus feet, one can understand the greatness of Your Personality. But those who speculate to understand the Supreme Personality of Godhead are unable to know You, even though they continue to study the *Vedas* for many years."

The *Katha Upanishad* (1.2.23) also relates, "The Supreme Soul can neither be attained by studying the *Veda*, nor by sharp intelligence, nor by hearing many discourses on the scriptures. However, the Lord reveals His original transcendental form to the soul who embraces Him within the heart as the only Lord and Master. That soul alone can attain Him--the Supreme Soul, the Personality of Godhead, the Lord of the heart."

Since Krishna is the Supreme Being and source of all enjoyment, it is in our best interest to engage in His service, for that will also connect us to Him and give us that great pleasure and bliss that we are always trying to find. That is the point of devotional service, called *bhakti-yoga*, which is the process of connecting (*yog*) with the Supreme through devotion (*bhakti*). In this way, our inherent loving propensity is directed toward the supreme lover and natural object of love, God. There is no better way of finding God than this. In other words, through devotion we do not try to see God, but we act in such a way that God sees us and reveals Himself to us. Then everything is accomplished. There can be no greater achievement in the human form of life than that. Everything else is temporary; it comes and goes. Only our spiritual achievements last eternally because they are connected with the immortal soul. Therefore, reawakening our relationship with the Supreme is the highest goal in human existence.

Since it is established in the Vedic texts that the Absolute is a person, then meditating on the personal form of God rather than the impersonal feature is the highest form of meditation. This is verified in *Bhagavad-gita* (12.2): "The Supreme Personality of Godhead said: 'He whose mind is fixed on My personal form, always engaged in worshipping Me with great and transcendental faith, is considered by Me to be the most perfect.'"

Herein, we can understand that realizing the Absolute Truth in the form of the Supreme Person is much easier and much more attractive than struggling to realize, meditate on, or merge into the great white light of the impersonal *brahmajyoti*, or some other non-personal aspect of God. By understanding the Supreme Personality, all other facets of the Absolute, such as the Brahman effulgence and Paramatma or Supersoul, are also understood. In fact, those who are absorbed in Brahman realization can easily become attracted to understanding the Supreme Personality as did such sages as Sukadeva Gosvami and the Kumaras, as noted in *Srimad-Bhagavatam*:

"Let me offer my respectful obeisances unto my spiritual master, the son of Vyasadeva, Sukadeva Gosvami. It is he who defeats all inauspicious things within this universe. Although in the beginning he was absorbed in the happiness of Brahman realization and was living in a secluded place, giving up all other types of consciousness, he became attracted by the most melodious pastimes of Lord Sri Krishna. He therefore mercifully spoke the supreme *Purana*, known as *Srimad-Bhagavatam*, which is the bright light of the Absolute Truth and which describes the activities of Lord Krishna." (*Bhag.*12.12.68)

Since Lord Krishna is the Supreme Personality, then naturally there are certain ways in which to understand Him. This is a science, which we can more deeply explain later. But for now we can offer a summary of the instructions that point the way. The main point of consideration is that if we are trying to understand Lord Krishna, then we need to know what pleases Him, which is something that we can find from His direct instructions.

The key is explained directly by Lord Sri Krishna Himself when he says: "Knowledge about Me as described in the scriptures is very confidential, and it has to be realized in conjunction with devotional service. The necessary paraphernalia for that process is being explained by Me. You may take it up carefully. All of Me, namely My actual eternal form and My transcendental existence, color, qualities and activities--let all be awakened within you by factual realization, out of My causeless mercy." (*Bhag*.2.9.31-32)

To start on this process, one needs to hear from one who knows and is acquainted with the qualities of Lord Krishna and can explain them to others. This is established in this famous verse:

> *yasya deve para bhaktir*
> *yatha deve tatha gurau*
> *tasyaite kathita hy arthaha*
> *prakashante mahatmanaha*

"Unto those great souls who have implicit faith in both the Lord and the spiritual master, all the imports of Vedic knowledge are automatically revealed." (*Svetasvatara Upanishad* 6.23)

Lord Krishna also says, however, that, "I am never manifest to the foolish and unintelligent. For them I am covered by My internal potency, and therefore they do not know that I am unborn and infallible." (*Bg*.9.25)

Lord Brahma concurs with this point and verifies the need for the performance of devotional service, in which he says to Lord Krishna, "My dear Lord, devotional service unto You is the best path for self-realization. If someone gives up that path and engages in the cultivation of speculative knowledge, he will simply undergo a troublesome process and will not achieve his desired result. As a person who beats an empty husk of wheat cannot get grain, one who simply speculates cannot achieve self-realization. His only gain is trouble." (*Bhag*. 10.14.4)

As Lord Krishna establishes the foundation for attaining the means to understand Him, He also explains how to begin the process. "Only by practicing unalloyed devotional service with full faith in Me can one obtain Me, the Supreme Person. I am naturally dear to My devotees, who take Me as the only goal of their loving service. By engaging in such pure devotional service, even the dog-eaters can purify themselves from the contamination of their low birth." (*Bhag*.11.14.21)

In his summary of the *Srimad-Bhagavatam*, Sri Suta Gosvami also explains the above point: "Remembrance of Lord Krishna's lotus feet destroys everything inauspicious and awards the greatest good fortune. It purifies the heart and bestows devotion for the Supreme Soul, along with knowledge enriched with realization and renunciation." (*Bhag*.12.12.55)

Lord Krishna continues His instructions to Arjuna: "My dear Arjuna, only by undivided devotional service can I be understood as I am, standing before you, and can thus be seen directly. Only in this way can you enter into the mysteries of My understanding. (*Bg*.11.54) For one who worships Me, giving up all his activities unto Me and being devoted to Me without deviation, engaged in devotional service and always meditating upon Me, who has fixed his mind upon Me, O son of Pritha, for him I am the swift deliverer from the ocean of birth and death. (*Bg*.12.6-7) All that you do, all that you eat, all that you offer and give away, as well as all austerities that you may perform, should be done as an offering unto Me. In this way, you will be freed from all reactions to good and evil deeds, and by this principle of renunciation you will be liberated and come to Me." (*Bg*.9.27-28)

Herein it is as if Lord Krishna is speaking directly to us, that if we follow through with this process, we will be successful even at the time of death, which is certainly the final test of life in whatever we may have done. This is the topmost process, through which steady progress will bring us to spiritual awakening. This is further related by Lord Krishna in His instructions to Brahma:

"The person who is searching after the Supreme Absolute Truth, the Personality of Godhead, must certainly search for it up to this, in all circumstances, in all space and time, and both directly and indirectly. O Brahma, just follow this conclusion by fixed concentration of mind, and no pride will disturb you, neither in the partial nor in the final devastation." (*Bhag*.2.9.36-37)

"By regularly hearing, chanting and meditating on the beautiful topics of Lord Mukunda with ever-increasing sincerity, a mortal being will attain the divine kingdom of the Lord, where the inviolable power of death holds no sway. For this purpose, many persons, including great kings, abandoned their mundane homes and took to the forest [for performing such spiritual pursuits]." (*Bhag*.10.90.50)

Here it becomes clear that for those who hear and chant the holy name and topics of Krishna, millions of grievous sinful reactions become immediately burned to ashes. Of course, the most important time for remembering the Lord and chanting His name is at the time of death. That is why it is said that those who chant "Krishna, Krishna" at the time the body expires become eligible for liberation.

The *GopalaTapani Upanishad* (1.6) states, "One who meditates on this Supreme Person, glorifies Him, and worships Him, becomes liberated. He becomes liberated."

In conclusion, Lord Krishna simply explains that, "Thus I have explained to you the most confidential of all knowledge. Deliberate on this fully, and then do what you wish to do. Because you are My very dear friend, I am speaking to you the most confidential part of knowledge. Hear this from Me, for it is for your benefit. Always think of Me and become My devotee. Worship Me and offer your homage unto Me. Thus you will come to Me without fail. I promise you this because you are My very dear friend. Abandon all varieties of religion and just surrender unto Me. I shall deliver you from all sinful reactions. Do not fear." (*Bg*.18.63-66)

THE RESULT OF FAILING TO KNOW KRISHNA

Failing to have enough faith in Lord Krishna, or in getting to know Him, is not quite the same as you might find in some other faiths or religions wherein they say you will go to eternal hell if you are a non-believer, or you are an infidel worthy of death, or whatever. But failing to investigate Him and realize what is our final destination is considered a waste of this particular life. Lord Krishna Himself explains:

"One may be well versed in all the transcendental literature of the *Vedas*, but if he fails to be acquainted with the Supreme, then it must be concluded that all of his education is like the burden of a beast or like one's keeping a cow without milking capacity." (*Bhag*.11.11.18)

"Those who worship the demigods will take birth among the demigods; those who worship ghosts and spirits will take birth among such beings; those who worship ancestors go to the ancestors; and those who worship Me will live with Me." (*Bg*.9.25)

In this way we can begin to see the futility of following some materialistic path or a secondary spiritual method without the process for reaching an understanding of Lord Krishna. "Among all the eternal, conscious beings, there is One who supplies the needs of everyone else. The wise who worship Him in His abode attain everlasting peace. Others cannot." (*Katha Upanishad* 2.2.13)

In this way, a person is allowed to proceed through life in the way he or she wants. Lord Krishna allows each person to develop in their own way, and to continue wandering throughout the universe and through various activities until they begin to wonder about the purpose of life, or become ready for a deep spiritual path. Materialistic activities are not the way to find everlasting peace, and most of us need to discover that for ourselves. However, a person cannot be helped until he or she is ready. So, until then, they may be offered the spiritual knowledge they need, but they must decide for themselves how much of it they wish to utilize. Just as when Sri Krishna spoke the whole *Bhagavad-gita* to Arjuna, at the end of it He asked Arjuna what he wished to do. He had to make up his own mind. He was not forced to do anything. In the same way, we can only offer this knowledge for the benefit of humanity, and they can decide what they wish to do, or how long they wish to continue their existence in the material worlds.

"They are truly ignorant who, while imprisoned within the ceaseless flow of this world's material qualities, fail to know You, the Supreme Soul of all that be, as their ultimate, sublime destination. Because of their ignorance, the entanglement of material work forces such souls to wander in the cycle of birth and death." (*Bhag*.10.85.15)

Therefore, regardless of what else we do, we should recognize how advantageous it is to add the process of engaging in devotional service to Lord Krishna in this lifetime. We may not even be able to become perfect at it, but it nonetheless accelerates our spiritual development. Otherwise, regardless of what else we have accomplished materially, our life remains incomplete. "Caught in the grip of ignorance, self-proclaimed experts consider themselves learned authorities. They wander about this world befooled, like the blind leading the blind." (*Katha Upanishad* 1.2.5)

It is only through this spiritual education that we can understand our real identity and transcendental nature beyond the body and all material activities. Without that, we remain ignorant of our true potential and the final shelter that is awaiting us in the spiritual domain.

KRISHNA'S ETERNAL SPIRITUAL ABODE

The Vedic texts describe that there are innumerable spiritual planets in the spiritual sky beyond this material creation, each having one of the unlimited forms of the Lord with countless devotees engaging in His service. In the centre of all the spiritual planets of Vaikuntha (meaning the spiritual sky where there is no anxiety) is the planet known as Krishnaloka or Goloka Vrindavana. This is the personal abode of the original Supreme Personality of God, Sri Krishna. Krishna enjoys His transcendental bliss in multiple forms on that planet, and all the opulences of the other Vaikuntha planets are found there. This planet is shaped like a lotus flower and many kinds of pastimes are taking place on each leaf of that lotus, as described in *Brahma-samhita*, verses two and four: "The superexcellent station of Krishna, which is known as Gokula, has thousands of petals and a corolla like that of a lotus sprouted from a part of His infinitary aspect, the whorl of the leaves being the actual abode of Krishna. The whorl of that eternal realm, Gokula, is the hexagonal abode of Krishna. Its petals are the abodes of *gopis* [friends] who are part and parcel of Krishna to whom they are most lovingly devoted and are similar in essence. The petals shine beautifully like so many walls. The extended leaves of that lotus are the garden-like *dhama*, or spiritual abode of Sri Radhika, the most beloved of Krishna."

The only business that Sri Krishna has in the spiritual realm is transcendental enjoyment. The only business of Krishna's eternal servants or devotees is to offer enjoyment to Him. The more enjoyment the devotees offer to Krishna, the happier He becomes. The happier Krishna becomes, the more His devotees become enlivened and taste eternal, transcendental ecstasy. In this way, there is an ever-increasing competition of spiritual ecstasy between Krishna and His parts and parcels, the devotees. This is the only business in the spiritual world, as confirmed in *Brahma-samhita*, verse 6: "The Lord of Gokula is the Transcendental Supreme Godhead, the own Self of eternal ecstasies. He is superior to all superiors and is busily engaged in the enjoyments of the transcendental realm and has no association with His mundane [material] potency."

Though it is not possible to experience spiritual pastimes or to see the form of the Supreme with ordinary senses, by spiritualizing our senses by the practice of devotional yoga we can reach the platform of perceiving the Supreme at every moment. At that time we start becoming Krishna conscious and can begin to enter into the pastimes of Krishna, although we may still be situated within this material body. If we become fully spiritualized in this manner, there is no doubt that when we give up this material body, we will return to the spiritual world. Until then, we can continue studying the Vedic texts to remember and be conversant about the beauty and loveliness of the spiritual world, as described as follows:

"Vrindavana-*dhama* is a place of ever-increasing joy. Flowers and fruits of all seasons grow there, and that transcendental land is full of the sweet sound of various birds. All directions resound with the humming of bumblebees, and it is served with cool breezes and the waters of the Yamuna River. Vrindavana is decorated with wish-fulfilling trees wound with creepers and beautiful flowers. Its divine beauty is ornamented with the pollen of red, blue and white lotuses. The ground is made of jewels whose dazzling glory is equal to a myriad of suns rising in the sky at one time. On that ground is a garden of desire trees, which always shower divine love. In that garden is a jewelled temple whose pinnacle is made of rubies. It is decorated with various jewels, so it remains brilliantly effulgent through all seasons of the year. The temple is beautified with bright-coloured canopies, glittering with various gems, and endowed with ruby-decorated coverings and jewelled gateways and arches. Its splendour is equal to millions of suns, and it is eternally free from the six waves of material miseries. In that temple there is a great golden throne inlaid with many jewels. In this way one should meditate on the divine realm of the Supreme Lord, Sri Vrindavana-*dhama*." (*Gautamiya Tantra* 4)

"I worship that transcendental seat, known as Svetadvipa where as loving consorts the *Lakshmis*, in their unalloyed spiritual essence, practice the amorous service of the Supreme Lord Krishna as their only lover; where every tree is a transcendental purpose-tree; where the soil is the purpose-gem, water is nectar, every word is a song, every gait is a dance, the flute is the favourite attendant, effulgence is full of transcendental bliss and the supreme spiritual entities are all enjoyable and tasty, where numberless milch-cows always emit transcendental oceans of milk; where there is eternal existence of transcendental time, who is ever present and without past or future and hence is not subject to the quality of passing away even for the duration of half a moment. That realm is known as Goloka only to a very few self-realized souls in this world." (*Brahma-samhita*, 5.56)

By studying and hearing about the beauty of the spiritual world, we will understand that everything we are looking for in life has its origin in that eternal realm. There, as it is described, one finds freedom from all pains and suffering, and the atmosphere is unlimitedly full of ever-expanding beauty, joy, happiness, knowledge, and eternal, loving relationships. In that realm, no one has the difficulties of maintaining a material body because everyone has spiritual forms. So, it is a world full of recreation only, without the struggle for maintaining our existence. There is never any hunger, and we can feast and never get full. Neither is there any lamentation over the past or fear of the future. It is said that time is conspicuous by its absence. Thus, the needs of the soul for complete freedom and unbounded love and happiness are found in the spiritual atmosphere. That is our real home.

CHAPTER THREE

The Avatars of Lord Krishna

As previously mentioned, the Supreme Being descends in various forms and incarnations. Actually, incarnation is not the accurate word, since it means to appear in the flesh. The Lord descends in His own spiritual form, and not in the material elements or flesh of this world. Thus, He descends and not incarnates. The proper name of such a descension of the Lord is the Sanskrit word *avatar*, though many times people use the word incarnation to mean the same thing. Each descension or *avatar* of the Lord has a specific mission, but primarily they help maintain the world and guide the living beings in life, and to attract them back to the spiritual domain.

To dispel the power of the illusory energy, the Lord maintains all of the planets in the universe and assumes roles or *avatars* to perform pastimes to reclaim those in the mode of goodness.[1] In this way, throughout the many millions of universes in which the Supreme Being appears, the purpose is to bring society to a higher understanding of its real purpose, at least those who are in the higher grades of consciousness and are receptive to understanding their spiritual relation with Him. He also sends His pure representatives and instructions in the authorized scripture to guide people. In either case, the purpose is the same, to point the suffering living beings back toward the spiritual world. Only there can the living beings find the true happiness for which they are hankering. That kind of happiness is not found in any part of the material universe.

The source of the various incarnations or *avatars* within this universe is the Lord of the universe, namely Garbhodakashayi Vishnu.[2] He is like the channel and through Him they all appear in this universe. All such expansions of Lord Krishna are residents of the spiritual world who are also called *avatars* when they descend into the material world.[3] And, as it says in the *Srimad-Bhagavatam* (1.3.26): "The *avatars* of the

Lord are innumerable, like rivulets flowing from inexhaustible sources of water."

There are six kinds of *avatars* of Krishna. These include those of Vishnu (*purusha-avatars*), pastime *avatars* (*lila-avatars*), *avatars* that control the modes of nature (*guna-avatars*), *avatars* of Manu (*manvantara-avatars*), *avatars* in different millenniums (*yuga-avatars*), and the empowered individuals (*avesh* or *shaktyavesha-avatars*).[4] However, Lord Krishna Himself descends to this world once in a day of Brahma to manifest His transcendental pastimes.[5] All other incarnations are potentially situated in the body of the primeval Lord Krishna. Thus, according to one's opinion, one may address Him as any one of the incarnations or *avatars*.[6] This is because all of the plenary expansions of the Supreme exist within the body of the original person. Thus, He can expand Himself as one flame from a candle lights another, but all such flames come from the original. Some say that Krishna is directly Nara-Narayana. Others say that He is Vamana, or the incarnation of Kshirodakashayi Vishnu, the Supersoul. None of these statements is impossible. Everything is possible in Krishna, for He is the primeval Lord.[7]

From Krishna comes innumerable incarnations, the most prominent of which are the *lila-avatars*, such as Matsya, Kurma, Varaha, Rama, etc. I will describe most of these later. There are also the qualitative incarnations who are in charge of the modes of material nature, such as Brahma, Vishnu and Shiva, along with the Manus and the *yuga-avatars*.[8]

The time and reason for these incarnations is that whenever and wherever there is a substantial decline of religion and a rise in irreligion, at that time Lord Krishna manifests Himself. In this way, in order to protect the *sadhus* (the pious), destroy the envious, and reestablish the principles of religion, He advents Himself millennium after millennium.[9]

Let us remember that Lord Maha-Vishnu is resting in His *yoga-nidra* trance, in which He manifests the material energy. He is also the seed of the other incarnations of the Supreme who appear in the material world. So, as it is described, you could say that the Lord is like a sleeping person who creates a separate world in His imagination and then enters His own dream and sees Himself within it.[10]

THE LORD APPEARS IN EACH UNIVERSE

Even though there are so many *avatars* of the Supreme Being and plenary expansions of Him who appear in this world, we have to be aware of how to distinguish who is and who is not an *avatar* or incarnation. As in other ages, an incarnation is accepted according to the directions in the scriptures.[11] In all descriptions of an incarnation, the scripture will provide the name of the father and the name of the place of birth in which the *avatara* will appear.[12] Such descriptions will also elaborate on His bodily symptoms and activities. Therefore, we must be able to recognize the characteristics of an *avatar* of God by such descriptions and must not be whimsical about accepting someone as an incarnation, or even a representative of the Supreme.[13] An actual incarnation of God never proclaims that He is God or an incarnation. The great Vedic texts have already recorded the characteristics of all the *avatars*.[14] In this way, not just anyone can claim to be God or an *avatar* without the proper qualities and references in the Vedic scripture that verify his appearance.

Whenever the Lord Sri Krishna desires to manifest Himself on earth, He first sends His respectable predecessors. These take the form of the incarnations of His father, mother, and spiritual master. They appear first in order to prepare the way for the Supreme Being's appearance.[15] These people, however, are the Lord's great devotees who serve Him by participating in His pastimes. Thus, though the Lord personally has nothing to do with this material existence, He comes to earth and imitates material life just to expand the varieties of ecstatic enjoyment for His devotees.[16] In this way, Krishna, the original Soul of all living beings, has appeared as an ordinary human being for the benefit of the whole universe and out of His causeless mercy. This He has done by the strength of His own spiritual potency.[17] Not only do the devotees enjoy Krishna's pastimes, but He also enjoys His transcendental activities in various forms in this material world, which cleans away all the unhappiness of those who joyfully chant His glories.[18]

In this way, Lord Krishna appears in each universe. When His activities are finished in one universe, He begins His pastimes in another. Thus, His eternal pastimes go on like this in the universes as long as the material manifestation continues. Furthermore, His eternally liberated devotees also follow Him from one universe to another to accompany Him in His blissful pastimes.[19]

The Supreme is also joined by those devotees who are nearly perfect in their spiritual consciousness. By joining the Lord's pastimes in another universe, and by their personal association with the Lord and His pure devotees, they can complete the necessary qualifications for entering directly into the spiritual atmosphere. This is how the Supreme Being displays the eternal pastimes of the spiritual domain within the material creation and attracts the materially conditioned souls to return to the eternal spiritual abode.

In this way, the consecutive pastimes of Krishna are manifest in one of the innumerable universes moment after moment. There is no possibility of counting the universes, but in any case some pastime of the Lord is being manifest at every moment in one universe or another.[20]

THE MAIN AVATARS OF THE SUPREME BEING

There are 22 main *lila-avatars* of the Supreme Being who appear throughout the ages. They all have specific forms or bodily features, and particular purposes for appearing. These are listed in the various Vedic texts, especially the *Puranas*, and Their many pastimes are explained in detail therein. But here we will provide a basic summary of Their activities and purposes.

The first of these incarnations are the four sons of Brahma, the Kumaras. They took a vow of celibacy and underwent severe austerities for realization of the Absolute Truth. They are considered empowered *jiva* souls, or *shaktyavesha-avatars*, whose mission was to teach the process of spiritual development.[21] Knowledge of spiritual truth had disappeared from the previous universal devastation and they helped re-establish it.[22]

Lord Varaha was the second *avatar* who appeared in the form of a huge boar. He lifted the earth planet out of the nether regions of the filthy waters of the universe, which was a suitable activity for a boar. He did this to counter the nefarious activities of the demons who had put the earth planet into jeopardy.[23]

The third incarnation was the empowered sage among the demigods, Devarshi Narada Muni. He collected expositions of the *Vedas* which dealt with the process of devotional service to Lord Krishna, and authored the great classic *Narada-pancharatna*. He also traveled by his mystic abilities throughout the universe singing the praises of the Lord and giving instruction on bhakti-yoga and how to attain real happiness. Thus, he has many disciples all over the creation.[24] Narada Muni had once been taught the science of loving service to the Supreme during the

The Avatars of Lord Krishna

Lord's Hamsavatara incarnation, the swan-like form of the Supreme, who had been very much pleased by Narada.[25]

In the fourth *avatar*, the Lord became the twin sons known as Nara and Narayana. They were born of Murti, the wife of King Dharma. They underwent severe austerities in the area of Badarikashrama (Badrinatha) in the Himalayas to demonstrate the process of controlling the senses for spiritual advancement.[26] The celestial beauties who were the companions of Cupid went to distract Narayana from His vows, but were unsuccessful when they could see many other beautiful women like them emanating from the Supreme Being. Everything comes from the Supreme, who remains unattached to all His manifestations.[27]

The fifth *avatar* was Lord Kapila, the foremost among perfected beings. He explained for the first time the system of the Sankhya philosophy and the way of understanding the Truth by the analysis of material elements.[28] He was the son of the sage Kardama Muni and his wife Devahuti. He also gave great expositions to his mother on the science of devotional service to the Supreme Lord. By that means she became cleansed of all material tendencies and achieved liberation.[29] This information is provided in detail in the *Srimad-Bhagavatam*.

The sixth *avatar* appeared as Dattatreya, the son of the sage Atri and his wife Anasuya, both of whom had prayed for an *avatar* to be their son. He had spoken on the subject of transcendence to Alarka, Prahlada, Yadu, Haihaya, and others.[30]

The seventh *avatar* was Yajna, the son of Ruci and his wife Akuti. During the time of Svayambhuva Manu there was no living entity qualified to take the post of Indra, the King of Heaven, on his planet Indraloka. So, Yajna took up the post of Indra and was assisted by His own sons, such as Yama, the lord of death, and other demigods to rule the administration over universal affairs.[31]

King Rishabha was the eighth *avatar* who appeared as the son of King Nabhi and his wife Merudevi. Again He demonstrated the path of spiritual perfection by performing yoga and instructing His sons in the process of *tapasya*, austerities for spiritual development. This path sanctifies one's existence and leads to eternal spiritual happiness. This process is followed by those who have fully controlled their senses and are honored by all orders of life.[32]

The Lord also appeared as the Hayagriva, the horse-headed, *avatar* in a golden color during a sacrifice performed by Brahma. When He breathed, all of the sweet sounds of the *Vedas* came out of His nostrils.[33]

The ninth *avatar* was Prithu, who accepted the body of a king. He had been prayed for by the brahmana priests to counteract the problems that had been brought on by impious activities of the previous king, Vena. Prithu made various arrangements to cultivate the land to yield various forms of produce.[34] Although King Vena was bound for hell due to the reactions of his misdeeds and the curse of the brahmanas, he was delivered by Prithu.[35]

After the time of the Chakshusha Manu there was a complete inundation over the whole world by water. Manu had been warned about this flood and built a ship in which he and his family survived. The Lord accepted the form of a huge fish to protect Vaivashvata Manu and guide the ship to safety on a huge mountain peak. This was the Matsya *avatar*. After the period of each Manu there is a devastation by water over the earth. The Lord then regularly appears to show special favor to His devotees and protect them from the devastation and allow society to start anew. In this way, He protects all of the living entities as well as the *Vedas* from destruction.[36] After the last flood, Manu and his family and the surviving living creatures again repopulated the earth. Local people of Uttarakhand in Northern India identify the Nanda Devi as the mountain peak in the story of the flood. Also, in the town of Manali in that region of northern India is the temple dedicated to Manu where his ship was said to have came to rest after the flood.

The eleventh *avatar* of the Supreme, as described in the *Bhagavata Purana*, was in the form of a huge tortoise, Kurma, whose main mission was to act as a pivot for the Mandara Hill, which was being used as a churning rod between the demons and demigods. The scheme was that the demons and demigods wanted to produce nectar from the ocean by this churning action which would make them immortal. Each side wanted to be the first to get it, and the back of Lord Kurma was the resting place for the hill.[37] As the mountain moved from side to side on the back of Kurma while He was partially asleep, He felt it as an itching sensation.[38]

As the twelfth *avatar*, the Lord appeared as Dhanvantari who produced the nectar that came from the churning action. He is considered the lord of good health. It is He who inaugurated the medical science in the universe.[39] The Lord accepted the thirteenth *avatar* by becoming Rohini, the most beautiful woman who allured the demons away from the pot of nectar and gave it to the demigods. Thus, the Lord prevented the havoc that would have taken place if the demons had gotten the nectar and became immortal.[40]

The Avatars of Lord Krishna 53

In the fourteenth *avatar*, the Lord appeared as Narashimhadeva, the half-man half-lion form that displayed the anger and power of the Supreme Being when one of His devotees, Prahlada, was in peril. The Lord placed the demon Hiranyakashipu on His lap and with His long fingernails tore apart the body of the atheist demon who had threatened the life of his son, Prahlada, who was a staunch devotee of the Lord.[41] This story has many twists and turns in it and is one of the most popular stories described in the *Puranas*.

As the fifteenth *avatar*, the Lord as Vamana assumed the form of a dwarf-brahmana. He appeared as the youngest son of His mother, Aditi. He visited the sacrificial arena of Bali Maharaja on the pretense of asking for a measly three steps of land. Bali quickly agreed, thinking that this dwarf could not take up much land. However, when Vamana took two steps, His body became so gigantic that it covered the whole universe. There was no where else to place His third step. So Bali, understanding that this was the Supreme Being, offered his own head. Thus, Vamana humbled Bali, who then became qualified to have his own planet.[42]

In the sixteenth *avatar*, the Lord accepted the mighty form of Parashurama and annihilated the wicked class of warrior kings twenty-one times in order to free the earth of the burden of these nefarious rulers. In this way, He could establish a noble administration.[43]

The seventeenth *avatar* was Srila Vyasadeva, who appeared as the son of Parashara Muni and his wife Satyavati. His mission was to divide the one *Veda* into various branches and sub-branches so the people who are less intelligent can more easily understand them.[44] IIe then composed the more important Vedic texts, culminating in his own commentary of the Vedic writing in the form of the *Srimad-Bhagavatam*. In this way, the one *Veda* became the four main *samhitas*, namely the *Rig*, *Yajur*, *Sama*, and *Atharva Vedas*. Then came the *Brahmana* texts, the *Vedanta Sutras*, the *Mahabharata*, and then the *Puranas*, of which Vyasadeva considered the *Bhagavata Purana* (*Bhagavatam*) the most important and complete.

It is also explained that the *Bhagavata Purana* is the literary incarnation of God, which is meant for the ultimate good of all people, and is all-blissful and all-perfect. It is considered that by faithfully reading the *Bhagavatam* from start to finish, a person will realize the Supreme, especially when this is combined with the process of self-realization through bhakti-yoga and regular chanting of the Lord's holy names. Sri Vyasadeva offered the *Bhagavata Purana* to his son after extracting the cream of all Vedic literature. This *Bhagavat Purana* is as brilliant as the sun, and has arisen just after the departure of Lord Krishna to His own abode. Persons who have lost their vision due to the dense darkness of this age of Kali can get light from this *Purana*.[45]

To explain further about Srila Vyasadeva, Jiva Gosvami quotes the *Vishnu Purana* (3.4.2-5) in his *Tattva-sandarbha* (16.2) that a different empowered *jiva* soul takes the position of Vyasadeva in each incarnation as a *shaktyavesha-avatara*. This takes place just as each Kali-yuga begins so that He can divide and categorize the Vedic knowledge for the benefit of the masses. So, Vyasadeva started doing this in every cycle of Kali-yuga many thousands of years ago. However, in this particular *divya-yuga* in which we are in, or cycle of the four ages, Lord Narayana Himself appears as Srila Krishna-Dvaipayana Vyasa (or Vyasadeva) to divide the Vedic literature into various branches. Therefore, in this age of Kali-yuga He is not simply an empowered living entity.

In the eighteenth *avatar*, the Lord appeared as King Rama. In order to please the demigods and mankind, He displayed His superhuman powers as the ideal king and killed the demon King Ravana.[46] This is one of the most popular stories in all of India that make up the great Vedic epic known as the *Ramayana*. Lord Rama appeared in the dynasty of Maharaja Ikshvaku as the son of Maharaja Dasaratha, with His internal potency and wife, Sita. Under the order of Dasaratha, Lord Rama had gone to the forest to live with Sita and His brother Lakshmana. While in the forest, Sita was kidnaped by the demon Ravana, which made way for the telling of the *Ramayana*. Being aggrieved, Rama went to search for Sita. With red-hot eyes, He looked all over India and on to the city of Ravana, which was on the island of Sri Lanka. All of the aquatics in the ocean were being burnt by the heat in His angry eyes, so the ocean gave way to Him. During the course of battle, proud Ravana was killed by the arrow from Lord Rama, who was then reunited with Sita.[47]

In the nineteenth and twentieth *avatars*, the Lord advented Himself as Lord Krishna and His brother Lord Balarama in the Yadu dynasty near the end of Dvapara-yuga. He displayed wonderful pastimes to invoke the attraction of the people and, again, to relieve the burden of the world of numerous demons and atheists.[48] Lord Krishna is directly the original Personality of Godhead, and Balarama is the first plenary expansion of the Lord. From Balarama comes all the other expansions of the Divine.

The next incarnation of the Lord appeared in the beginning of Kali-yuga as Lord Buddha, the son of Anjana, for the purpose of deluding the envious who had misused the Vedic path, and to preach a simple system of nonviolence.[49] At the time people in general were falling away from the proper execution of the Vedic system and had misused the Vedic recommendation of sacrifice and began offering and consuming animals. Buddha denounced all such actions and taught people simply to follow him and his teachings. Thus, he fooled the faithless people who then believed in Lord Buddha.

The twenty-second and final *avatar* of the Supreme will appear at the end of Kali-yuga, at the conjunction of the next *yuga*. He will take His birth as Kalki, the son of Yasha, when the rulers of earth will have degenerated into common thieves and plunderers.[50] At the time there will be no topics on the subject of God, nor any knowledge of religion. Then, rather than trying to teach or show the way of progress when people will be too retarded and slow minded to understand philosophy, He will simply slaughter the foolish rogues who wander the earth. This will take place about 427,000 years from now, according to the Vedic texts. [Details about Lord Kalki and His activities are provided in one of my previous books, *The Vedic Prophecies: A New Look into the Future*.]

As is summarized in the *Srimad-Bhagavatam* (1.3.28), all of these incarnations are either plenary portions or portions of the plenary portions of the Lord. Once again we have to remember the verse from the *Bhagavata Purana* (1.3.28):

> *ete chamsha-kalah pumsaha*
> *krishnas tu bhagavan svayam*
> *indrari-vyakulam lokam*
> *mridayanti yuge yuge*

"All of the (previously mentioned) *avatars* are either plenary portions or portions of plenary portions of the Lord, but Lord Sri Krishna is the original Personality of Godhead [from whom all other *avatars* and expansions of God appear]. All of them appear on planets whenever there is a disturbance created by the atheists. The Lord incarnates to protect the theists."

Also, as is further explained, "You should know Krishna to be the original Soul of all living entities. For the benefit of the whole universe, He has, out of His causeless mercy, appeared as an ordinary human being. He has done this by the strength of His internal potency.

"Those in this world who understand Lord Krishna as He is see all things, whether stationary or moving, as manifest forms of the Supreme Personality of Godhead. Such enlightened persons recognize no reality apart from the Supreme Lord Krishna." (*Bhagavata Purana* 10.14.55-56)

Although learned men discuss the birth and activities of the Supreme unborn, Lord of the heart, the foolish who have a poor fund of knowledge cannot understand the transcendental nature of the forms, names, and activities of the Supreme Being, who is playing like an actor in a drama.[51] However, only those who render favorable service to Lord Krishna can know the creator of the universe in His full glory, power and transcendence.[52]

THE MANU AVATARS

The Manus appear for certain durations during a day of Brahma. Brahma's day is calculated as 4,300,000 years (the time of one cycle of the four *yugas*) times 1,000. Within one day of Brahma there are only 14 Manus. The list of the 14 Manus in this universe are as follows: Yajna is Svayambhuva Manu, Vibhu is Svarocisha Manu, Satyasena is Uttama Manu, Hari is Tamasa Manu, Vaikuntha is Raivata Manu, Ajita is Ckakshusha Manu, Vamana is Vaivasvata Manu (the Manu of the present age), Sarvabhauma is Savarni Manu, Rishabha is Daksha-savarni Manu, Vishvaksena is Brahma-savarni Manu, Dharmasetu is Dharma-savarni Manu, Sudhama is Rudra-savarni Manu, Yogesvara is Deva-savarni Manu, and Brihadbhanu is Indra-savarni Manu. These fourteen Manus cover the 4,320,000,000 solar years of one day of Brahma.[53]

To understand more completely how long these Manus reign we can consider the following information. For example, there are four ages, namely Satya-yuga, Treta-yuga, Dvapara-yuga, and Kali-yuga, which comprise a *divya-yuga*, one set of the four *yugas*. Let's remember that Satya-yuga lasts 1,728,000 years, Treta-yuga 1,296,000 years, Dvapara-yuga 864,000 years, and Kali-yuga 432,000 years. That is a total of 4,320,000 years. A day of Brahma, called a *kalpa*, lasts for 1,000 of these cycles, and is thus 4,320,000,000 solar years. There are 14 Manus in each day of Brahma. Each Manu is said to exist for one *manvantara*, which is a period of time lasting 71 *divya-yugas*. Therefore, each Manu exists for roughly 306,720,000 years. Additionally, Brahma lives for 100 years, composed of 365 of such days in a year.[54] Of course, let us also remember that these beings live in the subtler dimensions where life goes on for much longer periods of time, and not in this earthly stratum.

From further analysis we can also discover the age of the earth from these Vedic calculations. The present Manu is the seventh in line, called Vaivasvata Manu, the son of Vivasvan. Twenty-seven *divya-yugas*, or cycles of the four *yugas*, of his age have now passed. So, 27 *divya-yugas* means 116,640,000 years. It is scheduled that at the end of the Dvapara-yuga of the twenty-eighth *divya-yuga* of the seventh Manu, Lord Krishna appears on earth with the full paraphernalia of His eternal spiritual abode, named Vrajadhama or Goloka Vrindavana. Brahma's day consists of 4,320,000,000 years. Six of these Manus appear and disappear before Lord Krishna takes birth. This means that 1,975,320,000 years of the day of Brahma have gone by before the appearance of Lord Krishna.[55] Therefore, this is also the age of the earth in this particular day of Brahma by these Vedic calculations. Science is sometimes surprised that such lengths of time were part of the ancient Vedic conception of the universe even hundreds of years ago.

THE YUGAVATARS

Getting back to the various *avatars* of the Supreme, we now come to the *yugavataras*. The *yugavataras* are divided by the millenniums in which they appear. They appear in a particular color according to the *yuga*. In Satya-yuga the color is white, in Treta-yuga the color is red, in Dvapara-yuga it is black, and in Kali-yuga the color is yellow or golden. For an example, in Dvapara-yuga Lord Krishna was a blackish color, while in Kali-yuga Lord Chaitanya had a golden complexion.[56]

In Satya-yuga the people were generally quite advanced in spiritual knowledge and could meditate upon Krishna very easily. During the time in the white incarnation, the Lord taught religion and meditation, and in this way showed His mercy to the people of that era. In the Lord's reddish incarnation during the Treta-yuga, He taught the process of performing great rituals and religious sacrifices. In Dvapara-yuga, the Lord appeared in His blackish form as Krishna and induced people to worship Him directly. Then in Kali-yuga the Lord appears in a golden color as His own devotee, showing others the spiritual process for this age. Accompanied by His personal associates, He introduces the process of *hari-nama-sankirtan*, or the congregational singing and chanting of the Lord's holy names, specifically in the form of the Hare Krishna mantra. He personally chants and dances in ecstatic love of God. Through this process He delivers this love of God to all. Whatever spiritual results are attained through the other processes in the previous three *yugas* can be easily achieved in Kali-yuga by the chanting of the holy names of Krishna. It is the easiest process for becoming freed from material existence and reaching the transcendental kingdom.[57]

THE SHAKTYAVESHA-AVATARS

The last kind of *avatars* are what is called the *shaktyavesha-avatars*. These are the living beings who are empowered by the Supreme to act in certain ways or accomplish a particular mission. Such *avatars* include the four Kumaras, Narada Muni, Lord Parashuram, and usually Lord Vyasadeva and Lord Brahma. The power of knowledge was given to the Kumaras. The power of devotion to the Lord was given to Narada. Brahma was, of course, empowered with the ability to create. Parashuram was given the power to kill the many rogues and thieves who were on the planet at His time. Whenever the Lord is present in someone by a portion of His various potencies that allow that person to do something wonderful and uplifting for the well-being of everyone, that living entity is considered a *shaktyavesha-avatar*--a living being invested with the Lord's special power.[58]

CONCLUSION

It is through these many *avatars* and expansion that the Lord maintains the universe and provides guidance to the living beings within it. To understand this knowledge is an important part in perceiving the plan behind the universe and our purpose in it, and it provides great benefits for all who hear it. As it is explained in the *Srimad-Bhagavatam* (8.23.30), "If one hears about the uncommon activities of the Supreme Personality of Godhead in His various *avatars*, he is certainly elevated to the higher planetary systems or even brought directly back to Godhead, the spiritual domain."

CHAPTER NOTES
1. *Srimad-Bhagavatam* 1.2.34
2. Ibid., 1.3.5
3. *Caitanya-caritamrita*, Madhya-lila 20.263-4
4. Ibid., Madhya-lila 20.245-246
5. Ibid., Adi-lila 3.6
6. Ibid., Adi-lila 2.112
7. Ibid., Adi-lila 2.133-115

The Avatars of Lord Krishna 59

8. *Srimad-Bhagavatam* 1.3.5.purport
9. *Bhagavad-gita* 4.7-8
10. *Srimad-Bhagavatam* 10.86.45
11. *Caitanya-caritamrita,* Madhya-lila 20.352
12. *Srimad-Bhagavatam* 2.7.2.purport
13. *Caitanya-caritamrita,* Adi-lila 14, 18.purport
14. Ibid., Madhya-lila 20.354
15. Ibid., Adi-lila 3, 93-94
16. *Srimad-Bhagavatam* 10.14.37
17. Ibid., 10.14.55
18. Ibid., 10.40.16
19. Ibid., 3.2.7
20. *Caitanya-caritamrita,* Madhya-lila 20.382
21. *Srimad-Bhagavatam* 1.3.6
22. Ibid., 2.7.5
23. Ibid., 1.3.7 & 2.7.1
24. Ibid., 1.3.8
25. Ibid., 2.7.19
26. Ibid., 1.3.9
27. Ibid., 2.7.6
28. Ibid., 1.3.10
29. Ibid., 2.7.3
30. Ibid., 1.3.11 & 2.7.4
31. Ibid., 1.3.12
32. Ibid., 1.3.13 & 2.7.10
33. Ibid., 2.7.11
34. Ibid., 1.3.14
35. Ibid., 2.7.9
36. Ibid., 1.3.15 & 2.7.12
37. Ibid., 1.3.16
38. Ibid., 2.7.13
39. Ibid., 2.7.21
40. Ibid., 1.3.17
41. Ibid., 1.3.18 & 2.7.14
42. Ibid., 1.3.19 & 2.7.17-18
43. Ibid., 1.3.20 & 2.7.22
44. Ibid., 1.3.21 & 2.7.36
45. Ibid., 1.3.40-43
46. Ibid., 1.3.22
47. Ibid., 2.7.23-5
48. Ibid., 1.3.23 & 2.7.26

49. Ibid., 1.3.24 & 2.7.37
50. Ibid., 1.3.25 & 2.7.38
51. Ibid., 1.3.35, 37
52. Ibid., 1.3.38
53. Ibid., 1.3.5.purport &
    Caitanya-caritamrita, Madhya-lila   20, 319-328
54. *Bhagavad-gita* 8.17 & *Srimad-Bhagavatam*.3.11.20 &
    Vishnu Purana, Book One, Chapter Three, p.35
55. *Caitanya-caritamrita*, Adi-lila 3, 7-10 &
    Srimad-Bhagavatam 4.30.49 purport
56. *Srimad-Bhagavatam* 1.3.5.purport &
    Caitanya-caritamrita, Madhya-lila 20, 329-333
57. *Caitanya-caritamrita*, Madhya-lila 20, 334-347 &
    Srimad-Bhagavatam 11.5.32, 36 & 12.3.51-2
58. *Caitanya-caritamrita*, Madhya-lila   20.369-73

CHAPTER FOUR

Lord Vishnu

Lord Vishnu is the all-pervasive Lord who expands into everything. He is the maintainer of the universe and the complete cosmic creation. He is called Vishnu because He overcomes all.[1] He represents *sattva-guna*, or the mode of goodness by which everything is sustained. He is also called Narayana, which means the shelter, resting place or ultimate goal of all living entities. It also means the one whose abode is the causal waters (Garbhodakashayi Ocean), and one who lives in the hearts of all living beings. It is this *sattva* nature, in the mode of goodness, which gives the living beings the tendency to grow toward a higher truth, the light, a more cohesive and intense reality. In this sense, Lord Vishnu is also called Hari, or one who removes the darkness of illusion. This illusion ultimately means the false idea that the living beings live separate from, or without connection to, the Lord.

References to the glories of Lord Vishnu are found in such early books as the *Rig Veda*. Many of them are in relation to His form as Vamanadeva, the dwarf incarnation who begged for only three steps of land from Bali Maharaja, and with those three steps covered the whole universe. A few of these verses are as follows:

"The gods be gracious unto us even from the place whence Vishnu strode, through the seven regions of the earth. Through all this strode Vishnu; thrice His foot He planted, and the whole was gathered in His footstep's dust. Vishnu, the Guardian, He whom none deceiveth, made three steps; thenceforth establishing His high decrees. Look ye on Vishnu's works, whereby the Friend of Indra, close-allied, hath let His holy ways be seen. The princes evermore behold that loftiest place where Vishnu is, laid as it were an eye in heaven. This, Vishnu's station most sublime, the singers ever vigilant, lovers of holy song, light up." (*Rig Veda*, 1.22.16-21)

A similar reference to Lord Vishnu's abode and His pastime as Vamanadeva is found in the *Rig Veda* (1.154.1-5). A few of the verses read as follows: "Him whose three places that are filled with sweetness, imperishable joy as it may list them, Who verily alone upholds the threefold, the earth, the heaven, and all living creatures. May I attain to

A standing image of Lord Vishnu located above one of the outside entranceways of the Large Vishnu temple in Sri Rangam, India.

His well-loved mansion where men devoted to the Gods are happy. For there springs, close akin to the Wide-Strider, the well of meath in Vishnu's highest footstep."

Another quote that shows Lord Vishnu's superiority over the demigods reads like so: "Far-shining, widely famed, going Thy wonted way, fed with the oil, be helpful, Mitra-like, to us. So, Vishnu, even the wise must swell Thy song of praise, and he who hath oblations must pay thee solemn rites. He who brings gifts to Him, the Ancient and the Last, to Vishnu who ordains, together with His spouse [Lakshmi], who tells the lofty birth of Him, the Lofty One, shall verily surpass in glory even his peer... The Sovran Varuna and both the Asvins wait on this the will of Him who guides the Marut host. Vishnu hath power supreme and might that finds the day... "[2]

Lord Vishnu is often portrayed resting on the huge serpent of Sesha. We see that the thousand heads of Sesha are all turned inward, representing a tranquil mind, and looking toward the Absolute Truth of Lord Vishnu. Lord Vishnu is also seen in the yogic sleep called *yoga-nidra*. The *yoga-nidra* (yoga or the root *yuj* meaning to connect or join) is a cosmic sleep wherein the Lord is focused on the Infinite Reality of His own identity.

Lord Vishnu is also seen standing on the whirl of a lotus flower with four hands, which represent the four directions and indicates His absolute power in the four corners of the universe. Each hand holds an item, such as a disc, lotus, conch, and mace. Of the four items, the conch represents the five universal elements. When the conch is blown, it is said to produce a sound related to the original vibration of universal creation, or *om*. The Lord also blows His conch in calling everyone to turn to the higher reality rather than remaining in the darkness of material existence. This calling is the inner voice which nudges all beings of conscience to seek the Absolute Truth. If man does not heed the call, then the Lord may still use His conch to cut asunder the ego and material attachments of those who do not turn toward the spiritual path.

The disc or *chakra* signifies the universal mind or awareness.[3] It rids all darkness wherever it appears, and thus shows the path to higher awareness. The disc is called Sudarshan, the limitless power and light that destroys all forms of ignorance. Thus, Lord Vishnu allows it to cut off the heads of envious demons. It has six spokes and shows the revolving nature of the universe (*maya*) around an unmoving and changeless center. The Sudarshana Chakra, when shown alone, is often viewed as a person with four, eight, or sixteen arms, holding such items as a bow, arrow, trident, noose, and a poker. These are said to represent the will and power of the Lord to not only create but to also destroy the universe.

The mace represents the cosmic intellect or knowledge. It is called Kaumodaki, meaning that which captivates the mind. It is also associated with time, which destroys all, and is thus also related to Kali, the power of time.[4] When pictured as a deity, it is viewed as a female with two hands, positioned in respect. The lotus being twirled in His hand shows the revolving or changing nature of the universe.[5] It also indicates the real purpose of human existence, which the Lord invites all to follow.

The Vaijayanti garland (garland of victory) with five rows of flowers that the Lord wears indicates the five senses and the Lord's illusory power which affect the senses.[6] Its fragrance represents the subtle elements found within the material manifestation. All this reflects the Lord's mastery of the whole universe, which is created out of the mixing or revolving of the five elements and the universal mind and intellect. The Srivatsa or lock of hair on the Lord's chest, which indicates the Goddess of Fortune, represents the products of the material creation, or the objects of enjoyment for which all living beings seek.[7] And the gem worn on His chest, called Kaustubha (Treasure of the Ocean), represents the one who enjoys these products. Thus, this world of the enjoyer and the enjoyed is but a piece of decoration for the Lord, a spark of His energy.

Lord Vishnu is also sometimes seen with additional items, such as a bow, called Sharnga. This represents the darker form of false-ego that makes one think he is nothing but the material body, not connected to the Lord. The arrows are the activities of the intellect, which can cut through false-ego when used properly. His fish shaped earrings represent the two processes of knowledge, such as through the *sankhya* (intellectual) and yoga (intuitive) methods. His armlets represent the three goals of worldly life, namely *dharma* (righteousness), *artha* (economic success) and *kama* (pleasure). Lord Vishnu's crown represents the highest and incomprehensible reality. The yellow cloth that He wears (Pitambara) is said to indicate the *Vedas*. Through the Vedic hymns the divine reality is revealed, just as the Lord's dark color can be seen through the cloth that He wears. And His sacred string, made of three threads, is said to indicate the three letters of the hallowed word AUM.

The various forms of Lord Vishnu are composed of the different arrangements of the four symbols He holds in His four hands. For example, in one form He holds the conch in His lower right hand, the disc in His upper right, the mace in His upper left, and lotus in the lower left. In this form He has the name of Keshava, meaning the Lord with long hair, according to the *Padma Purana* (Book Four, Chapter 79). In other forms, in which case He holds the items in different hands, He has the names that include, Narayana (the universal shelter), Govinda (saver of the Earth and protector of cows), Madhava (Lord of knowledge), Madhusudana (the destroyer of the demon Madhu), Trivikrama (the one who conquered the three planetary systems), Vamana (the dwarf incarnation), Shridhara (the possessor of fortune), Hrishikesha (Lord and controller of the senses), Padmanabha (whose navel produced the universal lotus), Damodara (who is self-restrained), Sankarshana (who reabsorbs), Vasudeva (one who dwells within), Pradyumna (who has the most wealth), Aniruddha (who no one can oppose), Purushottama (best of all men), Adhoksaja (the expanse of the universe), Nrisimha (the half-man and half-lion form), Achyuta (the inconceivable), Krishna (the dark and all-attractive one), Hari (He who removes obstacles or the sorrow of illusion), Janardana (He who gives rewards), and Upendra (the brother of Indra). Many other names of Lord Vishnu are found in the *Vishnu-sahasranam*, the Thousand Names of Vishnu, located in the *Anushasan Parva* (149.14-120) of the *Mahabharata*.

Lord Vishnu is also called Nilameghashyama for having a dark blue complexion. This represents a number of things, including pure consciousness, the infinite, and the all-pervading power.

At other times Lord Vishnu is seen resting on the coils of the serpent Shesha, also called Ananta. Sheshanaga, also called Anantasesha, is the expansion of Lord Balarama, Lord Krishna's brother, and serves the Lord in this way as the Lord's support and paraphernalia. Shesha has a thousand heads swinging to and fro over the form of Lord Vishnu, creating a shelter and couch for the Lord. Ananta means endless, and Ananta is endlessly singing the praises and glories of the Lord from His thousand hoods without ever reaching the end. His hoods are also supporting the many planetary systems in the cosmic creation that are orbiting throughout the universe above His heads. Ananta also means endless in terms of the endlessness of cosmic time. This is also represented by His thousand hoods as divisions of time. The material worlds are created within the element of time, and are thus sustained by time. During the process of the universal annihilation, time ceases to exist, in which case the material planets are also forced into obliteration.

Lord Shesha is often seen floating on the causal waters of the Garbhodaka Ocean, which exists on the bottom of the universe. Lord Vishnu is thus resting on Sheshanaga as They float on the ocean. At other times, They are viewed floating on the Kshiramudra, or an ocean of white milk. This represents the Prakriti or the ingredients of the unmanifest material nature in its purest form.

Sometimes, Lord Vishnu is also seen riding on his carrier bird, Garuda. This is a half-man and half-eagle bird, whose name means "Wings of Speech." It is described that he is huge and has a fierce expression. His color is that of molten gold. He has the head of an eagle with a red beak and feathered wings, and two arms like a man.[8] Different divisions of the *Vedas* are parts of the body of Garuda. The sound of his wings reflect the utterances of the Vedic hymns, which can carry a person to another world with the speed of light and the power of lightning. Thus, it is also the sound of the *Veda* that carries Lord Vishnu, and which can also transport Him into the hearts and minds of people.

According to the *Puranas*, Garuda is a son of Kashyapa and Vinata, who was a daughter of Daksha.[9] He is also the younger brother of Aruna. Garuda is known for his dislike of snakes, which he will eat. One reason for this is explained in the *Mahabharata* (1.20-35). Vinata once quarreled with her co-wife, Kadru, who was the mother of the serpent species known as nagas. It was from her that he inherited this hostility toward snakes. Then Garuda, with his wife Unnati, produced six sons, from whom descended all the bird species that eat snakes.

LORD VISHNU IS AN EXPANSION OF LORD KRISHNA

Many people think that Lord Vishnu is the source of all other *avatars* or incarnations of God. This is true, but not in the case of Lord Krishna. Lord Krishna is actually the source of Lord Vishnu. When Lord Krishna descends into this world, He appears as Himself and not as an expansion of Lord Vishnu. To verify this, let me present the following details.

It is explained that for the maintenance of the universe Lord Krishna descends in the form of Lord Vishnu, who is His personal plenary expansion and the director of the mode of goodness. Thus, Lord Vishnu is above the influence of the material energy. However, being in the category of *svamsha* (another form of God with unlimited potencies), Vishnu's opulences are almost equal to Lord Krishna's. Yet Krishna is the original person and Vishnu is His personal expansion. This can be compared to one candle lighting the flame of another. The second burns separately in a different position, but its illumination is equal to the original candle. In the same way, Lord Krishna, the Supreme Personality, expands Himself into the different forms of Vishnu, who are equally bright and powerful.[10]

Furthermore, it is described that outside the boundaries of the unlimited spiritual Vaikuntha planets is the transcendental sky known as the Brahman effulgence. Beyond that and in a small corner of it is the Karana or Causal Ocean, which is also spiritual.[11] This is what surrounds the innumerable material universes. Lord Vishnu in His form as Karanadakashayi Vishnu, or Maha-Vishnu, lies on the Causal Ocean and creates the universes merely by glancing upon the material nature. Thus, Lord Krishna personally has nothing to do with the material creation, nor does He ever come in touch with the material energy. He remains absorbed and unaffected in Goloka Vrindavan, the highest planet in the spiritual sky. The material energy never comes in contact with the spiritual world, nor even the Causal Ocean, as explained in the *Srimad-Bhagavatam* (11.22.17):

"In the beginning of creation nature assumes, by the modes of goodness, passion and ignorance, its form as the embodiment of all subtle causes and gross manifestations within the universe. The Supreme Personality of Godhead does not enter the interaction of material manifestation but merely glances upon nature. As the material elements, headed by the *mahat-tattva*, are transformed, they receive their specific potencies from the glance of the Supreme Lord, and being amalgamated by the power of nature, they create the universal egg."

Before the *mahat-tattva*, however, there is the *pradhana*, which is the sum total of all material energy in its subtle and undifferentiated stage. Material nature is always existing in its subtle form as the energy of the Lord. Sometimes, under the direction of the Supreme, it manifests its temporary existence in the form of the material cosmos.

In spite of the fact that everything comes from the Supreme Being, He is still aloof from it all. He does not disengage Himself from His eternal pleasure pastimes with His devotees in the spiritual realm. So, in the process of creating the material worlds, the Supreme expands Himself into various forms, which are His plenary parts. Krishna is the primeval Lord, the original Personality of Godhead, so if He wants He can expand Himself into unlimited forms with all potencies. They are no different from Him, but may exhibit differences in form.

It is explained that Lord Krishna first expands Himself into Baladeva, or Balarama, who is considered Krishna's second body and brother. Balarama assists in Lord Krishna's innumerable spiritual pastimes in both the spiritual and material realms.

Lord Balarama is also Lord Sankarshana, the predominator of

the creative energy. He creates and is the shelter of the material and spiritual worlds. By the will of Krishna and the power of the spiritual energy, Lord Balarama creates the spiritual world, which consists of the planet Goloka Vrindavana and the Vaikuntha planets.[12] Lord Balarama especially assists Lord Krishna in the creation of the material worlds. After Balarama has expanded Himself into Lord Maha-Sankarshana, He expands Himself into four different forms, including: 1) Karanadakashayi Vishnu [Maha-Vishnu], 2) Garbhodakashayi Vishnu [the expansion in each universe], 3) Kshirodakashayi Vishnu [the Supersoul in each individual], and 4) Sesha, also called Seshanaga. These first four plenary portions assist in the material cosmic manifestation. Sesha is Balarama's form who assists in the Lord's personal service. He is also called Ananta, meaning unlimited, because He assists the Lord in His unlimited variety of pastimes.[13]

All expansions of the Lord begin with Sri Krishna. For His pastimes in one of the highest levels of the spiritual realm, called Dvaraka, Sri Krishna expands Himself into Balarama, who then expands Himself into Pradyumna and Aniruddha. These four (Krishna, Balarama, Pradyumna, and Aniruddha) expand into a second quadruple which is present in the unlimited Vaikuntha planets of the spiritual sky. The second quadruple is known as Vasudeva, Sankarshana, Pradyumna, and Aniruddha. They are changeless, transcendental expansions of the Supreme Lord, Krishna. In this second quadruple, Vasudeva is an expansion of Krishna, and Sankarshana is a representation of Balarama.

Therefore, the center of the spiritual domain is Goloka Vrindavana, Lord Krishna's personal abode which is shaped like a huge lotus, where simple but deep loving devotion is the means of all spiritual relations. This is surrounded by the spiritual realm of Dwaraka, which is based on more opulent relations. Then, throughout the rest of the unlimited and effulgent spiritual sky are the spiritual Vaikuntha planets which are the residences of all the different forms of Krishna in His four-armed Vishnu expansions.

In the Vaikuntha sky there is the pure, spiritual creative energy called *Shuddha-sattva* that sustains all of the spiritual planets with the full opulences of knowledge, wealth, power, beauty, etc., all of which pervade the entire spiritual kingdom and are fully enjoyed by the residents there. This energy is but a display of the creative potencies of Balarama, Maha-Sankarshana. It is also this Sankarshana who is the original cause of the Causal Ocean where Karanodakashayi Vishnu (Maha-Vishnu) sleeps, while breathing out the seeds of innumerable universes. When the cosmic creation is annihilated, all of the materially conditioned, although indestructible, living entities merge back into the body of Maha-Vishnu where they rest until the time of the next creation. So, Balarama as Sankarshana is the origin of Maha-Vishnu, from who originates all of the potencies of the material manifestation.[14]

Therefore, to summarize, for His spiritual pastimes in the Vaikuntha realm, Lord Krishna has four original expansions, namely Vasudeva, Sankarshana, Pradyumna, and Aniruddha. Maha-Vishnu is an expansion of Sankarshana; Garbhodakashayi Vishnu is an expansion of Pradyumna; and Kshirodakashayi Vishnu is an expansion of Aniruddha.[15] These expansions are the basis of the whole cosmic creation, while Lord Krishna Himself remains in His own abode of Goloka Vrindavana, unless He personally descends into the material realm to display the attractiveness of His pastimes and the spiritual world to the materially conditioned souls.

THE FUNCTIONS OF LORD VISHNU

To begin explaining the purpose and function of these Vishnu expansions, the *Srimad-Bhagavatam* (2.6.42) describes that, "Maha-Vishnu (Karanadakashayi Vishnu) is the first incarnation of the Supreme Lord in the process of creating the material worlds. He is the master of eternal time, space, cause and effects, mind, elements, material ego, the modes of nature, senses, the universal form of the Lord (Garbhodakashayi Vishnu) and the sum total of all living beings, both moving and nonmoving."

It is further explained that Maha-Vishnu, who appears in the Karana Ocean and is an *avatar* of Lord Sankarshana, becomes the resting place of the *jiva-shakti*.[16] This is the collective energy of all the individual spirit souls, the *jivatmas*. "There is one marginal potency, known as the *jiva*. Maha-Sankarshana is the shelter of all *jivas*."[17] It is this Sankarshana who is the original source of all living entities because they are expansions of His marginal potency. Some become conditioned by the material energy while others are under the protection of the spiritual nature.[18]

Lord Maha-Vishnu is the source of thousands of *avatars* in His thousands and thousands of subjective portions or expansions. He is also the creator or source of countless individual souls. He is also known by the name of Narayana, meaning the shelter of all the individual *jiva* souls. From Him springs forth the vast expanse of water known as the spiritual Causal Ocean wherein the material creation takes place. Maha-

Vishnu then reclines in the waters of the Causal Ocean in a state of divine sleep, called *yoga-nidra*. Thus, it is said that the universal creation is but the dream of Maha-Vishnu.[19]

Then Maha-Vishnu lies down in the Causal Ocean, also called the Viraja River, which is the border between the spiritual and material worlds.[20]

Since the water of the Causal Ocean, known as the Karana Ocean, come from the body of Maha-Vishnu, it is completely spiritual. The sacred Ganga (Ganges River) is but a drop from that ocean, which has entered this universe and can purify the fallen souls.[21]

It is Lord Balarama who expands into the great serpent known as Ananta, or Seshanaga. He reposes on the Causal Ocean and serves as the couch upon whom Lord Maha-Vishnu reclines.[22] That Ananta-Sesha is the devotee incarnation of God who knows nothing but service to Lord Krishna. With His thousands of mouths He always sings the endless glories of Lord Krishna. He also expands Himself to serve as Lord Krishna's paraphernalia, including such items as the umbrella, slippers, bedding, pillow, garments, resting chair, residence, sacred *gayatri* thread, and His throne in the pastimes of Lord Krishna. Thus, He has attained and exhibits the ultimate end of servitude to Lord Krishna.[23]

At the time of creation, after the Supreme has been sleeping for some time, the first emanations from the breathing of Lord Maha-Vishnu are the personified *Vedas* who serve Him by waking Him from His mystic sleep. They begin to enthusiastically sing His glories, pastimes, and praises, just as a King is awoken in the morning by poets who recite his heroic deeds.[24] This shows the eternal nature of the Vedic literature. They are not merely the writings of men, but they are *shabda-brahma*, or eternal spiritual vibrations that exist before and after the material creation, and which emanate from the Supreme Lord.

In the *Srimad-Bhagavatam* (10.87.50) when the personified *Vedas* are offering their prayers to Lord Narayana [Maha-Vishnu], they relate His all-powerful position. "He is the Lord who eternally watches over this universe, who exists before, during and after its manifestation. He is the master of both the unmanifest material energy and the spirit soul. After sending forth the creation He enters within it, accompanying each living entity. There He creates the material bodies and then remains as their regulator. By surrendering to Him one can escape the embrace of illusion, just as a dreaming person forgets his own body. One who wants liberation from fear should constantly meditate upon Him, Lord Hari, who is always on the platform of perfection and thus never subject to material birth."

Once the Lord is awoken, He casts His glance upon the material energy of *maya*. This glance is how the Supreme impregnates material nature with all the original seeds of the living beings. Thus, the Lord does not personally touch the material energy, but by His functional expansion He places the living entities into the material nature by His glance. Then *maya*, the material nature, becomes agitated.[25] This functional expansion of the Lord then takes the form as Shiva, known in this activity as Shambhu. It is Shambhu who carries the living entities in the glance of the Lord into the material energy.

So, the Supreme Being in His feature as Maha-Vishnu impregnates the material nature by His glance [Shambhu]. Through this glance, which is the impregnation of consciousness, and by the influence of the time element, the innumerable living beings appear.[26] The Supreme Being then, out of His own body, sowed the seeds of universal manifestation within the *mahat-tattva*.[27] [The *mahat-tattva* is the essential seeds of the material ingredients in their undesignated form, and it is into that in which the living beings are injected by the glance of Maha-Vishnu.] In this way, the Lord, who is the controller of all energies, by His own potency creates eternal time, the fate of all living entities, and their particular nature [by which they become active within the newly formed cosmic creation]. At the end of the cosmic creation He again merges them back into Him.[28]

The *Srimad-Bhagavatam* (11.9.16-18) relates that the Lord of the universe, Narayana, Maha-Vishnu, is the worshipable Lord of all beings. With no other assistance, the Lord creates the universe by His own potency, and at the time of annihilation He destroys the universe through His expansion of time. At that time He withdraws the complete universe and all materially conditioned living beings back into Himself. In this way, His unlimited Self is the shelter and reservoir of all potencies. The Lord stands alone after the universal annihilation. He is the supreme worshipable object for all beings, such as liberated souls, demigods, and ordinary conditioned souls. He is eternally free from the material energy and constitutes the totality of spiritual bliss, which a person can experience by seeing the Lord's spiritual form. In this way, the Lord exhibits the full meaning of liberation.

The countless souls that appear within the material energy in the variegated species of life are all spiritual in their essential nature, they are all spiritual beings. However, they can also become deluded by the material energy. When they are thus deluded, they hanker for material activities and attractions. In order to accommodate this, the Supreme provides this material world as a playground in which they can work out their material desires. This means that regardless of species, whether it is Lord Brahma, or humans, animals, birds, or even tiny insects, material nature is the mother and the Supreme Lord is the seed-giving, universal Father.

After agitating material nature into three qualities, which are the modes of nature in the form of passion, goodness and ignorance, they become active and material nature begins to give birth to the total material energy known as the *hiranya-mahat-tattva*. This is the sum total of cosmic intelligence. Thus, material nature becomes agitated by the destinations of the conditioned souls as determined by the influence of the modes of nature.[29] Simply by the glance of Maha-Vishnu consciousness is created, which is known as the *mahat-tattva*. The predominating deity of the *mahat-tattva* is Lord Vasudeva, another expansion of Lord Krishna. This explains how the material energy is like the mother of the living beings while the Lord is the Supreme Father of everyone. Just as a woman cannot give birth without the contact of a man, or at least his seed, so material nature cannot create without the contact of the Supreme Being.

So, as it is continued to be described, first the total material energy is manifest, and from this arises the three types of egotism, which are the original sources of all the demigods [the minor controlling deities], the senses, and material elements. By combining the different elements, the Supreme Lord creates all of the unlimited universes. Once the material elements have been manifested, and the full potential for creating the universes has been established, the innumerable universes begin to emanate from the pores of the body of Maha-Vishnu, and from His exhalations. They appear just like atomic particles that float in sunshine and pass through a screen. When Maha-Vishnu inhales at the time of the universal annihilation, they return to His body. In this way, Maha-Vishnu is the Supersoul of all the universes.[30]

Brahma, the demigods, and each universe remain alive for the duration of one of His exhalations.[31] However, there is no limit to the exhalations of Maha-Vishnu.[32]

Garbhodakashayi Vishnu, who is known within the universe as Hiranyagarbha and Antaryami, the Supersoul, is glorified in the Vedic hymns. He is the master of each and every universe and shelter of the external or material energy. However, being transcendental, He is completely beyond the touch of the external energy.

Next is the third expansion of Vishnu, called Kshirodakashayi Vishnu, who is the incarnation of the quality of goodness. He is the universal form of the Lord and expands Himself as the Supersoul within

Lord Vishnu 73

A typical print of Lord Vishnu in His expansion as Garbhodakashayi Vishnu who expands into each universe, laying on the Sheshanaga serpent on the Garbhodaka Ocean, being served by Goddess Lakshmi, with the lotus sprouting from His navel, the top of which is where Lord Brahma appears to continue with the creation of the universe. The stem of the lotus holds the ingredients for the creation of the planetary systems that fill the universe.

every living entity. He is known as Kshirodakashayi Vishnu because He lies on the ocean of milk (*kshira*) on the island of Svetadvipa. These are the three expansions of Lord Vishnu who oversee and make the creation of the material worlds possible.[33]

Before the creation within the universe takes place and after the Lord enters the universe, there is a period of non-activity for one thousand celestial years. All of the living entities that have been injected into the *mahat-tattva* are divided among all the universes along with each expansion of Garbhodakashayi Vishnu, and all of them are as if dormant in the Lord until the birth of Lord Brahma. From Brahma all other demigods and living entities are born.[34]

Once all of the universes are created, which are unlimited, Maha-Vishnu expands Himself into unlimited forms and enters each universe as Garbhodakashayi Vishnu. Once He is in each universe, He sees that there is no place to reside. Then, after some consideration, He fills half of the universe with water from His own perspiration.[35]

On that water He creates his own residence as an expansion of Vaikuntha and rests in the waters on the bed of the great serpent, Lord Ananta, Seshanaga.[36] Although He appears to be in slumber, enjoying transcendental bliss in his internal potency, His eyes are slightly open. When He is ready to begin the act of creation, a golden lotus springs from his navel that becomes the birthplace of Lord Brahma. Within the stem of that lotus are the fourteen planetary systems.[37] Then Lord Brahma is manifested as described in the chapter on Brahma.

Not only do the creations and annihilations of the cosmos go on continually, but the maintenance of the universe also takes constant supervision. It is explained that as long as the Supreme Being as Maha-Vishnu continues to glance upon nature, the material world continues to exist. Thus, the variegated flow of universal creation perpetually manifests through procreation.[38] So, we can see that time and nature have no power to act independently, but are under the supervision of the Supreme.

However, it is also described that it is not only the material nature that is maintained, everyone in it is also given the ability to act and function through the power of the Supreme in His form as the Supersoul. He creates the entire variegated universe and then enters into it as the Supersoul. Through this means He provides the life force and consciousness of everyone, and, thus, maintains the creation. As Sri Krishna further explains, "As the mighty wind, blowing everywhere, always rests in ethereal space, know that in the same manner all beings rest in Me."[39] As the Supersoul, He also enters into each planet, and by

His energy they maintain their orbits.[40] Thus, the Lord's energy enters each universe, each planet, every living being, and even each atom, by which everything is appropriately manifested and maintained. Without this, everything would revert back to chaos and deterioration.

Another way that the Lord maintains the universe is by personally appearing within it, or by manifesting His plenary expansions. The scriptures proclaim that Lord Krishna descends to take away the burden of the earth. However, it is Krishna's expansion as Lord Vishnu who primarily engages in maintaining this universe. It is Lord Vishnu who makes the adjustments for the proper administration of the cosmic creation. When Lord Krishna personally appears, His primary mission is to simply display His transcendental pastimes and attract the conditioned souls for going back to the spiritual domain. However, since Lord Krishna is the source of all *avatars* and expansions of the Supreme, all other incarnations and forms of the Divine combine together within Him when He descends. In this way, all other *lila* or pastime incarnations, the *yuga-avatars*, the *manvantara avatars*, and as many other incarnations as there are, even Lord Vishnu, all descend into the body of Sri Krishna when He appears. Thus, He is the complete Supreme Personality and can do whatever He likes to exhibit His power and maintain the universe when He descends.[41]

The Supreme Being also sets up the universal demigods to continue overseeing the maintenance of the universe. For example, it is explained that Indra, after receiving benediction from the Supreme Lord, maintains the living beings by pouring sufficient rains all over the planets. Furthermore, in every *yuga*, the Supreme Lord assumes the form of Siddhas, such as Sanaka-kumara, to preach transcendental knowledge for the well-being of everyone. He also assumes the form of great saintly persons such as Yajnavalkya to teach the way of karma. He assumes the form of great souls, such as Dattatreya, to teach the system of mystic yoga. In the form of Prajapati Marici, the Supreme creates progeny; becoming the king, He kills rogues and thieves; and in the form of time, He annihilates everything. All of the different qualities of material existence are aspects and a display of the energy of the Supreme Absolute Truth.[42]

So, because of the benediction and power given by the Supreme to the demigods, they can provide the living beings with all necessities. However, Lord Krishna explains in the *Bhagavad-gita* (3.14-15) that all living entities subsist on food grains, which are produced from rains, which is manifest through the performance of spiritual activities prescribed in the spiritual writings of the Vedic scripture and the teachings of the Lord and great sages. Consequently, the all-pervading Transcendence is eternally situated in acts of sacrifice.

This is all a part of the process of how the Lord and His expansions of Vishnu maintain the world. As mankind engages in acts of sacrifice or spirituality, which simply means the worship, meditation and thoughts of the Supreme, the Lord and the demigods are automatically satisfied to supply everyone with all necessities of life. In this way, there can be proper cooperation between man, nature and God so that everyone can be peaceful and content with the facilities for living in this world.

CHAPTER NOTES
1. *Mahabharata*, 5.70.13
2. *Rig-veda* 1.156.1,2-4
3. *Vishnu Purana* 1.22.68
4. *Krishna Upanishad* 23
5. *Gopala-uttaratapini Upanishad* 55-57
6. *Vishnu Purana* 1.22.72
7. Ibid., 1.22.69
8. *Parameshvara Samhita* 6.269. 276-77
9. *Mahabharata* 1.32
10. *Caitanya-caritamrita*, Madhya-lila, 20.314-15 & *Brahma-samhita* 5.46
11. *Caitanya-caritamrita*, Adi-lila, 5.51
12. Ibid., Madhya-lila, 20.255-6
13. Ibid., Adi-lila, 5.4-6, 8-11
14. Ibid., Adi-lila, 5.41 & pur.
15. Ibid., Adi-lila, 2.56, pur.
16. *Jaiva Dharma*, Chapter 15, page 74
17. *Caitanya-caritamrita*, Adi-lila, 5.45
18. Ibid., Adi-lila, 2.36, pur.
19. *Brahma-samhita* 5.11-12
20. *Caitanya-caritamrita*, Madhya-lila, 20.268-271
21. Ibid., Adi-lila, 5.54
22. *Brahma-samhita* 5.47
23. *Caitanya-caritamrita*, Madhya-lila, 5.120-124
24. *Srimad-Bhagavatam* 10.87.12-13
25. *Caitanya-caritamrita*, Madhya-lila, 20.272
26. *Srimad-Bhagavatam* 3.5.26
27. Ibid., 3.5.27
28. Ibid., 2.5.21
29. Ibid., 3.26.19

30. *Caitanya-caritamrita*, Madhya-lila, 20.275-282
31. *Brahma-samhita* 5.48
32. *Caitanya-caritamrita*, Madhya-lila, 20.324
33. Ibid., Madhya-lila, 20.292, 294-5
34. *Srimad-Bhagavatam*, 3.6.6, pur.
35. *Caitanya-caritamrita*, Madhya-lila, 20.284-6
36. Ibid., Adi-lila, 5.95-101
37. Ibid., Adi-lila, 5.102-3
38. *Srimad-Bhagavatam* 11.24.20
39. *Bhagavad-gita* 9.6
40. Ibid., 15.13
41. *Caitanya-caritamrita*, Adi-lila, 4.8-11, 13
42. *Srimad-Bhagavatam* 8.14.7-9

CHAPTER FIVE

Lord Brahma

Lord Brahma represents the mode of *rajas*, passion, in which the propensity for creation is found. It is from Brahma that all forms of space, names, and forms manifest. Brahma also produced Sarasvati, the goddess of learning and knowledge. Brahma represents the essence of the *Vedas*, and Sarasvati represents their meaning. Thus, all knowledge and wisdom, in their manifest form, comes from them, after, of course, Brahma first received it from Lord Vishnu. Brahma is also wedded to Sarasvati because he must possess that spiritual understanding by which he is enabled to create.

Brahma is often pictured with four heads, each facing in one of the four directions. They are often seen with eyes closed in meditation. They represent several things, first of which is the four *Vedas*. They also represent the four *yugas* (divisions of the ages, namely Satya, Treta, Dvapara, and Kali-yuga). Brahma also has four arms, which indicate the mind, intellect, ego, and conditioned awareness. They are shown holding *japa mala* (rosary beads), a *kurcha* (a brush of *kusha* grass), *kamandalu* (a water pot), and a *pushtaka* (a book or four books), and sometimes, according to the image, a ladle and spoon. The rosary represents the passing of time, which Brahma controls, and the water pot represents the causal waters from which the creation has sprung and upon which it rests. The *kusha* grass, as well as the ladle and spoon, represent the Vedic process of sacrifice by which the living entities are properly sustained. The books represent knowledge or the four *Vedas*, of which he gives all forms of knowledge to the living beings. His hand gestures show the giving of blessings and granting protection.

He is also seen most often standing or sitting on a lotus, which comes from the navel of Vishnu. Or he is seen sitting on his carrier, a swan (*hamsa*), which is a symbol of knowledge. This also signifies that he moves about with the unique facility that a swan possesses. As a swan is said to be able to separate the milk when mixed with water, Brahma, as a being of higher awareness, can detect the one Supreme Reality that exists in the cosmic creation. Sometimes he is seen riding a chariot as it

Lord Brahma

is being pulled by seven swans, which signify the seven worlds or planetary systems. He often has a reddish complexion and usually has a beard, signifying the maturity of life.

Lord Brahma is the secondary creator after Lord Vishnu. He sits on a lotus flower that is rooted in the abdomen of Maha-Vishnu. Thus, Brahma is fixed in the Infinite Reality. Lord Brahma is manifested from Lord Vishnu to assist in the secondary process of the universal creation. Yet, this process of creation is described a little differently in various *Puranas*. This does not mean that they contradict each other. The pattern of creation can and does change as many as 25 different ways in the order of events that unfold in various *kalpas* or days of Brahma.[1] It changes depending on the different states of mind and consciousness Brahma enters as he creates the subsequent species, which may differ from one *kalpa* to the next.

Lord Brahma's other names include Hiranyagarbha (the golden embryo) and Prajapati (the progenitor). He is also called Svayambhu (self-born), Pitamaha (great patriarch), Adikavi (the first-seer), Lokesha (master of the world), Drughana (the undivided impulse), Nabhija (navel-born), and Abjaja (lotus born). He is sometimes called Visvakarma, who is the architect of the demigods or the universal architect, and who is an aspect of Lord Brahma.

Brahma is considered a universal creator, and thus is not a god of liberation or of material and heavenly facility. Therefore, he is not viewed as a god for much worship. And as we can see, there are very few Brahma temples in the world. However, in most major Vishnu or Shiva temples, there will be a shrine or an image of Brahma usually on the north wall, which is offered some daily worship.

There is one tale which explains why Lord Brahma is not worshiped much on Earth. Shortly after the creation of the universe, Brahma was sent to find the end of the *linga* of light, a shaft of light that extended from the top to bottom of the universe. Though he did not find it, he lied that he did. So, Lord Shiva cursed him that he would not be worshiped on Earth. However, in some of the *Puranas*, we do find that the demigods who act in accordance with universal management do offer prayers to Brahma.

Another reason why he is not so often worshiped in India is that the idea of creation of new thoughts is unwanted for a person who is trying to become spiritually advanced. The creation of thoughts, or in other words an uncontrolled mind that drags one deeper into material desires, is what helps veil the Absolute Truth from the seeker. The idea is that the seeker must control thoughts and the mind, or even rid oneself of unwanted desires, and maintain that mental state until the higher Truth is revealed. For this reason, Shiva and Vishnu are worshiped in preference to Brahma.

BRAHMA'S MAIN FUNCTION

Lord Brahma plays the part of manifesting the cosmic creation in the secondary phase of the creative process, after the first phase when Lord Vishnu manifests the material universes and ingredients. There are nine types or categories of creation that are described in the *Puranas*, and they are divided into two parts, primary and secondary. The primary part of creation is the *Prakrita-Sarga*, or the natural creation that comes about due to the interaction of the modes of material nature and the time element. The order of the *Prakrita-Sarga* generally begins with the manifestation of the *mahat-tattva*, or the seeds of the sum total of the material ingredients in its subtle form along with time. Due to the presence of the Supreme Lord, Maha-Vishnu, the modes of nature begin to interact. In the second stage of creation, the false ego is generated in which the material ingredients along with material knowledge and activities arise. In the third stage of creation, the elements, such as ether, air, fire, water, and earth, are generated along with the objects of the senses, such as what is seen, heard, tasted, touched, and smelled. In the fourth stage is the creation of knowledge and working capacity, or the working senses.[2]

In the fifth stage of creation, by the interaction with the mode of goodness, there is the manifestation of the controlling deities (*devas*), or what could be called the universal departmental managers. In the sixth stage of creation is the manifestation of ignorance or the principle of forgetfulness, which causes the conditioned souls to be bewildered as to what they really are, which is why they remain in illusion or darkness.[3] The five types of darkness are *tamasa* (ignorance), *moha* (delusion), *mahamoha* (great delusion), *andha-tamisra* (blinding darkness), and *avidya* (nescience).[4]

Now we come to the secondary part of creation, called the *Vaikrita-Sarga*, the creation from Lord Brahma. This is the process of creation that manifests not simply by the mixing of the modes of nature and various material ingredients, but directly by the superior power or guidance of Lord Brahma. All of the innumerable forms and types of bodies that manifest are for accommodating the different levels of consciousness of the living beings in the universe. These many forms are created out of the different levels of consciousness experienced by Lord Brahma through his creative meditation. He is able to create simply by the power of his mind. This is an example of how thoughts are actually things. They are vibrations that can produce effects. And when you have a mind as strong as Lord Brahma's, such thoughts will manifest forms. Thus, by his accepting different states of mind, material bodies were manifested that would accommodate the appropriate states of being of the innumerable living entities.

First from Brahma is the creation of all immovable objects and entities, called the seventh stage of the creative process. The eighth stage of creation involves the manifestation of the lower species of life. The ninth creative stage is that of the humans. The creation of the varieties of demigods, and those beings living in the astral planes, are considered the tenth level of creation. Finally, the appearance of the Kumaras is considered to be part of both the natural or primary creation and the secondary creation from Lord Brahma.[5]

HOW BRAHMA IS MANIFESTED FROM LORD VISHNU

As described in the Vedic texts, when the Lord as Maha-Vishnu expands Himself and enters each and every universe, He becomes known as Garbhodakashayi Vishnu, or Hiranyagarbha. He then expands further into the form known as Antaryami, the Supersoul. It is this Lord who is glorified by Vedic hymns. He is the master of each universe and the shelter of the external or material energy, although He remains beyond the touch of this energy.[6]

Before the universal creation takes place and after the Lord enters the universe, there is a period of non-activity for one thousand celestial years. All of the living entities that are injected into the *mahat-tattva* by Maha-Vishnu are divided among all the universes along with each of His expansions known as Garbhodakashayi Vishnu. All of these *jivas* or spirit souls remain as if dormant in the Lord until the birth of Lord Brahma. From Brahma all other demigods and living entities are born.[7]

Entering the universe, Lord Garbhodakashayi Vishnu finds only darkness with no place to reside. Thus, He considers what to do next. He then creates the waters of the Garbhodaka Ocean from the perspiration of His own body and fills half the universe. On that water He creates his own residence as an expansion of Vaikuntha and rests in the waters on the bed of the great serpent, Lord Ananta, Seshanaga.[8] Although He appears to be in slumber, enjoying transcendental bliss in his internal potency, His eyes are slightly open. When He is ready to begin the act of creation, a golden lotus springs from his navel which becomes the birthplace of Lord Brahma. Within the stem of that lotus are the ingredients that develop into the fourteen planetary systems.[9]

This is similarly described elsewhere as follows: Once Lord Vishnu desires to begin the act of creation, on which the Lord's attention is fixed, the subtle form of creation pierces through His abdomen, agitated by the material mode of passion. Then a golden lotus springs from His navel as He floats on the Garbhodaka Ocean. The lotus, called Brahmaloka or Satyaloka, becomes the abode of Lord Brahma. The golden color of the lotus represents the dim reflection of pure consciousness.[10] The lotus is the gigantic universal form of the Lord in the material world. This universal form becomes absorbed in Lord Vishnu at the time of dissolution and again reappears during creation. It is this lotus that contains the sum total of all fruitive activities of the conditioned living beings, the first of which is Lord Brahma who is generated in that lotus. It is also the seed from which all creation springs at the time of manifestation.

If the manifestation of this lotus is after a previous devastation, the golden lotus illuminates everything and dries up the waters of devastation. Then Lord Vishnu personally enters that universal lotus flower as the Supersoul. When it is thus impregnated with all the modes of material nature, the personality of Vedic wisdom, Lord Brahma, whom we call the self-born, is generated.[11]

In this way, the divine lotus became the birthplace of Lord Brahma who is well versed in the *Vedas*. The lotus is also spiritually related with all souls in the universe, the stem of which is where the fourteen planetary systems of the universe are generated.[12]

Although generally a *jiva* soul is given the position of the demigod Lord Brahma, if there is no such being suitable to occupy the post, then the Supreme Being again expands Himself to become Lord Brahma.[13]

Lord Vishnu maintains the universe, and through His form of Brahma He creates the functional universe, and in His form as Rudra [Lord Shiva] He brings about the destruction of the cosmic creation. Thus, only by the will of the Supreme is there creation, maintenance and dissolution of the complete cosmic creation, which are under the charge of these three personalities.[14]

The difference is that Lord Krishna expands Himself into His personal plenary form of Vishnu for the maintenance of the universe.

This is like the flame of one candle being used to light another candle. However, the second candle is as powerful as the first. Being the director of the mode of goodness, Vishnu is transcendental to the material energy. However, Lord Vishnu's opulences and potencies are not quite but almost equal to Krishna's.[15]

Regarding Lord Shiva, he is an assumed form of the Supreme Being, Vishnu, just as yogurt is a changed form of milk. Lord Vishnu assumes the form of Shiva for the special purpose of material transactions.[16] Lord Shiva is an associate of the external energy, the three modes of material nature. Therefore, he is absorbed in the material quality of darkness and the element of egotism. Lord Vishnu is transcendental to *maya* and her qualities, thus He is the Supreme Personality. The truth is that Lord Brahma and Lord Shiva are devotee incarnations who carry out the orders of the Supreme.[17]

Although Brahma lives for many millions of years, he lives only within the duration of one of the breaths of Maha-Vishnu. Such a lifetime is calculated to be equal to one *nimesha*, less than a second, for the Supreme Lord Maha-Vishnu.[18]

BRAHMA AND THE DAWN OF CREATION

The *Vishnu Purana* (Book One, Chapter Two) and the *Agni Purana* (17.2) explain that at the very beginning of creation there was neither day nor night, nor sky nor earth, nor darkness, nor light, nor any other things save only the One, Supreme, unapprehensible by intellect, along with Brahma, spirit, and the subtle energy of matter and time.

Although situated in the whorl of the lotus in which he was born, Brahma could not see the world. Therefore, he circumambulated all of space, and while moving his eyes in the four directions, he achieved four heads. Brahma could not understand anything about the creation, the lotus upon which he sat, nor himself. Then the air of devastation began to move the Garbhodaka Ocean, the water below him, and the lotus in great circles. Brahma began to wonder who he was, and how he came to be situated on top of the lotus. From where did it sprout, and what is the source that must be within the water? Brahma then entered the stem of the lotus, but try as he might he could not trace out the source. While searching in this way, Brahma realized his mortality and felt the fear of death in his mind. Then he retired to the lotus and simply contemplated on the Supreme in order to understand the ultimate cause of his existence.[19]

While thus engaged in thinking, Brahma twice heard two syllables of instruction from nearby. These syllables formed the word *tapa*, which means penance for spiritual realization. When he heard that sound, he searched all around but could find no speaker. So, he thought it best to sit down and attend to the performance of penance as he was told.[20]

Brahma then engaged in meditation until finally he had the required knowledge to see what he could not see before, which was the Supreme Being in his own heart.[21]

So, this is a great lesson. No one, not even the greatest of beings, can realize who they are by speculative knowledge, or by analyzing the surroundings in the universe. Only by the proper meditation and devotional surrender will the Supreme Being reveal Himself to us, by which we can understand who we are and our purpose in this material world.

The *Brahma-samhita* (5.23-26) also explains how Brahma, coming out of the lotus and being guided by divine potency, turned his mind to the act of creation under the impulse of impressions he had from previous lifetimes. [This also indicates that Lord Brahma is generally a powerful living being who is capable of the job, but when such a being is not available, Lord Vishnu takes up the position Himself.] Thus, he began to recall his purpose. However, he could see nothing but darkness in all directions and thus still felt confused. Then the goddess of learning, Sarasvati, the divine consort to the Supreme Lord, gave Brahma the *kama-bija* mantra: *Klim krishnaya govindaya gopi-jana-vallabhaya svaha*. She told him that he should practice spiritual association by means of this mantra to fulfill his heart's desires. Thereafter, he meditated by using this mantra, and by focusing his mind in this way: "There exists a divine lotus of a thousand petals, augmented by millions of filaments, in the transcendental land of Goloka. On its whorl, there exists a great divine throne on which is seated Sri Krishna, the form of eternal effulgence of transcendental bliss, playing on His divine flute resonant with the divine sound, with His lotus mouth. He is worshiped by His amorous milkmaids with their respective subjective portions and extensions and also by His external energy [meaning Durga, who stays outside the spiritual realm] embodying all mundane qualities."

Then the Gayatri mantra, mother of the *Vedas*, was imparted to Brahma from the sound of Sri Krishna's flute. Having been initiated with the Gayatri from the Supreme Being Himself, Brahma attained the status of twice-born, or having a spiritual birth. This was through the realization of the transcendental pastimes of Sri Krishna through the use

Lord Brahma

of the *kama-gayatri*. This is the highest Gayatri of all because it contains a meditation and prayer of the perfectly spiritual and sportive activities of Lord Krishna that are not found in other gayatris. The *kama-gayatri* is: *Klim kama-devaya vidmahe pushpa-banaya dhimahi tan no 'nangah prachodayat.*[22]

Enlightened by the recollection of that Gayatri, which embodies the three *Vedas*, Brahma became acquainted with the vast ocean of Truth. Then he worshiped Lord Krishna, the essence of all Vedic knowledge, with the hymn that makes up the major portion of the *Brahma-samhita*,[23] called the Govinda Prayers.

Being very much pleased with Lord Brahma because of his nondeceptive penance in bhakti-yoga, the Supreme Being, Lord Vishnu, presented His eternal and transcendental form to him.[24]

Thereafter, Brahma could see the gigantic lotus-like bedstead, which was the body of Seshanaga, on which the Personality of Lord Vishnu was lying alone. The rays of the jewels bedecking the body of Seshanaga dissipated the darkness of those regions. Lord Vishnu's unlimited spiritual body occupied the space of the upper, middle and lower planetary systems. He was self-effulgent and beautifully dressed and ornamented. He was decorated with valuable jewels and fragrant flowers. The Lord showed His lotus feet by raising them, which are the rewards of pure devotional service. The splendor of the transcendental rays from His moonlike toenails and fingernails looked like petals of a flower. His beautiful smile vanquishes the distress of His devotees, and His face was so pleasing because it dazzled with the rays from His lips and the beauty of His nose and eyebrows. As Lord Brahma, high in the lotus flower, thus saw the Lord, he simultaneously glanced over creation. He saw the lake in Lord Vishnu's navel and the lotus, as well as the devastating water below. All became visible to him. Lord Brahma, being thus surcharged with the mode of passion and the inclination to create, began to offer prayers to the Lord to acquire the necessary energy and creative mentality.[25]

Then Lord Brahma displayed his deep realizations about the purpose of life in the many prayers he offered to Lord Vishnu. After having prayed to the Supreme as far as his mind would permit, the Lord saw that Brahma was very anxious about planning and constructing the different planetary systems. Thus, He responded to Brahma in deep, thoughtful words, which removed all of the illusion that had arisen. He told Brahma, "Situate yourself in penance and meditation and follow the principles of knowledge to receive My favor. When you are absorbed in devotional service, in the course of your creative activities, you will see

Me in you and throughout the universe, and you will see that you yourself, the universe and all living entities are in Me. You will see Me in all living entities as well as all over the universe, just as fire is situated in wood. Only in that state of transcendental vision will you be able to be free from all kinds of illusion. I am the Supersoul of every individual. I am the supreme director and the dearest. People are wrongly attached to the gross and subtle bodies, but they should be attached to Me only. By following My instructions you can now generate the living entities as before, by dint of your complete Vedic wisdom and the body you have directly received from Me, the supreme cause of everything." Then the Supreme Being disappeared.[25]

Now that Brahma had the power to create, he began the process of manifesting the various living beings and objects of the universe from his own body and mind. This is described in many places in the *Puranas*, and in detail in Chapter Ten of the Third Canto of the *Srimad-Bhagavatam*.

It is also described that just before the creation of the universe, Lord Krishna had enlightened Brahma in his heart with the full *Srimad-Bhagavatam*. This was while Brahma was sitting on the huge lotus flower, frightened by the material existence before the process of creation had begun.[26] Only after having received this knowledge did Brahma realize how to proceed with the creation of the universe. Even afterwards, when it came time to manifest the Vedic sound vibration, the Supreme Lord had directly spoken the *Srimad-Bhagavatam* in summary to Brahma, who in turn then gave it to Narada.[27] It was Narada Muni who had played the role of spiritual master to Vyasadeva and gave the same *Bhagavatam* to him, which he then fully deliberated for the benefit of humanity. To do this, Brahma also created the Sanskrit alphabet in order to form the Vedic knowledge in spoken and later written forms.

More information on this process is supplied in the *Srimad-Bhagavatam* (12.6.43-46) which explains that it was from the *omkara* (*Om* mantra, seed of all things) that Lord Brahma created all the sounds of the alphabet, such as the vowels, consonants, semivowels, sibilants, and so on. Lord Brahma then made use of this collection of sounds and produced from his four faces the four *Vedas*, which then appeared along with *Om* and the seven *vyahriti* invocations. His intention was to propagate the process of Vedic rituals according to the different functions performed by the priests of each of the four *Vedas*. Brahma taught these *Vedas* to his sons, who were great sages among the brahamanas and experts in the art of Vedic recitation. They in turn took the role of *acharyas* [spiritual masters] and imparted the *Vedas* to their owns sons. In this way, throughout the cycles of the four ages, generation after generation of disciples–all firmly fixed in their spiritual vows–have received this Vedic knowledge by disciplic succession. At the end of each Dvapara-yuga, the *Vedas* and all related Vedic knowledge are edited into separate divisions by eminent sages [headed by Vyasadeva].

In this way, as previously explained, Lord Brahma is active during his day, which is equal to the length of time of one thousand cycles of the four *yugas*, Satya-yuga through Kali-yuga. Then he sleeps during his night, which is of the same duration. When he sleeps, there is a partial annihilation of the lower planetary systems below Brahmaloka, the residence of Brahma, which get submerged in the waters of devastation. Under the influence of the mode of darkness, the powerful manifestation of the universe merges into the darkness of night. The innumerable living entities stay merged in that darkness while everything remains silent. All three levels of planetary systems are out of sight, and the sun and moon are also dark. The process of the annihilation is caused by the flames emanating from Lord Sankarshana, Sheshanaga, who is lying on the Garbhodaka Ocean at the bottom of the universe. These flames produce the intense changes that cause the worlds to come to an end. Brahma then dreams about Lord Vishnu who gives him instructions about the recreation. When Brahma awakes, he reconstructs the devastated areas of the universe to start anew.[28]

CHAPTER NOTES
1. *Linga Purana* 40.86-92
2. *Srimad-Bhagavatam* 3.10.14-16
3. Ibid., 3.10.17
4. *Kurma Purana* 1.7.2
5. *Srimad-Bhagavatam* 3.10.18-29.
   Also described in *Vishnu Purana* (Book One, Chapter Five), *Padma Purana* 1.3.76-84, *Agni Purana* (Chapter 17 & 20), *Narada Purana*. 1.3.25-35, *Kurma Purana* 1.7.1-19, *Garuda Purana* 1.4.14-22, and others
6. *Caitanya-caritamrita*, Madhya-lila, 20.292-3
7. *Srimad-Bhagavatam* 3.6.6.purport
8. *Caitanya-caritamrita*, Adi-lila, 5.95-101
9. Ibid., Adi-lila, 5.102-3
10. *Brahma-samhita* 5.18 & *Srimad-Bhagavatam* 11.24.10
11. *Srimad-Bhagavatam* 3.8.14-15
12. *Brahma-samhita* 5.22 & *Caitanya-caritamrita*,
    Madhya-lila, 20.287-288

13. *Caitanya-caritamrita*, Madhya-lila, 20.305
14. Ibid., *Madhya-lila*, 20.288-291
15. Ibid., *Madhya-lila*, 20.314-316 & *Brahma-samhita* 5.46
16. *Brahma-samhita,* 5.45
17. *Caitanya-caritamrita*, Madhya-lila, 20.309-311, 317 & *Srimad-Bhagavatam* 10.88.3
18. *Brahma-samhita* 5.48 & *Srimad-Bhagavatam* 3.11.38
19. *Srimad-Bhagavatam* 3.8.16-21
20. Ibid., 2.9.6-7
21. Ibid., 3.8.22
22. *Brahma-samhita* 5.27
23. Ibid., 5.28
24. *Srimad-Bhagavatam* 2.9.4
25. Ibid., 3.8.23-33
26. Ibid., 12.13.10
27. Ibid., 2.7.51
28. Ibid., 3.11.22-30

CHAPTER SIX

The Identity of Lord Shiva and Goddess Durga

After understanding the information supplied so far, we can begin to see how the different Vedic gods have particular roles or functions, and represent or control different forces of nature. Thus, they are not all the same. They all have different potencies to do particular things in the arrangement and management of the universal creation. In this way, most of them have specific positions and purposes to help facilitate the cause for the creation, maintenance, and even the destruction of the universe.

The most prominent of all the Vedic gods consists of the Trinity of Vishnu, Brahma and Shiva. Brahma assists in creating the world, Vishnu maintains it, and Shiva helps in its annihilation. (I have dealt with this aspect much more extensively in my book, *How the Universe Was Created*, so I will not include that here.) Those that follow the Vedic path can generally be divided into three main categories; namely those who worship Shiva and are Shaivites, those who worship Shakti or the Goddess and are Shaktas, and those who worship Vishnu, the Vaishnavas. So, let us understand the identity and function of Lord Shiva and Goddess Durga.

* * *

One of the most significant of all the Vedic gods is Shiva. And one of the most noted of all the goddesses is Shiva's wife, Durga. They also go by many other names. For example, Durga is also called Parvati and Sati, which means chastity. The name Shiva means auspicious. Shiva is also known by many different names according to his function. When, for example, he expresses himself through space and time, he is known as Ishwara. He is called Sadashiva when he functions through air, which incorporates the principles of both sound and touch. Shiva is known as

Rudra when he operates through fire, which incorporates the principles of sound, touch and form.

Shiva is the embodiment and controller of *tama-guna*, the mode of darkness, inertia, and the tendency towards annihilation. This is how he assists in the destruction of the cosmic creation in the end times, as well as in the exhibition of continuous forms of death and destruction that we see every day. However, this demise and dissolution can also be viewed as a renewal, which is also considered to be a part of Shiva.

We can find additional characteristics of Lord Shiva in the *Srimad-Bhagavatam* (4.2.2) in which it states that Lord Shiva is the spiritual master of the entire world. He is a peaceful personality, free from enmity, always satisfied in himself. He is the greatest among all the demigods. He is the spiritual master of the world by showing how to worship the Supreme. He is considered the best of all devotees. Therefore, he has his own spiritual line or *sampradaya* called the Rudra-sampradaya that comes directly from him. These days it is found in the Vishnusvami-sampradaya, or the Vallabha-sampradaya.

Shiva is described as the most powerful, second only to Lord Vishnu.[1] In this way, he is not the Supreme, but is almost as powerful. Although he has nothing to attain in this material world, he is always engaged for the benefit of everyone in this universe, and is accompanied by his material and dangerous energies like goddess Kali and goddess Durga. They serve him by killing all kinds of demons and impious persons. War represents Kali's energy of devastation. Sometimes we see pictures of a fierce form of Kali standing with one foot on the body of Shiva. This is because Shiva sometimes has to lie down in front of her to pacify her from killing all the demoniac people in the world. In this way, Shiva controls the material energy. Lord Shiva is also in control of the destructive energy, *tamo-guna*, the mode of darkness, and is assisted by Kali and Durga in this purpose. Durga helps him in keeping the majority of the living beings in the darkness of ignorance. That is why Durga and Kali are described as dangerous potencies. Only those who are serious about spiritual life are protected from this darkness.

Shiva is often shown as a handsome young man, with long hair from which flows a spurt of the Ganga (Ganges) River (an emblem of purity) and in which is also a crescent moon. He is also white or light bluish in complexion, sometimes with a third eye between the eyebrows on the forehead, and usually with four arms (a sign of universal power) holding a Trishula (a trident, showing his ruling proficiency over the three modes of nature), the Damaru (small hour-glass shaped drum, the beating of which represents language or the alphabet), and exhibiting the

Lord Shiva on the left, with Goddess Parvati or Durga on the right, with little Lord Ganesh on their lap. Deities located in central Delhi.

mudras (hand positions) of Abhaya (protection) and Varada (giving blessings).

It is also said that Shiva's drum represents *srishti*, the creation; the *abhaya* hand (giving blessings) represents *sthiti*, or preservation; his foot that presses down symbolizes *tirobhava*, or the veiling effect; and the uplifted foot means blessings (*anugraha*), especially toward seeing through the veil of illusion caused by ego. When he is shown with an axe, it represents *samhara*, destruction.

Sometimes he is shown with eight, ten or even thirty-two hands. These represent his various potencies and contain such things as an Akshamala (rosary that signifies being the master of spiritual sciences), the Khatvanga (magic wand which shows his being an adept in occult sciences), a Darpana (a mirror showing that the creation is a reflection of his cosmic form), a *chakra* (disc), a noose, a staff, a bow, a Pashupata spear, a lotus, sword, and so on. He is often sitting on or wearing a tiger skin. The tiger skin represents his command over his desires, which often consumes common men like a tiger.

Shiva is often shown with serpents entwined around his arms, waist, neck, and hair. Snakes often invoke fear. So, this represents how Shiva is free from fear. The snake also signifies time. If a poisonous snake bites someone, it is only a matter of time before that person will die. And time catches up with everyone sooner or later. So, Lord Shiva is the Lord over time and death. These serpents also indicate that he is surrounded by death but beyond the power of it.

Shiva is also seen with ash from the cremation grounds smeared over his body. This is called *vibhuti*. It symbolizes death or detachment from the world and lust. It also indicates that our bodies, being inert matter in their essential form, will also become ashes when we die and if the body is cremated. Thus, we must rise above the bodily identification and become conscious of our real identity within. Ash is the sign of Shiva's complete renunciation of the world.

Sometimes Shiva is shown wearing a garland of skulls. The skulls are representative of his being the lord of destruction and the cyclical nature of the appearance and disappearance of the material creation.

One of the most beautiful forms of Lord Shiva is portrayed in his dancing position, known as Nataraja, the king of dancers. As Nataraja, Shiva holds his damaru drum in his upper right hand. This indicates *nada*, the sound of the universal development. In his other hand, he holds a flame of destruction. Together these indicate both creation and destruction, the counterpoints of all material existence. His right hand is also held in the position of blessing and protection. As Nataraja, he also wears the skin of a tiger, which he slew. This represents the ego, which will fight when attacked and must be killed by the knowledge of the guru, or the wisdom of Nataraja himself. As Nataraja, he is shown with one foot subduing or standing on the body of Mahamaya, the personification of the illusion which is the cause of all suffering. The other foot is raised upward, which represents the attainment of the *turiya* state beyond the states of waking, dreaming, deep sleep, and the influence of the mind and creation. Thus, he is completely free from all of these.

There are many stories that relate how and why Shiva appears the way he does. For example, Lord Shiva is shown at times with a third eye in between his eyebrows on his forehead. It is said that his third eye represents the eye of wisdom, or inner sight. The other two eyes represent the balanced form of love and justice. Thus, Lord Shiva is not too harsh nor too lenient, but views everything with the proper proportions of love, justice and inner knowledge. Together, Shiva's three eyes also represent the sun, moon and fire, the means by which the universe is illuminated. How Shiva got a third eye is explained that one day Shiva's wife Parvati covered Shiva's eyes with her hands and the whole world was enveloped in darkness. Then Shiva willed the third eye to manifest, which sent forth light, heat and fire.

Another story is that once when the heavenly Ganga River was descending onto the Earth, the weight of its force would have crushed the world, so Shiva accepted it on his head, wherein it stayed until it was ready to be released. The Ganga River is considered to have entered the universe when the Supreme Lord in His *avatar* as Vamanadeva kicked the outer shell of the universe with His toe, thus letting in some of the water of the Karanadakashayi Ocean, the spiritual water that surrounds the universe. This became the holy Ganga. Thus, it is considered the foot wash of the Lord. So, Lord Shiva keeps this water on his head.

Shiva's Ganga water is also said to represent the flow of knowledge and devotion to God. Shiva is known as the foremost devotee of Lord Krishna, Vishnu, or Lord Rama, which is one of the meanings of the spout of Ganga water on Shiva's head.

The *Bhagavatam* (10.41.15) relates: "The water of the river Ganga [Ganges] has purified the three worlds, having become transcendental by bathing Your [Lord Vishnu's] feet. Lord Shiva accepted that water on his head, and by that water's grace the sons of King Sagara attained heaven."

Another story is that during the time when the demons and demigods were churning the ocean of milk, many objects started to be produced from it. One was the moon, which Shiva took and placed in his hair. This represents the phases of the moon or the passing of time, which is but an ornament for Shiva since he is not affected by it. The crescent moon also signifies the happiness of life, especially when it is based on a spiritual purpose. The rays of the moon enhance one's inspiration and energy for spiritual life, just as it is said that the rays of the moon nourish the vegetable kingdom. It represents the cooling light of the knowledge of the Self, and the way life should be when lived in that knowledge.

Another object that appeared from the churning was the severe poison that Shiva drank to keep it from spreading. However, Parvati, being alarmed at this, grabbed his throat so it could not go down, which is where he kept the poison, and which made his throat turn blue.

Shiva is often portrayed standing next to or on his bull, Nandikeshvara or Nandi (meaning joyful). Symbolically, Nandi represents the animal tendencies, such as the urge for sex, which are tamed and docile by Lord Shiva's mastery over it. Thus, he rides on Nandi, who is obedient to Shiva's command. Nandi also represents strength and virility. He is often seen in temples of Shiva in a reclining position in front of the main shrine, gazing toward the image of Shiva. Nandi also represents the *jivatma*, the individual soul, and the animalistic impulses that will carry it away into material existence, unless such tendencies are curbed.

KRISHNA DEVOTEES ARE DEAR TO SHIVA
AND SHIVA IS DEAR TO THEM

Shiva works for the benefit of everyone, and tries to help the living beings make spiritual advancement. This is why he has his own line of disciplic succession. This is also why he says to the sons of King Pracinibarhi, "Any person who is surrendered to the Supreme Personality of God, Lord Krishna, the controller of everything, is very dear to me."[1]

The sons of the King were going to practice austerities to worship Lord Vishnu and while searching for a suitable place happened to find Lord Shiva. His bodily luster was like molten gold, his throat was bluish, he had three eyes, and was accompanied by musicians who were glorifying him. Shiva is the protector of the pious and those of gentle behavior. So, he was pleased to speak to the princes the way he did. He continued in this way:

"A person who is directly surrendered to Lord Krishna, or Vishnu, in unalloyed devotional service is immediately promoted to the spiritual planets. I, Lord Shiva, and other demigods attain these planets only after the destruction of the material world. You are all devotees of the Lord, and as such I appreciate that you are as respectable as the Supreme Personality of Godhead Himself. I know in this way that the devotees also respect me and that I am dear to them. Thus no one can be as dear to the devotees as I am."[2]

In this way, a devotee of Krishna does not disrespect Lord Shiva, but worships him as the greatest of devotees of Lord Krishna. A Krishna *bhakta* (devotee) also prays to Lord Shiva, but asks Shiva to assist him in attaining the favor of Lord Krishna, and not merely for material benefits. As we find in the Tulasi *Ramayana* (Uttara-Kanda, Doha 45), Lord Rama says "With joined palms I lay before you another secret doctrine: without adoring Sankara (Lord Shiva) man cannot attain devotion to Me." So, in this way, Shiva can assist us in attaining devotion to Lord Krishna and His expansions.

After Lord Shiva had spoken to the sons of King Pracinabarhi, he relates a particular mantra for their benefit, which is pure and auspicious for anyone who wants to attain the ultimate goal of life. This mantra is called Shiva's Song, and consists of verses 33 to 79 of the Twenty-fourth Chapter of the Forth Canto in *Srimad-Bhagavatam*. He starts his prayer with this verse:

"O Supreme Personality of Godhead, all glories unto You. You are the most exalted of all self-realized souls. Since You are always auspicious for the self-realized, I wish that You be auspicious to me. You are worshipable by virtue of the all perfect instructions You give. You are the Supersoul; therefore I offer my obeisances unto You as the supreme living bring."

Through the remaining 45 verses of this prayer, Lord Shiva praises the many qualities, characteristics, and powers of the Supreme Being in the form of Lord Krishna. At the end of many years in which the sons of the King, called the Pracetas, repeated this prayer everyday, Lord Vishnu Himself appeared to them. He said, "Those who will offer Me the prayers composed by Lord Shiva, both in the morning and in the evening, will be given benedictions by Me. In this way, they can both fulfill their desires and attain good intelligence."[3]

Also in the *Bhagavatam* (4.6.42-53) we can see Lord Shiva's greatness among the demigods. During the disastrous ritual of Daksha, who displayed great dislike toward Shiva and Shiva's wife, Durga (Sati) immolated herself in fire. Sati was Daksha's own daughter and could not tolerate the insults her father made toward her husband, Shiva. So, while in meditation she burst into flames. Thereafter, Lord Brahma and the demigods went to pacify Lord Shiva. Brahma consoled Shiva and addressed him as "My dear Lord," and called him the controller of the entire universe, the combination of mother and father of the universe, and the Supreme Brahman, beyond this creation. Therein we can see that Brahma, the partial creator of the universe, offers praises to Lord Shiva as a superior. This is to appease Lord Shiva, since it is known that his anger can annihilate the universe.

When the ritual was able to continue and Daksha offered the clarified butter with the mantras from the *Yajur Veda*, Lord Vishnu appeared there in His original form as Narayana. As described in the *Bhagavatam* (4.7.18-29), as soon as Lord Vishnu appeared, all the demigods, including Lord Brahma, Shiva, the Gandharvas and sages, immediately offered their respectful obeisances. In the presence of Lord Vishnu's glaring effulgence from His body, everyone else's luster faded. They all offered their prayers to Him. Therein, Lord Shiva addresses Lord Vishnu, "My dear Lord, my mind and consciousness are always fixed on Your lotus feet, which, as the source of all benediction and the fulfillment of all desires, are worshiped by all liberated sages because Your lotus feet are worthy of worship. With my mind fixed on Your lotus feet, I am no longer disturbed by persons who blaspheme me, claiming that my activities are not purified. I do not mind their accusations, and I excuse them out of compassion, just as You exhibit compassion toward all living entities."

After all the personalities had offered their prayers to Lord Vishnu, He replied to Daksha, "Brahma, Shiva and I are the supreme cause of the material manifestation. I am the Supersoul, the self-effulgent witness. But impersonally there is no difference between Brahma, Lord Shiva and Me. I am the original Personality of Godhead, but in order to create, maintain and annihilate this cosmic manifestation, I act through My material energy, and according to different grades of activity, My representations are equally named. One who is not in proper knowledge thinks that the demigods like Brahma and Shiva are independent, or he even thinks that the living entities are independent. A person with average intelligence does not think the head and other parts of the body to be separate. Similarly, My devotee does not differentiate Vishnu, the all-pervading Personality, from anything or any living entity. One who does not consider Brahma, Vishnu, Shiva or the living entities in general to be separate from the Supreme, and who knows Brahman, actually realizes peace; others do not."[4]

What this indicates is the interdependence of the demigods on Lord Vishnu. Lord Vishnu is the ultimate cause of the universal creation. Lord Brahma was born out of Lord Vishnu, and Lord Shiva was born from Lord Brahma, as will be explained. It is the energy that comes from Lord Vishnu, in the form of Lord Brahma and Shiva, that creates and annihilates the universe. Lord Brahma is manifested for the continuation of the creation, while Lord Shiva assists in the annihilation. In this way, they are interconnected and work together like parts of a single body. Yet, they all play distinct and significant roles in the affairs of the cosmos, but are dependent on Lord Vishnu. When we see that all living beings are expansions from the Supreme Lord and His energy, then one can achieve real peace.

In fact, it is said that these sages and devotees who see with such equal vision become worshipable by Lord Shiva, Brahma and Lord Vishnu. Once when Lord Shiva was traveling, he met the great sage Markandeya as he was coming out of his yogic trance. At that time, Markandeya offered prayers to Lord Shiva who blessed the sage and then asked if there were any benedictions that the sage wanted. As described in the *Bhagavatam* (12.10.19-22) Suta Gosvami said: "Lord Shiva, the foremost demigod and the shelter of the saintly devotees, was satisfied by Markandeya's praise. Pleased, he smiled and addressed the sage. Lord Shiva said: Please ask me for some benediction, since among all givers of benedictions, we three--Brahma, Vishnu and I--are the best. Seeing us never goes in vain, because simply by seeing us a mortal achieves immortality. The inhabitants and ruling demigods of all planets, along with Lord Brahma, the Supreme Lord Hari and I, glorify, worship and assist those brahmanas who are saintly, always peaceful, free of material attachment, compassionate to all living beings, purely devoted to us, devoid of hatred and endowed with equal vision. These devotees do not differentiate between Lord Vishnu, Lord Brahma and me, nor do they differentiate between themselves and other living beings. Therefore, because you are this kind of saintly devotee, we worship you."

LORD SHIVA'S POSITION

In the *Bhagavatam* (4.3.23), Lord Shiva himself tells his wife, Sati, that he is always engaged in worshiping the Supreme Personality known as Lord Vasudeva, Krishna, who is revealed in pure consciousness, by offering obeisances.

Herein, we can see that in actuality Lord Shiva is subordinate to Lord Vishnu, Krishna, in that he is also a part of Lord Krishna's universal form, as described in the *Bhagavad-gita* (11.15). Therein we find: "Arjuna said: My dear Lord Krishna, I see assembled together in Your [universal] body all the demigods and various other living entities. I see Brahma sitting on the lotus flower as well as Lord Shiva and many sages and divine serpents."

In the pastimes of Lord Krishna in Vrindavana, we find that Lord Shiva had also tried to enter the *rasa-lila* dance between Krishna and the *gopis*, the cowherd damsels. The Mahadeva Gopisvara temple in Vrindavana is said to mark where Lord Shiva desired to become a *gopi* in order to enter the dance with Lord Krishna. So, Lord Shiva was trying to enter into the most confidential pastimes and devotion of Sri Krishna.

In another light, Lord Shiva is Lord Krishna's brother-in-law. At the time of Krishna's birth pastime in Vrindavana, Yasoda bore a daughter, Katyayani or Durga, and Mother Devaki bore a son, Lord Krishna. To save Him from the nefarious King Kamsa, Krishna's father, Vasudeva, brought Krishna from Mathura to Gokul and exchanged Him with the daughter of Mother Yasoda, taking the daughter back with him. When King Kamsa came to get the newborn from Mother Devaki, the child rose into the air and exhibited her form as the eight-armed Durga and chastised Kamsa. Durga is Lord Shiva's wife, and in this pastime Lord Krishna's sister, so it can also be said that Shiva is the brother-in-law of Lord Krishna.

In another place in the *Bhagavatam* (8.12.10), when Lord Shiva was bewildered by the Supreme Lord's form as a beautiful woman, Mohini-Murti, Lord Shiva admits his weakness in being unable to fully understand the illusory nature of this material creation. "O My Lord, I, who am considered to be the best of the demigods, and Lord Brahma and the great rishis, headed by Marichi, are born of the mode of goodness. Nonetheless, we are bewildered by Your illusory energy and cannot understand what this creation is. Aside from us, what is to be said of others, like the demons and human beings, who are in the base modes of material nature [*rajo-guna* and *tamo-guna*]? How will they know You?"

Later, Lord Shiva, who is often pictured in meditation, explains to his wife who it is that he meditates on while in trance. He says, "O Goddess, You have now seen the illusory energy of the Supreme Personality of Godhead, who is the unborn master of everyone. Although I am one of the principal expansions of His Lordship, even I was illusioned by His energy. What then is to be said of others, who are fully dependent on maya? When I finished performing mystic yoga for one thousand years, you asked me upon whom was I meditating. Now, here is the Supreme Person to whom time has no entrance and who the *Vedas* cannot understand."[5]

Another time when Lord Shiva described his subservient position was when Lord Krishna was battling with Banasura, who was a devotee of Lord Shiva, and was cutting off Banasura's hundreds of arms that he had acquired as a blessing from Lord Shiva. When it looked like Banasura was about to lose his life, Lord Shiva, who had also been a part of the battle scene, approached Lord Krishna to pacify Him and spare Banasura's life. Therein (*Bhagavatam* 10.63.34-45) it is related, "Sri Rudra said: You alone are the Absolute Truth, the supreme light, the mystery hidden within the verbal manifestation of the Absolute. Those whose hearts are spotless can see You, for You are uncontaminated, like the sky." In the ten verses that follow, Lord Shiva also addresses Lord Krishna in other ways: "Your current descent into the material realm, O Lord of unrestricted power, is meant for upholding the principles of justice and benefitting the entire universe. We demigods, each depending on Your grace and authority, develop the seven planetary systems. You are the original person, one without a second, transcendental and self-manifesting. Uncaused, you are the cause of all, and You are the ultimate controller."

When Uddhava was praying to Lord Krishna, he said, "Even Lord Brahma and Lord Shiva act only as Your instruments in cosmic creation and annihilation, which are ultimately done by You, the Supreme Lord, in Your invisible aspect of time."[6]

One of the major differences between Shiva and Krishna is described as follows: "Sri Shukadeva Gosvami said: Lord Shiva is always united with his personal energy, the material nature. Manifesting himself in three features in response to the entreaties of nature's three modes, he thus embodies the threefold principle of material ego in goodness, passion and ignorance. The sixteen elements have evolved as transformations of that false ego. When a devotee of Lord Shiva worships his manifestation in any one of these elements, the devotee obtains all sorts of corresponding enjoyable opulences. Lord Hari, however, has no connection with the material modes. He is the Supreme Personality of Godhead, the all-seeing eternal witness, who is transcendental to material nature. One who worships Him becomes similarly free from the material modes."[7] Thus, a worshiper of Lord Shiva gets the results that are conditional to the affects of material nature, while a worshiper of Lord Krishna gets released from the material nature rather than receiving material opulences.

So, in this regard, Sri Shukadeva Gosvami said, "Lord Brahma, Lord Vishnu, Lord Shiva and others are able to curse or bless one. Lord Shiva and Lord Brahma are very quick to curse or bestow benedictions, my dear King, but the infallible Supreme Lord is not."[8]

Another aspect of understanding Shiva's position has to do with his purpose, which is connected with how he appeared. This is clearly explained in the ancient text of the *Brahma-samhita* (verse 15). Therein we find it said "The same Maha-Vishnu created [His next expansion of] Vishnu [Garbhodakashayi Vishnu] from His left limb, Brahma, the first progenitor of beings, from His right limb and, from the space between His two eyebrows, Shambhu [Shiva], the divine masculine manifested halo."

In an explanation of this, Srila Bhaktisiddhanta elaborates that when the mundane creation of the universe is manifested, then the principle of Shambhu in the form of Rudra is born from the space between the two eyebrows of Vishnu. Shambhu enshrines the principle of materialistic ego. This principle makes the living being identify with the material body, subject to the desires for material and bodily happiness. (*Brahma-samhita*, verse 16, purport)

So, the power of Lord Shiva comes from the potency of Lord Vishnu. This is described as follows in verse 10 of the *Brahma-samhita*: "The person embodying the material causal principle, viz., the great lord of this mundane world [Maheshvara] Shambhu, in the form of the male generating organ, is joined to his female consort, the limited energy [Maya] as the efficient causal principle. The Lord of the world Maha-Vishnu is manifest in him by His subjective portion in the form of His glance."

In this way, during the process of the material creation, and when Maha-Vishnu casts His glance onto the shadowy potency of Maya, Shambhu, lord of the *pradhana* (the unmanifest material ingredients), who is the same as Rudra, consummates his intercourse with Maya, the efficient principle of the cause of mundane energy. But Shambhu can do nothing independent of the energy of Maha-Vishnu, who represents the direct spiritual power of Krishna. In this way, the principle of the material creation is produced only when Maha-Vishnu, the plenary portion of Lord Krishna, is propitious towards the active endeavors of Maya, Shiva's consort, and the principle of mundane causality. (*Brahma-samhita*, verse 10, purport)

So, the difference between Maha-Vishnu and Shiva as Shambhu is more clearly described in the *Brahma-samhita* (verse 45) as follows: "Just as milk is transformed into curd by the action of acids, but yet the

Lord Shiva and Goddess Durga 101

effect curd is neither the same as, nor different from, its cause, viz., milk, so I adore the primeval Lord Govinda of whom the state of Shambhu is a transformation for the performance of the work of destruction."

Srila Bhaktisiddhanta adds clarification in the purport to this verse that Shiva is not a second Godhead other than Krishna. In fact, those who entertain such a discriminating sentiment commit a great offense to the Supreme Lord. The position of Shambhu is subservient to that of Govinda, Krishna. Hence, as the above verse indicates, they are not really different from each other. But as yogurt comes from its initial cause, so Shiva is manifest according to his initial cause, which is from Krishna through Maha-Vishnu. So, God takes a subservient position to His direct forms when He attains a distinct personality by the addition of a particular element of adulteration, which is the form of Lord Shiva or Shambhu, through which the Lord comes in contact with the material energy, since Maha-Vishnu never does touch the mundane energy. However, Shiva has no independent initiative or ability. This means that Shiva as Shambhu comes in contact with and interacts with the material energy as the agent of Maha-Vishnu, who does not come in such contact but only sets it all in motion.

Srila Bhaktisiddhanta further describes that in this way, Govinda manifests Himself as a plenary portion which, in this case, is a *guna-avatara* in the form of Shambhu, lord of *tamo-guna* or the mode of darkness... Thus, Shambhu, in pursuance of the supreme will of Govinda, works in union with his consort, Durga-devi, by his own time energy.

Therefore, the real difference between Govinda and Shiva or Brahma is that all the majestic attributes of God are fully present in the form of Govinda, Krishna. Shiva and Brahma are entities adulterated with mundane qualities, however slight they may be. Though Vishnu is also a divine appearance in the mode of goodness, still He is not adulterated. The appearance of Narayana as Maha-Vishnu, or as Garbhodakashayi Vishnu (Vishnu's expansion in each universe) and Kshirodakashayi Vishnu (Vishnu's expansion as the Supersoul within each living being), are examples of the ubiquitous function of the Supreme Divinity. Lord Vishnu is Godhead Himself, and the two other *guna-avataras* (Brahma and Shiva) and all the other gods are entities possessing authority in subordination to Him. The different expansions of the Supreme Being, Govinda, are the same as the identical light appearing in different candles, all shining by the spiritual potency of Govinda, Krishna. (*Brahma-samhita*, verse forty-six, purport)

This makes it clear that the forms and positions of Shiva and Brahma are eternal, but only in the context of the endurance of the material creation. Once the material creation is annihilated, their forms and positions are no longer needed. Lord Shiva is the lord of *tamo-guna* and material nature, but not of the spiritual world. It is only Lord Krishna who is described as the Supreme Being and controller of both the spiritual and material energies.

It is explained further by Srila Bhaktisiddhanta that Lord Krishna has sixty divine qualities in their fullest measure. While 50 of the divine qualities of the individual *jiva* souls are present along with five additional qualities in Lord Brahma. Yet in Shiva these fifty-five qualities are also present but in greater degrees than in Lord Brahma. (*Brahma-samhita*, verse 49, purport)

Thus, the position of Lord Shiva has been described relative to his purpose and function within the material creation, and his form is but an expansion of Lord Krishna. [More about Lord Shiva's real position and identity is explained later in the section of this chapter called "How Shiva and Durga Are Considered the Mother and Father of the Universe".]

HOW LORD SHIVA APPEARED IN THIS WORLD

The previous paragraphs point out how Lord Shiva participated in the creation process from Maha-Vishnu as Shambhu. But it is also related how Lord Shiva appeared in this universe in his personal form from Lord Brahma. It is explained in the *Bhagavatam* (3.12.4), that in the beginning of the creation process, Lord Brahma manifested four great sages named Sanaka, Sananda, Sanatana, and Sanat-kumara. Brahma expected them to assist in filling the universe with varieties of living beings. However, they were unwilling to adopt materialistic activities because they were highly elevated beings. Brahma requested that they begin to produce progeny, but they refused because they were already attached to Lord Vasudeva, the Supreme Lord, and were focused on achieving liberation, *moksha*. So, they expressed their unwillingness, which made Lord Brahma extremely angry.

The anger that was generated in the mind of Lord Brahma, though he tried to control it, came out from between his eyebrows. Immediately there was produced a child of mixed red and blue color. This child immediately began to cry and requested to Lord Brahma, "O destiny maker, teacher of the universe, kindly designate my name and place." Lord Brahma then pacified the boy and said, "O chief of the demigods, you shall be called Rudra because you have cried so anxiously." Then Brahma gave Rudra the following places for his residence: the heart, the senses, the life-air of the body, the sky, the air, the fire, water, earth, sun, the moon, and austerity. He then told Rudra that he would be known by eleven other names: Manyu, Manu, Mahan, Shiva, Ritadhvaja, Ugrareta, Bhava, Kala, Vamadeva, and Dhritavrata. These names represent the other aspects of Lord Shiva, each having different appearances and activities. Rudra is often shown as tall, well built, with long hair, wielding the thunderbolt, bow and arrow. He is viewed as the protector of humanity against its enemies. He is also known as an excellent physician and has numerous medicines that can cure diseases. Brahma also told Rudra that he would have eleven wives, namely Dhi, Dhriti, Rasala, Uma, Niyut, Sarpi, Ila, Ambika, Iravati, Svadha, and Diksha.

Brahma then told Rudra to accept these names and wives, and that since he was one of the masters of the living beings, he should now increase the population on a large scale. Rudra then created many offspring that resembled him in color, strength and furious nature. They were unlimited in number, and when they gathered together, they attempted to devour the universe. Brahma, becoming alarmed at the situation, then requested Rudra not to generate living beings of this nature. It would be better if Rudra engaged himself in penance, or meditation, which is auspicious for all. Through penance he could create the universe as it was before. By penance only can one approach the Supreme Lord, who is within the heart of every living being and at the same time beyond the reach of the senses. Thus, Rudra accepted the advice of his father, Brahma, and went to the forest to perform austere penances. This is why we so often see Shiva pictured in the mountain forests engaged in meditation.

Some of Shiva's other names include Dakshinamurti, meaning a universal teacher. Then there is Trilochana (Three-eyed), Nila-kantha (Blue-throated), Pancha-anana (Five-faced), Chandrashekhara (Moon-crested), Gangadhara (Bearer of the Ganga), Girisha (Mountain Lord), Jatadhara (Wearer of matted hair), Sthanu (Immutable), Visvanatha (Lord of the Universe), Bhairava (the Terrible, destructive aspect of Shiva), Bhutesha or Bhuteshvara (Lord of ghosts or elements), Hara (remover of death), Shambhu (abode of joy), Shankara (giver of joy), Bhava (existence), Mahadeva (great God), Ashani (thunderbolt), Isha or Ishana (the ruler), Pashupati (the herdsman or friend of animals), Mritunjaya (conqueror of death), Aghora (non-fearful), Ugra (the fearful), Bhima (the tremendous), Rudra (Lord of tears), as well as Shuli,

Maheshvara, Ishvara, Sharva, Khandaparashu, Mrida, Krittivasas, Pinaki, Pramathadhipa, Kapardi, Shrikantha, Shitikantha, Kapalabhrit, Vamadeva, Mahadeva, Virupaksha, Krishanuretas, Sarvajna, Dhurjati, Nilalohita, Smarahara, Bharga, Tryambaka, Tripurantaka, Antakaripu, Kratudhvamsi, Vrishadhvaja, Vyomakesha, Umapati, Ahirbudhnya, Ashtamurti, Gajari, Mahanata, and others. The 1000 names of Shiva can be found in Chapter 17 of the Anushasana Parva of the *Mahabharata*, as well as in the *Linga Purana* (1.65-98).

SHAIVISM

Shaivism is one of the major traditions of the Vedic system, and centers around the worship of Lord Shiva. Those who accept Shiva as the supreme deity are called Shaivites. Its origin predates recorded history, but references to the worship of Shiva can be found in the *Vedas* and *Puranas*.

You will notice that a devotee of Shiva in India usually wears Vibhuti or *bhasma*, the sacred ash, on his forehead, and Radraksha *mala* around his neck and elsewhere. The Rudraksha or Rudra bead represents the third eye on Lord Shiva's forehead. The Shaivite should worship the Shiva *lingam* with the leaves of the Bilva trees, and his meditation should consist of chanting the Panchakshara, "Om Namaha Shivaya".

The philosophy of Shaivism covers a wide range of Hindu thought, from idealistic monism to pluralistic realism, depending on the locality. As it changed through the years, a number of Shaivite sects were established, and the Pasupatas are considered the earliest. The Shaiva cults have had great popularity with village people throughout India, and use a form of asceticism for their means of spiritual advancement. This includes rising above anger and greed, engaging in deep meditation, and concentrating on the repetition of the sacred syllable *om*. Many Shaiva ascetics can be recognized by their long matted hair, which may also be wrapped and piled up on the head in a bun. They often wear a horizontal, three-lined *tilok* mark on their forehead. Many initiates and *naga babas* also smear their bodies with ash that come from the sacred fire that they often have in their camp, or from crematoriums. They chant mantras to become free from the bondage of material existence, and sometimes dance and sing to induce trance-like states. Some of their practices have been rather unorthodox, depending on the school of thought, and, thus, some have met with opposition at various times. Much information about the practices of Shaivism is given in the *Shiva Purana*.

Lord Shiva and Goddess Durga

The Pasupatas were the earliest sect of Shaivism. They based their ideas on two works, both said to be by Kaundinya: the *Pasupatasutra* (written around 100-200 CE) and the *Pancarthabhasya* (400-600 CE). They expanded primarily into Gujarat. The Pasupatas accept the idea of a Supreme controller, but do not use the *Vedas*. They establish the existence of the Supreme through inference and say that the Supreme, who they accept as Lord Shiva, is not the original cause of the material world, but is the operative cause in that he simply used the material ingredients which already existed to form the cosmic manifestation. Therefore, through a combination of the potency of Lord Shiva and the material energy, generally regarded as Shakti or Mother Durga, the universe is created.

The conclusive Vedic literature, however, maintains that demigods such as Lord Brahma and Lord Shiva are created by and subordinate to Lord Narayana, Vishnu, who is the creator of the material worlds and all ingredients thereof. The *Varaha Purana*, *Bhagavata Purana*, *Vishnu Purana*, and many others specifically state that Narayana is the Supreme Personality, and from Him Brahma was born, from whom Shiva was born. Therefore, the demigods are not the Supreme but only dependent agents of the Supreme who work under His direction. This is confirmed in many verses throughout the Vedic literature. Although in some places we may find that demigods like Shiva, Ganesh, Surya, Indra, etc., are described as the ruler and creator of all, we should understand that almost all prayers to the demigods use such terms. But the words should be taken in their etymological sense referring to Narayana, or Vishnu, who is the source of the power that the demigods have. Shiva's name as Pasupati means "Lord of all souls," Ganesh means "Lord of all beings," Surya means "the goal of the wise," Indra means "the supreme ruler," all of which ultimately refer to the Supreme Lord and that these demigods are His agents and represent the power of the Supreme.

The *Vedanta-sutras* point out various contradictions in the philosophy of the Pasupatas or Shaivites (*Vedanta-sutras* or *Sri Bhasya* 2.2.35-41). It concludes that if one is serious about attaining spiritual enlightenment and liberation, he must avoid this questionable philosophy, for in spite of the uncommon austerities and lifestyle of the Shaivites, their destination after death is not certain. The reason is that, though they may worship Shiva as the Supreme Being, they generally believe that God is an unembodied void into which they try to merge. Many of them accept Shiva or any other deity as simply being a material manifestation of that void or Brahman. Thus, their understanding of the

Absolute Truth is faulty, and the process they use for spiritual realization is misdirected.

We should point out, however, that the Vedic literature establishes Lord Shiva as one of the topmost devotees of Lord Vishnu or Krishna. Shiva is often pictured in meditation, and many verses from the *Puranas* explain that he is always meditating on the Supreme, Sri Krishna. This means that Shiva is a Vaishnava of the greatest caliber. Furthermore, he is also one of the most important demigods in the universe. Therefore, as long as one understands Lord Shiva's real position and avoids the impersonalistic philosophy that most Shaivites follow, there certainly is no harm in worshiping or offering respects to Lord Shiva or visiting the temples dedicated to him. In this case, worshiping Lord Shiva is simply offering respects to a superior devotee of God who can help one along the way. In fact, as we have explained earlier, respect for Shiva is beneficial for such advancement.

There are many other sects of the Shaivites besides the Pasupatas. The Pratyabhijna Shaiva sect is from Kashmir. They were systematized by Vasugupta (800 CE) based on the *Shivasutra* and *Spandakarika*. The latter was expanded by the commentaries of Somananda, Utpaladeva, Abhinavagupta, and Kshemaraja, who wrote the summary teachings in his *Pratyabhijnabridaya*.

The Virasaiva or Lingayatas was another sect. There was little notice of this sect until Basava, a brahmana from Kannada developed it. They may have developed from the Kalamukhas and worshiped the *linga*.

The Shaiva Siddhantas was another sect in South India, having originated in the 11th and 13th centuries. They used Sanskrit texts, but these were later overshadowed by the Tamil texts of the Nayanmar poets, which lent to its *bhakti* or devotionally oriented system.

Additionally, there was also the Lakulisha Pasupatas who were also ascetics. The Kapalikas dwelled in the cremation grounds. Kalamukhas were ascetics similar to the Pasupatas. The Kashmir or Trika Shaivites had a three-fold concept of God: namely Shiva, the *shakti* energy, and the *anu* or individual. The *smarta* or orthodox of Shaivism practiced the *varnashrama* system as enunciated in the *smriti* literature and the *Manu-samhita* and *Kalpa Sutra*. The Natha or Kanphata yogis were a Shaiva sect said to be founded by Goraknatha. This blended the Pasupata system with Tantric practices and hatha yoga.

Shaivism essentially consists of believing and accepting that Shiva is the Absolute, that he is transcendental to time and space, and pervades all energy and existence. Shaivites believe that once the influence of *maya* and karma are removed, they will be free from the bondage that prevents them from perceiving that their spiritual identity is equal to Shiva. They chant obeisances to Shiva on a regular basis, such as "Om Namaha Shivaya," or simply "Namashivaya." Shiva is known to bless his devotees with material opulence if he is pleased. And he can be easily pleased or quickly angered. Yet, many people offer worship of some kind to Shiva and Durga generally in hopes of acquiring blessings for material facility.

The basic process of Shaivism, summarized as follows, particularly of the Saiva Siddhanta school, consists of: 1) maintaining virtue, 2) doing service and worship, 3) yoga, meditation, 4) acquiring knowledge, and then attaining enlightenment and Self-realization.

To elaborate a little, the first step includes maintaining virtue and purity, which means to cause no injury to any creature, do no stealing, and maintain honesty, truthfulness, proper conduct, patience and dedication, compassion, and control of the appetite. However, these are the basics of karma-yoga as well as the building blocks of any spiritual process.

The second step includes maintaining discipline in *sadhana*, or in one's spiritual practice and habits. This is when we control the mind and absorb our consciousness in the higher purpose of life and activities. This is also called *kriya*, regulated exercises or methods. There is also worship of the image of the divine or the deity to invoke the dormant spiritual love within us. Going to the temple or *ashrama* to participate in the *puja*, worship, and to joyfully absorb oneself in hearing the Vedic wisdom and chanting or singing is also included.

The third step includes the performance of yoga in which a person practices *pranayama* and *pratyahara*, breath control to steady the mind and senses, and withdraw them from external distractions. Then through concentration and meditation the practitioner becomes aware of God within. Through this practice, the *kundalini* may also become active, rising through the *chakras*. One's doubts, faults, mental weaknesses and ignorance, even past karma, become reduced. Then ecstasy and the divine energy are aroused. Ultimately, this is meant to give way, with practice, to *nirvikalpa samadhi*, or the experience of the timeless and formless Parashiva.

The fourth step is when a person becomes enlightened and Self-realized. In this sate, divine wisdom is a part of one's every move. Though still living in this mortal world, the person knows and also perceives that he is not of it. He is of a different, transcendental nature. This is a result of all his practice, austerity, *sadhana*, and devotional love. No more does such a yogi experience the limitations of the mind or ordinary intellect. He is free of it, or liberated, a *jivanmukta*, a liberated soul.

This process, as described in the above paragraphs, includes the basic steps that you will find in most forms of yoga, no matter whether it is applied directly to Shaivism or not. However, in this day and age, being able to take this system to its full perfection is not easy, and to attempt it thinking one can do so may be misleading. Nonetheless, as anyone can see, the basic steps of this process include qualities and practices that can enhance anyone's life and assist in whatever spiritual path is being pursued.

THE SHIVARATRI FESTIVAL

One festival that all worshipers of Shiva take part in is Shivaratri. The night of Shiva is a festival that is held in the typical pattern of preparation, purification, realization, and then celebration. On the day of the festival, people will fast and spend the day focused on Shiva, meditating and chanting "Om Namaha Shivaya." Thus, offering their obeisances to Lord Shiva, the mind is held in such single-pointed concentration throughout the day. Then at the stroke of midnight Shiva is said to manifest as the inner light of purified consciousness. This climax at night represents our overcoming the dark ignorance and reaching the state of purified spiritual knowledge. Therein we conquer the influence of the mind and senses, exhibited by staying awake all night, and enter the state of steady awareness wherein there is spiritual awakening. If one can follow this process, then he or she can experience the real meaning of Shivaratri.

THE SHIVA-LINGAM

One thing you may be questioning is why Lord Shiva is so often represented as a *lingam*. *Linga* basically means a sign or symbol. So, the *lingam* is essentially a symbol of the shapeless universal consciousness of Lord Shiva. "Shiva" also means that in which the creation lies dormant after the annihilation. So, one explanation is that the *lingam* is a

Above: A line of *lingas* around the large Shiva temple in Tanjore, India.
Bottom: A *linga* being worshiped with Ganga water, Khajurao, India.

representative of the dormant universal consciousness in which all created things rest after the cosmic annihilation. It also represents the *pradhana*, the potential but unmanifest ingredients of the material world. Another explanation is that Shiva means auspicious. So, the *linga* is the shapeless symbol for the great god of auspiciousness. It is intended to bring the shapeless unknown into our attention.

The *yoni* upon which the *lingam* often sits represents the manifest universal energy. From the unmanifest comes the manifest energy, through which all other things are created. The *yoni*, which is a symbol of Shakti, combined with the *lingam*, is a symbol of the eternal union of the paternal and maternal principles, or the positive and negative, or the static and dynamic energies of the Absolute Reality. It is the communion of the eternal consciousness and dynamic power of the Shakti, the source of all actions and changes. It is also the symbol for the creation of the universe through the combination of the active energy of Lord Shiva and his Shakti. This is how Lord Shiva and Durga are considered the parents of the universe. The symbolism of the *lingam* and *yoni* also represents the base of the spine, meaning the Muladhara *chakra*, upon which the *kundalini* is resting, waiting for awakening.

There are a few versions according to the *Puranas* of why Shiva is worshiped as a *lingam* and how this happened, of which I will relate one. There was a great sacrificial ceremony that was going to take place many hundreds of years ago. The great sage Narada Muni was invited to it and asked who would receive the effects of the sacrifice. No one could answer, so the sages who were present asked him who should receive it. Narada said that Sri Vishnu, Brahma and Shiva were all eligible, but they would have to find out which one had the most patience and purity to be the receiver of the sacrifice. So, he chose the great sage Brighu to learn the answer.

Brighu had many mystic powers and was able to travel to the domain of the demigods. So, first he went to see Lord Brahma, but Brahma was preoccupied and did not notice Brighu's presence. Feeling insulted, Brighu cursed Brahma, "You are so proud of your power of creation, you did not notice my arrival. For this you shall have no temples on earth." Thus, there are very few temples of Brahma on earth. Next, Brighu went to see Shiva in Kailash, but Shiva also did not notice Brighu's arrival. Brighu, again feeling offended, cursed Shiva to be worshiped only as a *lingam* on earth. This is the reason why Lord Shiva is primarily represented and worshiped as a *lingam* on this planet instead of a personalized deity.

Then, to continue the story, Brighu went to see Lord Vishnu, who also did not recognize Brighu's presence. Brighu was so angered that he went forward and kicked Vishnu's chest. Lord Vishnu apologized if He had hurt Brighu's foot and began praising Brighu. Brighu immediately felt pleased and could understand that Vishnu was actually the most qualified to receive the offerings from the sacrifice. However, Lakshmidevi, the goddess of fortune and Lord Vishnu's wife, was very displeased by Brighu's action and, therefore, does not bestow much mercy on the brahmanas who, as a result, are often without much money.

To explain the shape of the *lingam*, a Baana *linga* is egg-shaped and is meant to show that Ishvara has neither beginning nor end. The Lingobhavamurti form of the *linga* is said to be the prime manifestation of the form of the formless, which Shiva is said to have manifested exactly at midnight on Shivaratri. This is why everyone stays up until midnight and then worships that form during the Shivaratri festival. A representation of the Lingobhavamurti can often be found in a niche on the outside wall of the sanctum in any important Shiva temple.

The *lingas* in the temples are often formed in three parts. The lowest part is the base square called the Brahmabhaga or Brahma-pitha, which represents the creator Brahma. The next part in the middle is the octagonal Vishnubhaga or Vishnu-pitha, which signifies Lord Vishnu the sustainer. Both of these parts form the pedestal. The top cylindrical portion is the Rudrabhaga or Shiva-pitha, which is also called the Pujabhaga since this is the worshipable part. The top portion is also meant to symbolize the projecting flame of fire. This flame also represents the destructive aspects as well as the preserving power of God.

There are twelve important Jyotirlinga or self-manifesting *linga* temples scattered across India. They are found at Kedarnatha, Kashi Visvanatha, Somnatha, Baijnath, Ramesvare, Ghrisnesvar, Bhimasankar, Mahakala, Mallikarjuna, Amalesvar, Nagesvar, and Tryambakesvar. The five Pancha Bhuta Lingas in India are located at Kalahastisvar, Jambukesvar, Arunachalesvar, Ekambesvara at Kanchipuram, and Nataraja at Chidambaram. The temple of Lord Mahalinga at Tiruvidaimarudur (Madhyarjuna) is also a great temple in South India.

The reason Lord Shiva is often worshiped by pouring Ganges water over the *lingam* is that it represents the Ganges descending from heaven on to Shiva's head. The legend is that when the Ganges first began to flow to the earthly planet from the heavenly region, the force of it would have destroyed the earth. To prevent this, Lord Shiva agreed to let the river first fall on his head before it formed into a river. It is also explained that when worshipers pour milk or Ganga water on the *linga*, it represents the pouring of ghee on the sacred fire in the fire ceremony, or *yajna*. This is the symbolic offering of ourselves to God.

One story in connection with the Shiva *linga* is found in the *Linga Purana*. It describes that once Lord Brahma, the god of creation, and Lord Vishnu, the God of protection, engaged in an argument on who was greater. When those two great gods were fighting between themselves, Lord Shiva appeared as a huge pillar of fire that spread across the universe. He told Brahma and Vishnu that whoever finds the head or foot of his form of flame would be considered greater. Then Brahma took the form of a swan and set out to reach the top of the flame. Vishnu took the form of a boar to seek out the foot of the fire. But in spite of their efforts, they could not succeed in finding the limits. They realized their mistake and the peerless greatness of Lord Shiva. This shows how Shiva cannot be approached through ego, but responds with love to those who surrender to him. In this pastime, Lord Shiva appeared in the form of the fiery *lingam* for their benefit. So, they were considered blessed with additional insight for worshiping that oldest form of him. This form of Shiva who appeared from the flame is called Lingodbhava. This story is found in the *Shiva Purana* and other texts.

This further helps to show how the *lingam* is not formless nor really a form, but a symbol for the divinity of Lord Shiva. In Sanskrit, *linga* also means "mark." It is a mark or symbol of Lord Shiva in the same way that large puddles of water is an indication of heavy rains. It is an inference for something else, like the form of that which is formless and omnipotent.

THE GODDESS DURGA

Worship of the Goddess goes back at least 4000 years in India, and further back to the Vedic times. Durga is the Goddess of the universe, and Parvati, the wife of Lord Shiva, is a form of Durga. She has up to 64 different forms, with different names for each form. Each form represents a different pastime, power, or aspect of the Goddess. Some of the names of these forms of Durga are Ambika, Bhadra, Bhadrakali, Aryadurga, Vedagarbha, Kshemakshemakari, Naikabahu, Bhagavati, Katyayani, and others, such as Sati, which means chastity. In her gentle aspects she is worshiped as Kanya, Kamakshi, or Mukamba. Uma (Parvati) is the maiden name for the consort of Lord Shiva. She represents matter (*prakriti*). Shiva is the god of destruction, which has no meaning without objects to destroy. Thus, he is paired with Uma.

The *Narada Purana* (1.3.13-15) lists many other names of

Lord Shiva and Goddess Durga 113

A deity of Goddess Durga, multi-armed which chows her weapons and powers, wearing red cloth, and riding her lion carrier, in a temple in South Delhi.

Durga. Since she is considered one of the energies of the Supreme Lord, she is regarded as His *shakti*, and is called Uma, Bharati, Girija, and Ambika. The great sages designate her as Durga, Bhadrakali, Chandi, Mahesvari, Kaumari, Vaishnavi (supreme potency of Lord Vishnu), Varahi (potency of Lord Varaha, an *avatar* of Krishna), Aindra, Shambhavi, Brahmi (connected with Lord Brahma), Vidya (spiritual knowledge), Avidya (nescience), Maya (the illusory energy of the Lord), and Para Prakriti (the Supreme Primordial Nature).

Other aspects of Durga are accompanied by a different name and often a story for each name. We will not relate each story, but some of the additional names can be summarized. These include Lalita, who is a beautiful Goddess, living eternally in the city of Shripura on Mount Meru with her spouse, Shiva Kameshvara. Annapurna is the form of Parvati who blesses the household with food. Aparajita means Durga as the invincible. Bala means the child. Bhadrakali is one of the aspects of Mahakali and the form that sprang from her wrath when her husband, Shiva, was insulted by Daksha, and who fought along with Virabhadra, the embodiment of Shiva's wrath, to destroy Daksha's sacrifice. Bhairavi is the Devi as the power to cause terror, one of the ten aspects of Shiva's energy. Bhavani is another name. Bhutatma is the Mother of the Bhutas or ghosts. Dakshayani is Durga as the daughter of Daksha. Gauri, means yellow or golden wife of Shiva. Indrakshi has eyes similar to Lord Indra's, and is often worshiped by Indra. She can also alleviate the incurable diseases when pleased by nice hymns. Jagadhatri is the one who sustains the world. Katyayani is the Devi who was once born as the daughter of Kata. Parvati is the daughter of Parvata, the personification of the Himalaya. Rudrani is wife of Rudra. Tripura Bhairavi is the *shakti* of Shiva when he is the ruler of death.

Durga is often pictured as a beautiful woman in red cloth. She may have four, eight, ten, eighteen, or twenty hands and three eyes. Items in her hands can include a conch, disc, trident, bow, arrow, sword, dagger, shield, rosary, wine cup, and bell, all of which represent her different potencies. She may also be standing on a lotus or riding a lion. The lion represents power, but also the animal tendency of greed for food and other sensual objects. Her riding on the lion represents that she keeps all such tendencies under complete control.

The full details of Durga can be found in the *Devibhagavat*, or another text called the *Durgasaptashati* which can be found as part of the *Markandeya Purana*. The name "Durga" means one who is difficult to know. Yet, being the mother of the universe, she can be approached through love. Love is also natural for her to give to her children.

Durga is the personification of the material energy, in which all materially conditioned living beings are absorbed in thoughts, actions and identity. She is also considered the power of sleep, or the *yoga-nidra* in which Lord Vishnu rests between creative cycles. She is also the personification of wisdom and knowledge. Her energy permeates the universe. She also embodies sacrifice or penance and the highest knowledge. She is most beautiful, but at the same time fierce and terrible. She can dispel difficulties as well as kill the demons.

Another of her popular forms is Mahishasuramardini. In this form she is often pictured with eight arms, each with a weapon, and in the process of killing the demon Mahishasura in his form as a bull. She was generated out of the anger and powers of the gods, namely Vishnu, Shiva, Brahma, and others. And their weapons became her weapons. Thus, riding on her fierce lion, she fought and killed Mahishasura and his army. This demon represents the egotistical propensity that brute strength is all that is needed to acquire selfish desires. While fighting amongst the gods, he was succeeding, until their combined powers and will to fight was manifest in the form of the Devi as Mahishasuramardini, who then killed the demon.

Symbolically, Durga destroys the buffalo demon which represents *tamo-guna*, the dark quality of laziness, ignorance and inertia. So, she destroys the *tamo-guna* within each of us, which can be very difficult to overcome. Another one of her qualities is her wrath, which sometimes manifests as war. Such war cleanses the world of the many negative elements that accumulate from a sinful society.

Later, when the gods were challenged by the demons Shumbha and Nishumbha, they went to petition the Goddess again. This time, from the side of Parvati, she manifested herself as Kaushika Durga, also called Ambika. Ambika's beauty attracted the demons who then wanted to marry her. She vowed to marry the one who could defeat her in battle, but all such attempts were disastrous. Even with the assistance of giants like Dhumralochana, Chanda, Munda, and Raktabija, they were unsuccessful.

Then from the forehead of this Durga manifested the fierce, dark goddess Kali, who became known as Chamunda for beheading the demons Chanda and Munda. When she fought with Raktabija, it took a special endeavor because of his powers that caused each drop of his spilled blood to become another demon. It was Kali who managed to drink all of his flowing blood and prevent any additional demons from manifesting. Thus, Durga was able to kill him. She then easily killed Nishumbha, but Shumbha accused her of accepting help. The Devi then withdrew all her emanations into her one form, and then proceeded to battle and kill Shumbha.

Durga is also called Vaishnavishakti, the creative power from Lord Vishnu, the original cause. She is also called Vindhyavasini (the one who lives in the Vindhya mountains), Raktadanta (the one with the red teeth), Shatakshi (who is liked to having one hundred eyes), Shakambhari (who gives the life-force of vegetables), Durgaa (the slayer of the demon Durga), Bhima (the ferocious), and Bhramaramba (one who is liked to having a form of bees).

Devi is also manifested as Maheshvari, which, according to the three modes of material nature, also manifests as Mahakali, Mahalakshmi and Mahasarasvati. These are different than the goddesses Lakshmi and Sarasvati, which will be discussed later. In the aspect of Mahakali she is considered the personification of the *tamo-guna*, or mode of darkness and sleep or inertia. She is also *maya*, the illusory energy of Lord Vishnu. Thus, this *maya* must be removed for us to awaken to our real spiritual identity. It is within this *maya* in which the seeming powers of evil and divisiveness exist. She is often pictured as blue in color with ten hands, each holding a different weapon, including a sword, disc, mace, arrow, bow, iron club, lance, sling, a human head, and a conch.

Mahalakshmi is the aspect of *raja-guna*, the passionate nature. In this aspect she is seen as red in color, signifying the will to fight evil forces. She has eighteen hands, holding a rosary, pot, club, lance, sword, shield, conch, bell, wine cup, trident, noose, and disc. She is the one who killed Mahishasura.

Mahasarasvati represents the *sattvic* aspect, or that of goodness and purity. She is light in color and has eight hands that hold a bell, trident, plough, conch, pestle, disc, bow, and arrow. She is the manifestation of beauty, work and organization. It is she, as Kaushika Durga, who manifested from Parvati. She is the one who destroyed the demons known as Dhumralochana, Chanda, Munda, Raktabija, Nishumbha, and Shumbha, all of which are certain aspects of the principle of ego.

Kali is another form of the goddess that is often seen in temples and pictures. She is usually pictured as nude except for being covered by her scattered hair. She has a dark complexion. She wears an apron of human hands and a garland of human skulls, and sometimes carries a human head in one hand, freshly severed and dripping with blood, and a long chopper in another hand. The other two hands are giving blessings and offering protection. Her tongue is protruding, dripping with blood. She is also often seen in a cremation ground or in a battlefield amidst dead and mutilated bodies. Sometimes she is standing on the white or bluish body of her spouse, Shiva. He supplicates her in this way to keep her from destroying everything.

The meaning of all this is that, first of all, Kali represents time, Kala, which devours everything in its terrifying ways. She is naked because she is free from the veil of ignorance that the universe represents, which hides our real spiritual identity. She is black because she represents *tama-guna* or the void which has swallowed everything, including space, time, and the ingredients of material nature. Her apron of hands indicates that she is pleased with the offerings of our work, so she wears them. It also represents the inward potential for outward manifestation waiting to take place. Her disheveled hair simply represents her freedom to go and do as she likes. The garland of 50 skulls represents the 50 letters of the alphabet or sound, from which the whole material manifestation has sprung, and which is now in a state of destruction indicated by her wearing them. Though she is an awesome form, she is also offering freedom from fear by her hand gestures.

A further explanation of why Goddess Kali stands on Shiva is that once Kali engaged in a battle in which she destroyed all the demons. She danced in victory to such an extent that the worlds started to shake in destruction. Everyone became concerned and Shiva came to appease her from further dancing. Yet, she was so worked up that she could not notice or listen to him. So, Shiva laid like a corpse at her feet to absorb the shock of her movements, and when she finally noticed that she had stepped on her husband, she put her tongue out in shame.

THE IDENTITY OF DURGA AND DIFFERENCE BETWEEN MAHAMAYA AND YOGAMAYA

Being the personification of the material energy, Durga is also the maidservant of Lord Krishna, and conducts herself in accordance to the will of the Supreme. Her shadow is the material energy, *maya*. In this form of Durga, she is pictured as a beautiful demigoddess with ten arms, representing the ten types of material activities. She rides on her lion, indicating her heroic activities. She is the subduer of vices, represented by the image of her trampling the demon Mahishasura. She is the mother of her sons Kartikeya and Ganesha, representing beauty and success. She is armed with twenty weapons, denoting the various pious activities enjoined by the *Vedas* for the suppression of vices. She also holds a snake, which signifies destructive time. The word *durga* also means a prison house or a fort. So, the material world is like a prison from which it is hard to escape. "Dur" means difficulty and "Ga" means going. So, it is very difficult to escape from this material world without undergoing many hardships. But one who takes shelter of the spiritual potency can get free from the illusory nature of the material world. Thus, when the living beings forget their spiritual nature and the service of the Supreme Being, Krishna, they are confined in the material prison of the universe. This is the aspect of the cosmic creation which is presided over by Durga. However, those who are devotees of the Lord and who are on the spiritual path to regain their real nature are free from this prison-like environment of the universe. Durga does not affect them.

The spiritual form of Durga is *Yogamaya*. The external form of Durga is *Mahamaya*, the illusory energy. The spiritual form of Durga who functions on the platform of *shuddha-sattva*, pure transcendental existence, is understood to be Krishna's sister, known as Ekanamsha or Subhadra.[9] The name Subhadra means auspicious. So, Subhadra also paves the way for the devotee's spiritual progress by supplying that which is auspicious and taking away all that is inauspicious. This is the spiritual form of Durga, the shadow of whom is the external material energy.

We should note, however, that Durga works in the material world. Subhadra plays the part of Lord Krishna's sister and is the internal or spiritual energy, and does not work as Durga in the material world. So, originally their energy is one and the same, but through her expansion as Durga she works in a different capacity within the material realm.

Furthermore, higher than Subhadra is Radharani, Lord Krishna's consort and the quintessence of spiritual energy. She is the personification, essence, and origin of Lord Krishna's pleasure potency, *hladini-shakti*. This pleasure potency of Lord Krishna expands to become Radharani for the sake of the most intimate spiritual pastimes in Goloka Vrinadavana, the topmost spiritual planet. This potency expands further into the forms of Krishna's queens in the other Vaikuntha planets, and also as His sister, Subhadra, for other purposes and pastimes. And Durga is an expansion of this internal or spiritual energy. In this way, Durga also can be considered an expansion of Radharani. Therefore, Radharani is the source of the pleasure essence in the spiritual dimension, while Durga provides the means for all pleasure in the material realm.

So, herein we can understand that *mahamaya* in the material world is an expansion of *yogamaya* in the spiritual world. The difference in function is that *yogamaya* manages the spiritual sky, and in her partial expansion as *mahamaya* she manages the material world. *Yogamaya* covers the devotees in the spiritual world so that they can forget the Lord's greatness and engage in loving pastimes with Him as His friends, parents, servants, and so on without being overwhelmed by His omnipotence. *Mahamaya* in the material world, on the other hand, keeps the living entities forgetful of their true eternal nature as long as they have no spiritual inclination. It keeps them superficially content with material happiness. So, *yogamaya* helps bring the devotees together with the Supreme Being in various relationships while *mahamaya* keeps them separate, or at least makes it seem they are separate through the principle of forgetfulness.

THE TWO ENERGIES OF MATERIAL AND SPIRITUAL

Another way to understand this is that there are two divisions of energy, the material and spiritual. The original energy is the spiritual, in which is the *hladini-shakti* potency of Krishna, which is His pleasure potency. It is this pleasure potency from God through which all spiritual joy and happiness are felt. This is also the original form of Durga who is nondifferent from this spiritual energy, but Durga is her form in the material world. The partial expansion of the *hladini-shakti* potency is *mahamaya*, which also acts like a covering for the *hladini-shakti* potency, which is also the pleasure of our spiritual nature and connection with the Supreme. In the material world she bewilders the conditioned souls so they can think they are happy in material pursuits. In this way, the materialists remain covered over by their attraction to their desires for sense pleasure due to *mahamaya*, and the devotees and transcendentalists become absorbed in spiritual pleasure through *yogamaya*, or the *hladini-shakti*. It is through *yogamaya* that the religious become happy or joyous in their spiritual pursuits and liberated from the material realm. This is the work of Subhadra who provides what is auspicious and takes away what is inauspicious for the sincere seekers on the spiritual path. Thus, the material energy is like a testing ground that must be passed before one can gain entrance into the spiritual world. It also protects the spiritual atmosphere from those who are not sincere. This is also one of the functions of Durga.

In the *Brahma Vaivarta Purana* (*Krishna-Janma-Khanda*, 118.35) Durga talks with Shiva about how she is an expansion from the highest realms and explains herself in this way: "I am Mahalakshmi in Vaikuntha, Srimati Radha in Goloka, Shivaa [connected with Shiva] in the region of Shiva, and Sarasvati in the abode of god Brahma." Thus, from the highest levels of the spiritual domain she expands herself to include all other *shaktis* or potencies.

The *Narada Purana* (1.3.27) also explains that in regard to Lord Vishnu, "His Shakti is the great Maya, the trustworthy upholder of the universe. In view of its being the material cause of the universe, it is [also] called *prakriti* by scholars."

This illusory energy, *maya*, plays an important part in the creative process of the cosmic manifestation. In the *Srimad-Bhagavatam* (3.5.25), Maitreya explains to Vidura that the external energy works as both cause and effect in the cosmic manifestation. This external energy is known as *maya* or illusion, and through her agency only is the entire material manifestation made possible.

Maya is the external energy of the Lord and is divided into two parts. *Maya* is the efficient cause, and the other part are the ingredients that create the cosmic manifestation, known as the *pradhana* or *prakriti*.[10] The *Srimad-Bhagavatam* (10.63.26) relates that in the *pradhana* aspect, *maya* is composed of time, activity, providence (the destiny of the conditioned souls) and nature. These along with the vital force or energy, the subtle material ingredients, and the material nature, known as the field of activity for the conditioned souls, and the eleven senses (the senses of perception and organs of action) and five elements (earth, air, fire, water, and ether), are the ingredients of *maya*. Thus, Lord Krishna is the creator and *maya* only helps Him as an instrument. It is this *maya*, or material nature, which the Lord glances over which becomes agitated, and into which the Lord injects the seed of life as the original living entities. Thereafter, due to the reactions of the Lord's glance and His energy that mixes with *maya*, the material energy gives birth to the myriad universes.[11]

So, *maya*, or material nature, is merely the secondary cause of the creation. Nonetheless, it serves two purposes: It contains the subtle material elements, and then through the changes that take place causes the material manifestation. The *Brahma-samhita* (5.19) also explains that the primary material elements were originally separated. Then through the spiritual power of the Supreme, in His knowledge potency, *maya* was moved. It is through this combination of the efficient or spiritual potency in conjunction with the inactive material causal principles of *maya* that the elements and the different entities develop into a state of cooperation. Thus, it is by this combination of energies that the material creation can manifest, and the spiritual living beings appear as the materially conditioned souls within the material elements of the creation. In a graphic description, it is explained that *maya* appears like a huge pot filled with the innumerable universes that are like mustard seeds within it.[12]

Another function of *maya* is to cover the living beings with the material energy, and, thus, keep them in illusion as to what is their true identity. This sort of forgetfulness is one of the main principles of the material world, without which the living beings could not engage in material life. After all, if it was too obvious to the living beings that they are spiritual entities, they would not be satisfied with material pursuits or the engagement of bodily sense pleasures. So, to help provide a playground for the materially conditioned souls who are rebellious and want to live outside of God's kingdom, this forgetfulness must be there. This is the third function of *maya*, which covers the living entity in this way. As explained in the *Srimad-Bhagavatam* (8.14.10), "People in general are bewildered by the illusory energy [*maya*], and therefore they try to find the Absolute Truth, the Supreme Personality of Godhead, through various types of research and philosophical speculation. Nonetheless, they are unable to see the Supreme Lord."

This is further explained as follows: The internal potency of the Supreme Lord is spiritual. The marginal potency consists of the living beings who can lean toward either the spiritual or material energy. The third potency of the Lord is the material energy itself, *maya*, also called nescience or darkness. It is this *maya* which makes the living entity godless and fills him with the desires for fruitive activity and sense pleasure. Thus, because of being influenced by the nescient potency, which covers his spiritual position, he suffers the threefold miseries of material existence.[13] These three kinds of miseries of material existence include those that come from the body itself, those caused by other living beings, and those problems caused by natural occurrences.

Because of being illusioned like this, the living entities cannot understand the truth of the creation and, thus, they wander throughout the material world for many lifetimes. However, the living beings are independent in determining whether they want to engage in material or spiritual activities. Misusing this independence to turn toward the dark side separates the living beings in varying degrees from the spiritual light. Yet, when the living beings turn toward God and work to regain their spiritual nature, they can return to their normal spiritual state of being and be relieved of material existence.

Actually, the spiritual living beings are merely covered by this cloud of *maya*, which affects their consciousness. Therefore, the goal of any genuine spiritual path is simply to remove this cloud and the influence of the illusory energy. If a religious system cannot do that, then it is incomplete.

The *Brahma-samhita* (5.44) also explains that *maya* is like the shadow of the Lord's *chit* or knowledge potency, and is also worshiped in the form of Durga, the creating, preserving, and destroying agency of this material world.

THE SHAKTAS AND TANTRISM

The Shakta tradition is another of the three major traditions of the Vedic culture. The power or energy of Shiva is Shakti, the embodiment of power. She is the power and support of the entire universe. Thus, she is the Universal Mother. He who worships Shakti or the divine feminine energy is a Shakta. In this tradition Shiva represents the eternal consciousness, while Shakti represents mind and mater. The Shaktas are those who believe that the original active and creative principle of existence is the divine energy called *shakti*. Shakti is the feminine energy inherent in everything throughout the universe and is considered the companion of Lord Shiva in her personified form.

The original ideas of the Shakta belief can be traced back to the *Rig Veda* and other later works. However, the *Vedanta-sutras* (2.2.42-45) point out some essential faults with the Shakta philosophy. For example, to consider that Shakti or energy alone can be the independent cause of the world is not a complete understanding. The reason is that energy alone cannot create without the cooperation, direction, and facility from the energetic, which, in this case, is the Creator or Supreme Being. Energy must have a source, meaning the energetic. Thus, as we have explained in the previous section, this Shakti is ultimately the energy of the Supreme Lord. She is not nor can be the sole cause of the world. She works most closely with the energy of the Lord in the form of Lord Shiva.

The Supreme is the energetic or source and controller of the energy, just as the powerhouse is the source of the electrical energy that is controlled to illuminate so many light bulbs. Thus, energy cannot exist without the energetic. Therefore, the followers of the Shakti cult who have imagined that energy is the cause of the world are not supported by conclusive Vedic authority. It is not possible that merely by energy alone all the elements of the universe can be produced. In the same manner, we do not see a woman produce children without the contact of a man. Only through the energy given by the seed of a man can there be conception in a woman. Similarly, only if Shakti or nature is controlled and directed by the contact of the *purusha*, God, can there be the organized formation of the material elements. In this way, everything proceeds from the Supreme Being, as explained elsewhere in Vedic literature, and Shakti is not independent.

The Shaktas are divided into two groups, one called the Right-hand, the other called the Left-hand group. The Right-hand or *dakshinachara* are the ascetic group, while the Left-hand or *vamachara* are those who combine their yogic exercises with practices that are often considered more unorthodox, called the *panchamakara*, or the five "M"s. These are *madya* (wine drinking), *mamsa* (meat-eating), *matsya* (fish), *mudra* (parched grain), *maithuna* (ritual sex), and also ceremonial songs. In most cases, the drinking of wine, eating meat, and sexual activities are meant to be used as part of a sacrificial rite in the worship of goddess Kali or Durga.

Tantraism is linked with yoga and the magical formulas of the *Atharva Veda*. The ascetic process of the Tantric path is very similar to the raja yoga and kundalini yoga systems. But before going on to the advanced stages, one must perfect the basics, such as simplicity, kindness, devotion, prayer, and self-analysis, along with the *yama* and *niyama* principles as described in raja yoga.

Tantra is a path meant to utilize all the sciences to develop psychic power, understand reality, and expand one's awareness in all states of consciousness. In this way, all levels of consciousness are to be explored by performing various kinds of exercises and techniques. However, the training and procedures that some Tantric yogis may have to do as a sign of advancement can be a dreadful experience for one who is psychologically unprepared. Detachment from the body and advancement on the path is attained by the performance of what most people would consider unusual if not bizarre practices. In Tantrism, particularly the Left-hand path, progress and liberation are achieved primarily through direct experience rather than through meditation. The ingredients and experiences in the rituals are also to induce different levels of consciousness.

Once the Tantric yogi has mastered all the basic requisites of yoga, such as the sitting postures, controlling the external and internal organs, and keeping the mind from all material attractions and repulsions, then he can continue with more arduous austerities. He may be instructed to go to the cremation grounds and search through the ashes to find and eat particular parts of a corpse that do not burn. He must do this without the slightest disgust. These more extreme practices were mostly for the adepts who were experienced in the Left Hand path. These would induce a deep level of detachment from praise, pride, or even shame or disgust, and all that might keep one from entering the Supreme bliss. These practices are metaphorically called "removing a thorn with a thorn." It is to break social norms in order to transcend limitations of body consciousness and attain Shiva. The path of the Right Hand Tantric is not as extreme and uses tamer or more harmless symbolism in rituals, or ignores the severe rituals altogether.

Some of the Tantric followers also practice magic and alchemy in their techniques. It is well known that Tantrics who know the art of magic can possess amazing but dark powers. The apparel of such sorcerers usually include items like flayed animal or human skin as coverings, necklaces of teeth or bone, a girdle of snake skin, and they sometimes cover themselves with the ashes of cremated bodies or the dirt from an exhumed corpse. Elements used in their rituals may consist of charred bones, eyeballs, fat, marrow, and even excrement from corpses, along with mantras used to call or address the dead or even demons and ghouls. The Tantric may also make a human skull into his eating bowl, or the top of a monkey skull as a drinking cup. The human thighbone is also used among some as a horn for calling spirits. With these kinds of items they perform ceremonies such as the black ritual that is a secret and dangerous short path to attaining occult power.

One ritual on this path in Tibetan is called the *chod*, in which the Tantric practitioner goes to the crematorium and invites spirits to feast on his body, which symbolizes destruction of ego, pride, selfishness, fear, etc. The Tantric should be so focused on this that he can actually hear the ghouls masticating as they devour his flesh. After the spirits have dined and departed, the Tantric, recovering from the ordeal, mentally reassembles his bones and organs until he is whole again. Another aspect of this black ritual is known in Tibet as *rolangs*, in which the Tantric, through occult powers, animates a dead corpse by calling spirits to possess it and then asks it questions or uses it for magical purposes.

If the yogi remains sane and continues on the Left-hand Shakta or Tantric path, he may also try to perform the sex ritual. In this case, the Tantric yogi worships the woman as a representation of Shakti and accepts the role as Shiva and has intercourse with her, but does not ejaculate any semen. The Tantric controls his mind and senses, and during intercourse constricts his stomach muscles in particular ways so that he takes in the fluid and energy released by the woman. Thus, he keeps the combination of his male energy and the female energy at the base of his spine. By combining the male and female energy in such a way, the practitioner is said to get special power and enlightenment. This is also supposed to help awaken the *kundalini* at the base of the spine when it is time for the yogi to begin meditation. However, some descriptions of these sex practices are very strange, and the texts that describe them are quite graphic. It has also been said that even Marco Polo, while witnessing these Tantric practices and acts of sorcery during his explorations of the world, did not consider it fit to give a full account of what he saw. This, however, is only one aspect of the Tantric cult. Other more prominent techniques include mantra, *pranayama*, meditation, etc, as has already been described.

These days in the West people use certain Tantric practices as an excuse to simply engage in sex in the name of so-called spiritual exercises, religion or yoga. Although they hardly know anything about the real Tantric practices or bother to reach any of the initial yogic qualifications one must attain, they are very eager to engage in so-called Tantric sex with the hopes of increasing the duration of their orgasm. This, however, was the exact opposite of the real purpose of the ritual. Extended orgasm is considered to deplete the yogi of his mystic powers and mental and psychic capacity. Even Buddhist texts mention that keeping the seed (semen) is life, while the falling of the seed is death. In this way, by retaining one's semen, a man can become very powerful.

THE TANTRAS

When explaining the *Tantras*, the root *tan* means to expand. Thus, *tantra* means to expand the meaning of the Vedic knowledge. The *Tantras* are the texts studied by those, especially amongst the Shaiva and Tibetan Buddhist Vajrayana cults, who worship Shakti, the Goddess personification of the universal feminine energy. These *Tantras* can be dialogues between the goddess Durga and Shiva. When the Goddess asks Shiva questions, they are called *Agamas*, and when Shiva asks the Goddess questions, they are *Nigamas*. The *Agamas* contain descriptions of a variety of topics such as deity making, temple and altar construction, etc. They may also elaborate on the five main topics which include the creation, universal annihilation, worship of the gods, the attainment of the six superhuman faculties, and the main methods of meditation that bring union with the Supreme. Certain *Tantras* also contain magical or mystical formulas that some practitioners use for their own purposes.

The *Tantras* generally accept Shakti as the creative force, worshipable as an aspect of the Divine but inseparable from the masculine principle, which is called Brahman by some and Shiva by others. However, the *Tantras* are often composed of irregular Sanskrit to obscure their secrets in the language. Also, in order to allow only the initiates to understand it's meaning, some of them used much erotic symbolism and esoteric terminology. This has led to a misunderstanding of its ideology as well as its practices, especially among westerners who perceive an overabundance of sexual connotation in it, which is not really there.

It is not easy to date the formation or appearance of the *Tantras*. It is suggested that they were predominately developed in North India and Assam. Some scholars have not been able to determine whether Tantrism originated in Buddhism or Hinduism, but evidence suggests that Tantrism was first systematized by particular Buddhist schools. This systematization seemed to have resulted in dividing Buddhism into several major and minor groups because of philosophical differences. All such groups assisted in laying the groundwork for various radical ideas, among which was Tantrism. Tantrism greatly influenced the Vajrayana and Mahayana sects. Some scholars date the Buddhist *Tantras*, like the *Hevajra*, to sometime earlier than 400-700 CE. Other *Tantras* include the *Nityashoda-shikarnava*, *Yoginihridaya*, *Tantraraja*, and *Kularnava*, all dated between 1000-1400 CE, and the later *Mahanirvana Tantra*. However, those *Tantras* that are related to the older Vedic texts had to have been of an earlier date. For example, the *Narada-Pancharatra* is said to have been spoken by Lord Shiva to Narada Muni, and later compiled by Srila Vyasadeva 5,000 years ago.

There are, however, different *Tantras* for different people. There are specific *Tantras* for those who are in the mode of darkness or *tamo-guna*, others for those in the mode of passion or *rajo-guna*, and still more for those in the mode of goodness, *sattva-guna*. There are the Shaiva *Agamas*, the Shakta *Agamas*, and the later Tibetan Buddhist *Agamas*, as well as the *Linga, Kalika* and *Devi Puranas*. The *Agamas* are divided in four parts: metaphysical knowledge, yoga, ritual practices, and conduct. There are 28 Shaiva *Agamas*, 77 Shakta *Agamas*, and 108 Pancharatra or Vaishnava *Agamas*. The Vaishnava *Tantras* include the *Narada-pancharatra, Pancharatra, Vaikhanasa*, the *Gautamiya Tantra, Brihad-Gautamiya Tantra*, and others like the *Lakshmi Tantra*. These contain rules and regulations for engaging in the process for purifying the mind of the stumbling blocks of material attachments and for fixing the consciousness on the qualities and spiritual pastimes of the Supreme. The *Narada-Pancharatra* deals with Lord Krishna and some about Radha. Ramanuja wrote his *Agama-pramanya* to show the Vedic connection of the Vaishnava *Pancharatra* texts.

The difference in the Vaishnava *Tantras* from the *Tantras* of the Left-hand Shaktas is that they remove the illusion that the physical body is the self, along with the need for performing unorthodox bodily activities for spiritual advancement, while the Left-hand Shaktas are attached to the means of using the body to attain magical powers, rapid illumination, wealth, high position, or quick liberation. To be successful on the Left-hand path is very difficult and the aspirant can rarely persevere to the end. As we can easily see from our partial description of the Tantric Left-hand path, such philosophy and activities are deeply imbedded in the mode of darkness, *tamo-guna*. This may be the level of experience that some people need in this life, but by tampering with this path, one usually increases his illusion, selfishness and pride, or it can bring disease, evil-mindedness, even insanity, and sometimes sudden death. This is not surprising since what is associated with the dark modes produces intense, dark, or questionable results.

The Vaishnava *Tantras*, on the other hand, are aimed at bringing one to a higher state of consciousness, a loftier awareness of our real identity as spiritual beings and our relationship with God without the unorthodox activities. It enables one to feel an inner joy and happiness by reawakening one's awareness of his or her spiritual identity. Soon the obstacles or material attachments and desires that seemed insurmountable have no effect. A serious follower can feel himself progressing very rapidly. As a person attains a higher spiritual taste, he becomes less concerned for bodily attractions and is content in any situation, whether it be in gain or in loss. His unity with God increases and he becomes perfectly satisfied. In this way, he soon leaves material consciousness behind and through his spiritual realizations reaches the perfectional stage of life.

HOW SHIVA AND DURGA ARE CONSIDERED THE MOTHER AND FATHER OF THE UNIVERSE

Since it is the glance of the Supreme Being over the energy of Durga, *maya*, which sets in motion the creation of the universes, Durga is therefore known as the Universal Mother.[14] This is why when people speak of the material nature, it is always referred to as a female, as "she", Mother Nature, and as the Goddess. And the essence of Mother Nature in the Vedic tradition is represented as Durga. She is united with her husband, Lord Shiva, who is then considered the father of the universe.

It is explained in the *Vayu Purana* that Shiva is an expansion of

Sadashiva, who is a direct expansion of Lord Krishna. Sadashiva appears in order to perform various pastimes. Sadashiva is a resident of one of the eternal Vaikuntha planets of the spiritual world. His consort there is Ramadevi, a form of Lakshmi. She expands into *mahamaya* in the material worlds, where she is then known as Durga. Thus, the spiritual Sadashiva and Ramadevi again become related as Shiva and Durga, who are the origin of material nature.

The part that is played by Lord Shiva during the creation is more fully explained in the *Brahma-samhita* (5.6-8). Therein it states that Lord Krishna, the Lord of Gokula, the topmost planet in the spiritual sky, is the Supreme Godhead, the very Self of eternal ecstasies. He is busily engaged in the enjoyments of the transcendental realm and has no association with the mundane, illusory material energy. He does not stop His spiritual engagements. When He intends to create the material manifestation, He merely sends His glance over the deluding energy in the form of His time potency. Krishna's expansion in the form of Maha-Vishnu in the Causal Ocean carries this glance to the material energy. This glance from Maha-Vishnu is the efficient cause of the creation. The dim halo of this glance, the reflected effulgence, is Shiva in his form as Shambhu, who is the symbol of masculine mundane procreation. It is through this form of Shiva that the Supreme Lord associates with the material energy. In his role as Shambhu, he is the principle by which Maha-Vishnu impregnates the material nature with the seeds of the innumerable living entities. Otherwise, the Supreme Being has no association with the material energy.

The *Brahma-samhita* (5.10) goes on to explain that it is Shambhu, Maheshvara, who is the dim reflection of the Lord's glance, and lord of the *pradhana* who embodies the seed of all living beings. The *pradhana* is the unmanifest material ingredients that later form the cosmic manifestation. It is Shambhu who comes forth from the glance of the Lord. Shambhu is created from the space in between the two eyebrows of Maha-Vishnu. Furthermore, Shambhu then joins with *maya* in the form of the male organ or power of regeneration. But he can do nothing independent of the power of Maha-Vishnu, who represents the direct spiritual power of Krishna. Therefore, the necessary changes in the material energy cannot happen unless facilitated by the will of the Supreme Lord, Krishna. (*Bs*.5.15)

As further described (*Brahma-samhita* 5.16), the function of Shambhu in relation to the conditioned souls is that the mundane egoistic principle has originated from Shambhu. What this means, without trying to get complicated about it, is that the tendency for the individual living being to forget his spiritual identity comes from Shambhu. This forgetfulness makes the individual in this material world want to be an enjoyer of the material experience. This is because he thinks he is the material body. This false identity makes all conditioned souls want to continue with their existence in the temporary, mundane world. This is the function of Shambhu, Shiva, in relation with the Supreme Lord Krishna's creative process. This principle of forgetfulness is then carried further by *mahamaya*, Durga, as previously explained.

However, to make it more clearly understood, Shiva is an expansion of the Supreme Lord, Krishna, as described above. He is not a second god that acts in place of Krishna. Those who think he is make an offense against the Supreme Being. Neither is he a *jiva*, a marginal spirit soul. As clearly explained in the *Brahma-samhita* (5.45), just as milk is transformed into curd by the action of acids, it is nonetheless neither the same as nor completely different from its cause, namely milk. So, the primeval Lord Govinda is from whom the state of Shambhu is a transformation for the work of destruction.

In other words, Lord Krishna manifests His energy through Maha-Vishnu whose glance produces the form of Shambhu, Shiva, in order to perform various tasks without having to give up His completely spiritual activities or come into direct contact with the material energy. It is through Shiva that the Supreme Being associates with His material energy in the form of *maya*. He does not do so directly. Thus, Shiva is not really different from Krishna, yet remains subservient to Him. The difference is like that of yogurt and milk. Yogurt is simply a changed form of milk, different in function simply by adding a certain acid. Similarly, the Supreme Being expands and changes into the distinct personality of Shambhu by the addition of a certain adulterated element to perform a particular function connected with the material energy. It is also this form of Shambhu from whom Rudra, another form of Shiva, is created from Lord Brahma later on in the creative process. [This is more thoroughly discussed in my book *How the Universe was Created*.]

So, here we have learned another aspect of how the spiritual energy expands to create the material energy. Thus, ultimately, everything comes from Lord Krishna. It is He who expands into the forms of Maha-Vishnu and then Shiva and Durga, who are considered the indirect mother and father of the universe, and are themselves expansions of Sadashiva and Ramadevi from the spiritual Vaikuntha worlds.

HOW LORD SHIVA ASSISTS IN THE UNIVERSAL DESTRUCTION

Another point, as previously mentioned, is that within the glance of Maha-Vishnu over *maya* is the element of time, which starts the agitation within the energy of *maya*, or the *pradhana*. This is what starts the process of creating and separating the various material elements. This element of time has been identified as Shambhu, the personality of the destructive principle. It is also this Shambu in the form of Rudra who later appears at the end of time to bring about the destruction of the universe.

So, Shiva is considered to be an expansion of the Supreme Lord Vishnu, Krishna, and is called Hara as such, and is transcendental to the material qualities. However, in his activities of destroying the world at the end of time, he is in touch with the mode of ignorance, or *tamo-guna*, and then he is considered as one of the living entities, called Rudra.

It is further explained that Lord Krishna expands a portion of His plenary portion, Lord Vishnu, who assumes the form of Rudra when it is time to dissolve the cosmic manifestation. Lord Vishnu does this for accepting the association of the material mode of ignorance. Thus, Rudra is but another expansion of the *energy* of Lord Krishna, although not a personal expansion. Rudra has various forms, which are transformations brought about by the different degrees of association with *maya*. Although Rudra is on a higher level than the *jiva-tattvas*, the individual living beings, he still cannot be considered a personal expansion of Krishna. Thus he is considered like an empowered *jiva*.[15]

Although many people worship Lord Shiva, Shiva worships Lord Krishna. The *Shiva Purana* states that Shiva is the Supreme, however, this is in regard to his power over the material world. After all, it is he who assists in the annihilation of the material creation, so he has power over the universe. But no scripture ever says that Shiva is the Supreme Lord of any of the Vaikuntha planets or of Goloka Vrinadavana, or any part of the spiritual domain. Such precincts belong only to Lord Krishna and His personal expansions. That is why Lord Shiva is always pictured absorbed in meditation. He is meditating on Lord Sankarshana, who is represented by the snakes on Shiva's body. Since Shiva is the origin of the mundane egoistic principle, one who is a worshiper of Lord Shiva as a devotee of Sankarshana can be freed from the false, material ego.[16]

Shiva is often pictured doing his Tandava dance of destruction. He is seen with four hands and one leg up, as an expert dancer, and one

Lord Shiva as Nataraj, king of dancers, doing his Tandiva dance that facilitates the destruction of the universe. This deity is located in the Government Museum in Delhi.

leg dancing on a small person called the Apasmara-purusha. In two of his hands he holds the damaru drum and fire. The drum represents sound which is supported or carried by ether. This is a sign of further creation after the annihilation or destruction. Fire represents the Pralayagni, or the fire of universal destruction. Thus, Shiva holds the symbols of cyclical universal creation and annihilation. The other two hands represent protection and blessing for those who take refuge of him or his spiritual knowledge. The Apasamara upon whom Shiva stands symbolizes the ignorance that makes us lose our clarity and consciousness of our real identity. This also signifies our succumbing to the process of death without spiritual preparation. Shiva is shown dancing on this ignorance for the good of the devotees who take refuge.

How Shiva assists in the cosmic annihilation is described in the *Puranas*. This process of cyclical destruction at the end of each day of Brahma is explained in the *Vishnu Purana* (Book Six, Chapters Three & Four). It states that at the end of 1,000 cycles of the four *yugas*, which is known as one day of Brahma called a *kalpa*, the earth is almost exhausted. A great scarcity of food ensues, which lasts 100 years. Because of the lack of food, all beings become weak and slow, and finally perish entirely. Lord Vishnu then assumes the character of Rudra (a form of Lord Shiva), the destroyer, and descends to reunite all of His creatures within Himself. He enters into the seven rays of the sun, causing all moisture in the oceans, rivers, soil, and living bodies to evaporate. The whole earth is dried up. Thus fed with abundant moisture the seven rays dilate into seven suns, the radiance of which glows everywhere and sets the three planetary systems and the lower system of Patala on fire. The three planetary systems become rugged and deformed throughout their mountains, rivers, and seas as they are consumed by these suns. The earth alone remains, destitute of moisture, resembling the back of a turtle.

Then Lord Hari, in the form of Rudra, who is the fire of time, destroyer of all things, becomes the scorching breath of Ananta Sesha, Sankarshana, and reduces the lower planetary system of Patala to ashes. The great roaring fire makes its way up through the universe to earth and destroys it. A vast whirlpool of flame then spreads to the higher region of the demigods and puts them all to ruin. The three planetary systems appear like a frying pan surrounded by flames that consume all things. The inhabitants of the upper planetary systems then mystically move higher to Maharloka, and when that becomes too hot, those who desire final liberation depart for the higher regions of Janaloka.

Elsewhere in the *Bhagavatam* (5.25.3) it explains how Lord

Shiva plays a significant role in the final and ultimate annihilation of the universe, which takes place at the end of Brahma's life of one hundred of his years. "At the time of devastation, when Lord Anantadeva [Ananta Sesha, Sankarshana] desires to destroy the entire creation, He becomes slightly angry. Then from between His two eyebrows appears three-eyed Rudra, carrying a trident. This Rudra, who is known as Sankarshana, is the embodiment of the eleven Rudras, or incarnations of Lord Shiva. He appears in order to devastate the entire creation."

The *Brahma Purana* (124.16) describes how it is the imperishable Lord Krishna who assumes the form of Rudra to bring all the elements and living beings back into Himself in the process of annihilation.

After Shiva appears in this way, he begins to do his dance of dissolution, dancing wildly to the beat of his drum. "At the time of dissolution, Lord Shiva's hair is scattered, and he pierces the rulers of the different directions with his trident. He laughs and dances proudly, scattering their hands like flags, as thunder scattered the clouds all over the world."[17] Lord Shiva's dancing causes such a commotion that it brings in the clouds that cause the universe to become inundated with water, which is what happens next as the process of annihilation continues (which I have fully described in my book, *The Vedic Prophecies*).

LORD SHIVA'S ULTIMATE SPIRITUAL ADVICE

In the *Sri Sanatkumara-samhita*, from the ancient *Skanda Purana*, we find a conversation between the great sage Sri Narada and Lord Sadashiva, the master of the demigods. Starting at text number 26 to text 30, Narada Muni asks Lord Sadashiva, "O master please tell what method the people of Kali-yuga may adopt to easily attain the transcendental abode of Lord Hari [Krishna]. O Lord, what mantra will carry the people from this world of birth and death? So everyone may benefit, please tell it to me. O Lord, of all mantras what mantra needs no *purashcharana*, no *nyasa*, no yoga, no *samskara* [processes of purification or initiation], and no other thing? A single utterance of the Lord's holy name gives the highest result. O master of the demigods, if I am competent to hear it, please kindly tell me the Lord's holy name."

In texts 31-35, Lord Sadashiva gives his answer: "O fortunate one, your question is excellent. O you who wish for the welfare of all, I will tell you the secret *chintamani* [wish-fulfilling] jewel of all mantras. I will tell you the secret of secrets, the most confidential of all confidential things. I will tell you what I have not told either the goddess or your elder brothers. I will tell you two peerless Krishna mantras that are the crest-jewels of all mantras. One is:

"'Gopijana-vallabha-charanau sharanam prapadye.' (I take shelter of the feet of He who is the *gopi*'s beloved, Krishna.) This mantra has three compound words, five individual words and sixteen syllables.

"The second mantra is: 'Namo gopijana-vallabhabhyam.' (Obeisances to the divine couple, Sri Sri Radha-Krishna, who are dear to the *gopis*.) This mantra has two words and ten syllables.

In texts 36-41, Lord Sadashiva continues: "One who either with faith or without faith once chants this five-word mantra resides among Lord Krishna's *gopi*-beloveds. Of this there is no doubt. In chanting these mantras there is no need of *purshcharana*, *nyasa*, *ari-shuddhi*, *mitra-shuddhi*, or other kinds of purification. In chanting these mantras there is no restriction of time or place. All, from the lowest outcaste to the greatest sage, are eligible to chant this mantra. Women, shudras, and all others are eligible. The paralyzed, mute, blind, and lame are eligible. The Andhras, Hunas, Kiratas, Pulindas, Pukkashas, Abhiras, Yavanas, Kankas, Khashas, and all others even if born from sinful wombs are also eligible. They who are overcome with pride and ego, who are intent on committing sins, who are killers of cows and brahmanas, and who are the greatest of sinners, are also eligible. They who have neither knowledge nor renunciation, they who have never studied the *shruti-shastra* and other scriptures, and all others, whoever they may be, are also eligible to chant these mantras."

Then in texts 42-48 Lord Sadashiva explains who is not eligible and who should not be told these sacred mantras or the purpose of them: "Anyone who has devotion to Lord Krishna, the master of all masters, is eligible to chant these mantras, but they who have no devotion, even if they may be the greatest of sages, are not eligible. They who have performed many *yajnas* (rituals), given charity, visited all holy places, been devoted to speaking the truth, accepted the renounced order, traveled to the farther shore of the *Vedas* and *Vedangas*, devotedly served the brahmanas, taken birth in good families, and performed austerities and vows, but are not devoted to Lord Krishna, are not eligible to chant these mantras. Therefore these mantras should not be spoken to one who is not devoted to Lord Hari, nor to one who is ungrateful, proud, or faithless, nor to an atheist or a blasphemer. One should not speak these mantras to one who does not wish to hear them, nor to one who has not stayed for one year in the speaker's ashrama. One should carefully give these mantras to one who is free from hypocrisy, greed, lust, anger, and

Lord Shiva and Goddess Durga   135

The height of meditation, Sri Sri Radha and Krishna, as described by Lord Shiva. Here they share a swing in Their pastimes in Vrindavana.

other vices, and who is sincerely devoted to Lord Krishna. The sage of this mantra is Lord Sadashiva. The meter is Gayatri. The deity is Lord Krishna, the beloved of the *gopis*. The purpose is to attain service to dear Lord Hari."

In text 53 Lord Sadashiva says: "By once chanting this mantra one attains success. Of this there is no doubt. Still, for the purpose of chanting *japa* one should chant this mantra ten times daily."

In texts 54-77 of the *Sri Sanatkumara-samhita*, Lord Sadashiva describes the most nectarean meditation of the mantras, after which he continues with many additional topics in regard to the pastimes of Radha and Krishna and the importance of the land of Vrindavana:

"O best of brahmanas, now I will tell you the meditation of this mantra. I meditate on two-armed Lord Krishna, who is dark like a monsoon cloud, dressed in yellow garments, garlanded with forest flowers... crowned with a peacock feather, and garlanded with lotus whorls, whose face is splendid like ten million moons, whose eyes move restlessly... whose forehead is marked with the *tilaka* of sandal paste and musk... who is splendid with earrings like two rising suns, whose perspiration-anointed cheeks are like two glistening mirrors... who with raised eyebrows playfully glances at His beloved's face, the tip of whose graceful raised nose is decorated with a glistening pearl... whose bimba-fruit lips are splendid in the moonlight of His teeth, whose hands are splendid with bracelets, armlets, and jewel rings... who holds a flute in His left lotus hand, whose waist is splendid with a graceful belt, whose feet are splendid with graceful anklets... whose eyes are restless with the nectar of amorous pastimes, who jokes with His beloved, making Her laugh again and again... and who stays with Her on a jewel throne under a *kalpa-vriksha* [wish-fulfilling] tree in Vrindavana forest. In this way one should meditate on Lord Krishna and His beloved."

"On the Lord's left side one should meditate on Sri Radha, who is dressed in blue garments, who is splendid like molten gold... who with the edge of Her garment covers Her graceful lotus smile, whose restless chakori-bird eyes dance on Her beloved's face... who with Her forefinger and thumb places betel nuts and crushed betel leaves in Her beloved's lotus mouth... whose full, raised breasts are decorated with a glistening pearl-necklace, whose waist is slender, whose broad hips are decorated with tinkling ornaments... who is decorated with jewel earrings, finger rings, toe rings, bracelets, armlets, and tinkling golden anklets... whose limbs are graceful with the best of beauty, who is always in the prime of youth, and who is always plunged in the nectar of bliss. O king of brahmanas, Her friends, whose age and qualities are like Hers, devotedly serve Her with *chamaras*, fans, and other articles."

"Please hear, O Narada, and I will tell you the meaning of these mantras. The material world is manifested by the Lord's *maya* potency and other external potencies. The spiritual world is manifested by the Lord's *chit* [spiritual knowledge] potency and other internal and everlasting spiritual potencies. The protector of these potencies is said to be the *gopi* Sri Radha, who is Lord Krishna's beloved. The transcendental goddess Sri Radha is the direct counterpart of Lord Sri Krishna. She is the central figure for all the goddesses of fortune. She is the pleasure potency of Lord Krishna. The wise say that She is the pleasure potency of Lord Krishna. Durga and the other goddesses in the world of the three modes are a million-millionth part of one of Her expansions. She is directly Goddess Maha-Lakshmi and Lord Krishna is Lord Narayana. O best of sages, there is not the slightest difference between Them. O best of sages, what more can I say? Nothing can exist without them. This universe made of spirit and matter together is Their potency. She is Durga and Lord Hari is Shiva. Lord Krishna is Indra and She is Shachi. She is Savitri and Lord Hari is Brahma. She is Dhumorna and Lord Hari is Yama. O Narada, please know that everything is Their potency. Even if I had many hundreds of years, I could not describe all Their glories." Thus, Lord Shiva encourages everyone in the most potent and practical way for making rapid spiritual development

CHAPTER NOTES
1. *Srimad-Bhagavatam* 4.24.22-28
2. Ibid., 4.24.29-30
3. Ibid., 4.30.10
4. Ibid., 4.7.50-54
5. Ibid., 8.12.43-44
6. Ibid., 10.71.8
7. Ibid., 10.88.3-5
8. Ibid., 10.88.12
9. Ibid., 10.22.4, pur.
10. *Caitanya-caritamrita*, Adi-lila, 5.58 & Madhya-lila, 20.271
11. Ibid., Cc.Adi-lila, 5.64-66
12. Ibid., Madhya-lila, 15.176
13. Ibid., Madhya-lila, 6.154-156
14. Ibid., Madhya-lila, 21.53
15. Ibid., Madhya-lila, 20.307-8
16. *Srimad-Bhagavatam* 3.2.21,pur.
17. Ibid., 4.5.10

CHAPTER SEVEN

The Goddesses

We have already discussed Goddess Durga and her many manifestations in the previous chapter. So, in this chapter we will turn our attention to the other main goddesses, such as Lakshmi, the goddess of fortune, and Sarasvati, the goddess of learning, and Srimati Radharani.

LAKSHMI

Goddess Lakshmi is the consort and *shakti*, or potency, of Lord Vishnu. Lakshmi, or Sri when she is especially known as the goddess of beauty (though sometimes considered to be separate entities), is the goddess of fortune, wealth, power, and loveliness. Wealth means not only money, but also the higher values and qualities of life. The power of the mind and intellect is also a must if one wants to be truly wealthy, which includes spiritual wealth. These are prerequisites to attaining spiritual knowledge. This is why Lakshmi is worshiped in the second set of three days during the Navaratri festival before the worship of Sarasvati, which is explained later.

As the spouse of Lord Vishnu, she appears whenever He does in each of His appearances, such as Vamana, Parashurama, Rama, or Krishna. In each of these appearances, she appeared as Padma or Kamala, Dharani, Sita, and Queen Rukmini respectively. They are inseparable.

Lakshmi is seen as exceptionally beautiful, standing (or sometimes sitting) on a lotus with four hands, two of which hold lotus flowers, and the lower right offering blessings of fortune, and the lower left held in the upright *mudra* or posture of benediction or blessings. The lotuses she carries in her hands represents that the realization of the Self is the supreme goal of life. They also indicate the various worlds and living beings in different states of development or evolution. Sometimes she may be holding a potted coconut in one hand, which is another representation of Lakshmi. However, when she is in the company of

Lord Vishnu, she can be seen with either two or four hands. Her four hands indicate the four main blessings of human existence, namely *dharma* (acts of righteousness and duty), *artha* (wealth), *kama* (sensual pleasures), and *moksha* (final liberation). She always wears a lotus garland, and is often seen with elephants on either side of her offering items such as garlands or pouring pots of water over her, which in turn may be presented by celestial maidens. Her complexion is often dark, or white, pink, or golden yellow. When her complexion is dark, it represents her connection with Lord Vishnu. When she is seen as golden yellow, it represents her as the source of all fortune and wealth. When it is white, she is seen as the highest mode of nature from which the universe has sprung. And when seen as pinkish, it represents her mood of mercy or compassion toward all creatures since she is also the mother of all beings.

Occasionally you can see her in a temple of her own, rather than accompanying Lord Vishnu. When this is the case, she is seen sitting on a lotus throne with her four hands holding a *padma* (lotus), *shankha* (conch shell), *amritakalasha* (pot of nectar), and a *bilva* fruit. The pot of nectar indicates the blessings of immortality. The fruit that she holds represents the results of our labors or actions, which comes from her blessings. When such fruit is a coconut, it indicates that she is the source of the three levels of creation, namely the gross, subtle, and the imperceptible. If it is a pomegranate, it means that all the worlds are under her influence, which she is beyond. And if the fruit is the *bilva*, which is healthy but not very appetizing, then it means the blessings of *moksha*, liberation.

When she is shown with eight hands, she also holds a bow, arrow, mace, and disc. However, this is actually an aspect of Durga as Mahalakshmi.

There are not many temples that are dedicated exclusively to Goddess Lakshmi. She is usually given a spot next to Lord Vishnu, or a small shrine in one of the temples. Yet, in some rare temples dedicated to Lakshmi you can see her on a central throne, and her eight other aspects or expansions as well, four on either side of her. These have different four hands holding various combinations of objects representing her different powers. The most popular of these is Gajalakshmi, shown with four arms, sitting or standing on an eight-petaled lotus. This aspect of her is most often seen when positioned above door frames of houses or temples. When seen with two hands, she is known as Samanyalakshmi and Indralakshmi.

Other names for Lakshmi include Hira (jewel), Indira (powerful one), Jaladhi-ja (ocean-born), and Lokamata (mother of the world). However, she is also called Chanchala, which means fickle or never in one place for long. This signifies that fortune or wealth often does not stay with anyone for extended lengths of time. Only with the greatest of respect for Lakshmi will she stay in one's household. This means not only offering her worship, but also taking care of not letting her go too easily by spending money on unnecessary items or projects.

In some depictions of her, she is seen riding an owl, which in Sanskrit is *uluka*, another name for Indra, the king of heaven. Thus, she rides on the king of the *devas*, the holder of all the material wealth and power that a living being could want in this world, which is still not the spiritual world.

In her first incarnation, Lakshmi was the daughter of the sage Bhrigu and his wife Khyati. She was later born from the milk ocean when it had been churned by a cooperative effort of the *devas* (demigods) and *asuras* (demons). This can be read in the *Bhagavata Purana* in Canto Eight, Chapters Six, Seven and Eight. In summary, the demons and the demigods had been struggling with each other. Because the demigods had offended and been cursed by the sage Durvasa Muni, they had lost their heavenly kingdom when they were defeated by the demons. Thus, the demigods went to Lord Brahma to explain the situation. They all in turn went to offer prayers to Lord Vishnu, who, being pleased with them, advised them what they should do. Carrying out these instructions, the demigods made a truce with the demons so they would work together to churn the huge ocean of milk, by which the nectar of immortality would be produced, which they all naturally wanted. Many other things would also come from this churning, such as a powerful poison that Lord Shiva would ingest. Thereafter, among the other things, was Lakshmi, the goddess of fortune. She was worshiped by the great sages and demigods, but she could find no one to be her husband, so she selected Lord Vishnu who gave her a place to always stay.

SARASVATI

The literal meaning of the name Sarasvati is the one who gives the essential knowledge (*Sara*) of our own Self (*Sva*). The goddess Sarasvati is also considered the Goddess of Learning, or of education, intelligence, crafts, arts, and skills. As she is the consort of Brahma, who is considered the source of all knowledge, Sarasvati is knowledge itself.

The Goddesses

Thus, many students or even scholars may worship her for her blessings. She is, therefore, depicted as white in complexion, and quite beautiful and graceful.

She is often depicted sitting on a lotus, which symbolizes that she is founded in the experience of the Absolute Truth. Thus, she not only has the knowledge but also the experience of the Highest Reality. She holds in her four hands a vina instrument, an *akshamala* (prayer beads) in the right hand, and a *pustaka* (book) in the left, which represents the knowledge of all sciences. Holding the book or scriptures in one hand also indicates that this knowledge alone can bring us to the Truth. The vina shows the beauty of learning the fine arts. Playing her vina, she tunes the mind and intellect with her knowledge, and thus the seeker can be in harmony with the universe. The prayer beads represent all spiritual sciences, like meditation and *japa* (chanting the holy names of God), and, being held in the right hand, that it is more important than the secular knowledge contained in the book in her left hand. Her four arms represent her unrestricted power in the four directions. She also represents creativity, or the combination of power and intelligence, the basis of creativity.

Her name literally means the one who flows, which can be applied to thoughts, words, or the flow of a river. She is the deity of a river in the *Rig Veda*. Her other names include Sarada (giver of essence), Brahmi (wife of Brahma), Mahavidya (holder of supreme knowledge), Bharati (eloquence), Maha-vidya (transcendent knowledge), Arya (noble one), Maha-vani (the transcendent word), Kamadhenu (like the wish-fulfilling cow), Dhaneshvari (the divinity of wealth), and Vagishvari (mistress of speech). It is through speech that knowledge manifests in action. It is through her that language and writing is revealed.

She is also occasionally shown with five faces and eight hands, representing her additional powers. Other objects that she may hold include the *pasha* (noose), *ankusha* (goad), *chakra* (disc), *padma* (lotus), *trishula* (trident), and *shankha* (conch). Sometimes she is also seen riding on a swan, the carrier of her spouse, Brahma. At other times she is seen riding on a peacock or sitting with one nearby. The peacock represents the worldly beauty, which can distract the spiritual aspirant. The swan signifies the acquisition of wisdom and knowledge because of its ability to separate milk from water when eating, and thus acquire only the milk.

Sarasvati is also the *shakti* or power and consort of Brahma, the secondary creator of the universe. Thus, she is also considered a mother of the universe. In this way, she is also connected with fertility.

MEANING OF NAVARATRI

Nava means nine and *ratri* means night. So, Navaratri literally means nine nights. It is during these nine nights of festivities that the goddess is worshiped in her different forms of Durga, Lakshmi, and then Sarasvati. Durga is worshiped during the first three nights of the festival because of her destructive aspect. She destroys the *anarthas* or unwanted barriers that hold us back from our true spiritual potential. She reduces the evil tendencies in the mind, which is the meaning of *durgati harini*. Thus, she is worshiped to relieve us of our destructive qualities of desire, lust, passion, greed, anger, etc. Without removing these obstacles, the spiritual unfoldment cannot take place.

The next step is to apply the positive process of adding the qualities we need. So, Lakshmi is worshiped over the following three nights. She gives one the wealth of good qualities, such as love, goodness, compassion, forgiveness, cooperation, nonviolence, devotion, purity, and the like. Virtue is the true wealth, which is given by Lakshmi. This is not merely the wealth of riches and possessions, but the real wealth that can propel us toward the spiritual goal. These positive uplifting qualities replace the bad ones that were removed by Durga.

At this point the seeker can become fit for the philosophical study and contemplation that is required. Then Sarasvati, the goddess of knowledge, is worshiped the remaining three nights. Sarasvati gives one the intelligence, knowledge and wisdom by which spiritual realization is possible. She represents the highest knowledge of the Self. By invoking her blessings, she plays her well-tuned vina of knowledge and insight, which can then tune our mind and intellect for working in harmony with the world and the purpose of our existence. Then our spiritual practice, study and meditation become effective for producing the victory of rising above the influence of our mind and senses. Then we can perceive our real identity as a spiritual being and a part of the spiritual dimension, free from illusion.

After having removed our impurities, gained the proper virtues, and then acquired the knowledge of the Self, then the last day is called Vijayadashami, or the day of victory over our minds and the lower dimension after having worshiped the goddess in her three forms. The celebrations of Navaratri are held at night because it represents our overcoming the ignorance of the mode of darkness, the night of *tamoguna*.

So, such festivals are performed in these phases: 1) preparation, 2) purification, 3) realization, and 4) then celebration. It represents one's progress toward the real goal of life. First the mind must be purified of all unwanted thoughts and habits. Then it must become focused on one's concentration of the Supreme. As the knowledge of our spirituality of the Self and our connection with the Supreme Being becomes revealed, then there is realization. When such realization has been reached and the ego destroyed, then there is celebration. Living life on the basis of spiritual realization means that life is a constant joy and celebration.

Vijayadashami is also known as Dusserha, which is observed throughout India and every Indian community. So, everyone worships the goddesses and studies the sacred texts and purifies their minds and homes. Vijayadashami or Dusserha is celebrated because on the tenth day of the battle between Rama and the demon Ravana, Rama killed Ravana and rescued Sita. Thus, it is the day of victory, or Vijay (victory) Dashami (tenth day). On that day there is often a huge bonfire in which people burn the effigy of the demon Ravana, which also represents the destruction of the false ego. In this way, Navaratri and Vijayadashami is a festival that shows the process by which humanity can reach the perception of God. It incorporates the means and worship by which one can purify themselves of the ten sins, meaning the sins committed by the ten active senses. It is the process of purification through which one is meant to become free of the dictates of the mind and the temporary world of sense objects, which paves the way for one to enter into the transcendental experience.

What this shows is that all aspects of the Vedic process, whether we are familiar with them or not, and no matter whether they be austerities or festivities, are ultimately meant to be a vehicle by which we can transcend the mind, senses, and the temporary material world and enter into the Supreme Reality wherein we can reestablish our lost relationship with the Supreme Being.

GAYATRI

Gayatri is the goddess that is the personification of the sacred Gayatri mantra, which is chanted three times a day. She shares that with the goddesses Savitri and Sarasvati. Gayatri has four faces, and four or ten arms and rides a swan. She presides over the morning chanting of the prayer, and also over the *Rig Veda* and the sacred fires called the Garhapatya. These were the sacred fires that the three *varnas* known as the brahmanas, kshatriyas, and vaishyas were meant to keep in their homes for the performance of sacred rituals. Then Goddess Savitri presides over the noon chanting of the prayer. She has four faces with twelve eyes, four arms, and has a bull for a carrier. She also rules over the *Yajur Veda* and the Dakshina fire, while Sarasvati rules over the evening rendition of the prayer and the *Sama Veda*.

SRIMATI RADHARANI

Srimati Radharani is the Supreme Goddess. She is most always seen with Lord Krishna. It is described that She is the Chief Associate and devotee of Lord Krishna, and topmost of all goddesses. Her name means that She is the most excellent worshiper of Lord Krishna. However, She is also an expansion of the Lord's energy. Since She is also an extension of Krishna, She is the feminine aspect of God. Thus, in the Gaudiya Vaishnava tradition, God is both male and female. They are One, but Krishna expands into two, Himself and Radharani, for the sake of divine loving pastimes. If They remained as One, then there would be no relationship, no pastimes, and no dynamic exchange of love. (*Caitanya-caritamrita*, Adi-lila, 4.55-56)

Actually, if we all remained merged or amalgamated into one single force or light, then there is no further need of anything else. There certainly would be no need for the material manifestation to provide the innumerable conditioned souls with the means to seek out the way to satisfy their senses, minds, emotions, desires for self-expression, intellectual pursuits, and on and on.

So, similarly, the spiritual world is the manifestation wherein all souls have the opportunity to engage in a multitude of pastimes in loving relationships in full spiritual variety, without the many hindrances we find in this material world. The only difference is that the spiritual world is centered around the Supreme Being. And that Supreme Personality has expanded Himself into Radharani for exhibiting the supreme loving relationship, in which many others assist Them.

In the *Brihad-Gautamiya Tantra*, Radharani is described as follows:

devi krishna-mayi prokta
radhika para-devata
sarva-lakshmi-mayi sarva
kantih sammohini para

The Goddesses

"The transcendental goddess Srimati Radharani is the direct counterpart of Lord Sri Krishna. She is the central figure for all the goddesses of fortune. She possesses all the attractiveness to attract the all-attractive Personality of Godhead. She is the primeval internal potency of the Lord."

The *Brihad-Gautamiya Tantra* goes on to explain that Radha is known as the Supreme Goddess, the source of all abundance and beauty, and has the power to enchant all. Her whole existence is pervaded by Sri Krishna. So, in this way, She is the Supreme Goddess of love because She is the consort of Lord Krishna, who is the Supreme God of love.

To explain further, Srimati Radharani is also the source of the other goddesses, who are expansions of Her. Just as Lord Krishna is the source of all other expansions and *avatars* of God, Radharani is the source of all other expansions of the energies of God, the *shaktis*, or other goddesses. Thus, Vishnu, Rama, even Shiva are all expansions of the one Supreme Being, and similarly Lakshmi, Sita, and even Durga are all expansions of this Supreme Feminine form of God, Radharani.

It is explained that the beloved consorts of Lord Krishna are of three kinds, namely the goddesses of fortune or Lakshmis, His queens, and the milkmaids of Vraja called the *gopis*. All of them proceed from Radharani. The Lakshmis are partial manifestations, or plenary portions, of Srimati Radharani, while the queens in Vaikuntha and in Dvaraka are reflections of Her image. The Vraja-devis or *gopis* are Her expansions and assist in the increase of *rasa*, or the divine loving pastimes. Among them there are many groups that have various sentiments and moods, which help Lord Krishna taste the sweetness of the *rasa* dance and other pastimes. (*Caitanya-caritamrita*, Adi-lila. 4.75-81)

"Among the *gopis* of Vrindavana, Srimati Radharani and another *gopi* are considered chief. However, when we compare the *gopis*, it appears that Srimati Radharani is most important because Her real feature expresses the highest ecstasy of love. The ecstasy of love experienced by the other *gopis* cannot be compared to that of Srimati Radharani." (*Ujjvala-nilamani* 4.3 by Rupa Gosvami)

Radharani has many names according to Her qualities and characteristics. Some of the names that Radharani is known by include Govinda-anandini--She who gives pleasure to Govinda [Krishna]; Govinda-mohini--She who mystifies Govinda; Govinda-sarvasa--the all-in-all of Lord Govinda; Shiromani Sarva-kanta--the crown jewel of all the Lord's consorts; and Krishnamayi--the one who sees Krishna both within and without. She is also called Radhika in the *Puranas* because Her worship [*aradhana*] of the Lord consists of fulfilling His desires.

Aradhana is the root of the name Radharani, which indicates one who excels in worshiping the Lord. She is also called Sarva-lakshmi, the original source of all the goddesses of fortune. This also means that She is the supreme energy of Lord Krishna, and represents His six opulences which include fame, fortune, strength, wealth, knowledge, and detachment. She is also known as Sarva-kanti, which indicates that all beauty and luster rest in Her body, and all the Lakshmis derive their beauty from Her. It also means that all the desires of Lord Krishna rest in Srimati Radharani. As Lord Krishna enchants the world with His beauty and charm, Sri Radha enchants Him. Therefore She is the Supreme Goddess. Sri Radha is the full power, and Lord Krishna is the possessor of full power. (*Cc.*Adi-lila, 4.82, 84, 87-96) Thus, the two are non-different, as the sunshine is non-different from the sun, or as the energy is non-different from the energetic or source of energy.

In this way, without Radha there is no meaning to Krishna and without Krishna there is no meaning to Radha. Because of this, in the Vaishnava tradition we always pay respects first to the Lord's internal energy in the form of Radha, and then to the Lord. Thus, They are referred to as Radha-Krishna, or in other names as Sita-Rama, Lakshmi-Narayana, and so on. In this way, Radha and Krishna are one, but when Lord Krishna wants to enjoy, He manifests Himself as Radharani. Otherwise, there is no energy in which Krishna can attain pleasure outside Himself.

To understand Himself through the agency of Radha, or the *hladini-shakti*, the Lord manifests Himself as Lord Chaitanya, who is Lord Krishna but with the super-excellent emotions of Radharani's love toward Lord Krishna. This is because the Lord accepts a position and the emotions of a devotee in order to fully taste His own sweetness.

It is also described that the potency of love of God is called *hladini*, the Lord's pleasure potency. Whenever the Lord wants to enjoy pleasure, He exhibits His own spiritual potency known as *hladini*. And the essence of that love is in the emotion called *bhava*. The ultimate development of that emotion is *mahabhava*, or great *bhava*. Mahabhava is full of the pleasure potency, and it is an exhibition of the highest love for Lord Krishna. Sri Radharani is the embodiment of that transcendental consciousness found in *mahabhava*. Her mind, senses, and body are steeped in that highest sort of love for Krishna. She is as spiritual as the Lord Himself. In fact, being the personification of the *hladini-shakti*, the pleasure giving energy of the Lord, She is the only source of enjoyment for the Lord. This pleasure potency manifests spiritually as Radharani in a way that attracts even Lord Krishna. He takes no pleasure in anything material. The Lord could never enjoy anything that is less spiritual than Himself. Therefore Radha and Krishna are identical. Then She expands Herself into different forms, known as Lalita, Visakha, and Her other confidential associates that increase the mood of divine love. However, being the Lord's *hladini* feature, She is also the ultimate source of all happiness for all the living beings. In other words, everything that gives pleasure and happiness within the spiritual or the material worlds is because of Her and the energy that emanates from Her. (*Cc*.Adi-lila.4.68-72) That same pleasure potency expands and spreads throughout the spiritual worlds, and then descends into the material creation into the many forms of happiness that is experienced by the conditioned soul, though it may be called by different names and perceived in assorted ways. Since we are all parts and parcels of the Lord, we also have that pleasure potency within us to a minute degree. But we are trying to enjoy it in the material world. Therefore we are like sparks that are dying out because we have left our place which is in the blazing fire of Lord Krishna's association.

The Hare Krishna mantra also directs one's attention and devotion to Radha as well as Krishna. Radha is also known as Mother Hara, which is the name Hare in the vocative form within the mantra. So, in chanting Hare Krishna, we are first approaching the Lord's internal potency and asking Radha to please engage us in the service of Lord Krishna. Concentrating on Krishna through His names is one form of that service. In other words, it is through Radha that one more easily attains Krishna and service to Krishna. This is the advantage of approaching Lord Krishna through Radharani.

The descriptions of the beauty of Radharani are wonderfully poetic and descriptive. Actually, the residents of Vrindavana care more for Radharani than they do for Lord Krishna. They know that Krishna can be influenced through Radharani. They know that Radha can bring one to Krishna. She is also the compassionate nature of the Lord, and, thus, more easily approached than trying to reach Lord Krishna directly. And when we read these descriptions of Radha, it is no wonder why they are devoted to Her. For example, it is explained that Srimati Radharani has unlimited transcendental qualities, of which twenty-five are principal. These include: 1) She is very sweet. 2) She is always freshly youthful. 3) Her eyes are restless. 4) She smiles brightly. 5) She has beautiful, auspicious lines. 6) She makes Krishna happy with Her bodily aroma. 7) She is very expert in singing. 8) Her speech is charming. 9) She is very expert in joking and speaking pleasantly. 10) She is very humble and meek. 11) She is always full of mercy. 12) She is cunning.

13) She is expert in executing Her duties. 14) She is shy. 15) She is always respectful. 16) She is always calm. 17) She is always grave. 18) She is expert in enjoying life. 19) She is situated in the topmost level of ecstatic love. 20) She is the reservoir of loving affairs in Gokula. 21) She is the most famous of submissive devotees. 22) She is very affectionate to elderly people. 23) She is very submissive to the love of Her friends. 24) She is the chief *gopi*. 25) She always keeps Krishna under Her control. In short, She possesses unlimited transcendental qualities, just as Lord Krishna does. (from *Ujjvala-nilamani, Sri-radha-prakarana* 11-15)

In describing Srimati Radharani, it is also said in the *Vidagdha-madhava* (1.32) by Rupa Gosvami, "The beauty of Srimati Radharani's eyes forcibly devours the beauty of newly grown blue lotus flowers, and the beauty of Her face surpasses that of an entire forest of fully blossomed lotuses. Her bodily luster seems to place even gold in a painful situation. Thus, the wonderful, unprecedented beauty of Srimati Radharani is awakening Vrindavana."

"Although the effulgence of the moon is brilliant initially at night, in the daytime it fades away. Similarly, although the lotus is beautiful during the daytime, at night it closes. But, O My friend, the face of My most dear Srimati Radharani is always bright and beautiful, both day and night. Therefore, to what can Her face be compared?" (*Vidagdha-madhava* 5.20)

"When Srimati Radharani smiles, waves of joy overtake Her cheeks, and Her arched eyebrows dance like the bow of Cupid. Her glance is so enchanting that it is like a dancing bumblebee, moving unsteadily due to intoxication. That bee has bitten the whorl of My heart." (*Vidagdha-madhava* 2.51)

Many of the great spiritual preceptors in the Vaishnava line have written books to explain and glorify the divine love between Radha and Krishna. Some of them are Jayadeva, Bilvamangala, Rupa Gosvami, Sanatana Gosvami, Krishnadasa Kaviraja, Raghunatha dasa, Ramananda Raya, Prabhodananda Sarasvati, Bhaktivinoda Thakur, and others.

This devotional love for God, which is considered the highest development of spiritual awakening, has been eloquently expressed for many years in art, such as paintings, dance, poems, music, etc. Such saints who are noted for their songs on the love of Sri Krishna include Chandidas, Jayadeva, Surdas, Mirabai, Tulasidas, Tukaram, Narottama dasa Thakura, and many others.

There is much more to be known about Srimati Radharani, but this should suffice for now. Thus, the spiritual exchange of divine love between Radha and Krishna is the display of the internal energy of the

Lord, and is very confidential and difficult to understand. No materialist can begin to understand this topic of the relationship between Radharani and Lord Krishna. But the more we awaken our dormant love for God, which is a natural state of being for a fully awakened soul, then the more we can comprehend and actually enter into such spiritual loving exchanges.

CHAPTER EIGHT

Ganesh and Murugan

Ganesh and Murugan are the sons of Lord Shiva. Ganesh is the more popular, and it seems that these days people from all around the world are aware of Ganesh as a god of good luck and the remover of obstacles. You can find images and the knowledge of Ganesh throughout Southeast Asia, China, Japan, and the South Pacific islands. However, there are many details that may not be so well known, unless you are a part of the Vedic tradition. Murugan is another son of Shiva, and most popular in South India. In this chapter we will provide an introduction to the characteristics and meaning of the symbols of these two demigods.

GANESH

Ganesh is also called Ganapati. This means lord of the Ganas who are the lesser demigods or attendants who control the function of the sense organs. According to Karapatri's *Sri Bhagavat-tattva* (p. 638), the word *gana* means a collection of something that can be counted or comprehended. In this way, Ganapati is also the lord or ruler of categories. He is also known as the Lord of thresholds or entrances into new dimensions. He is the remover of obstacles or obstructions. So, it is not unusual, especially in India, that as we enter a new space or house we may see an image of Ganesh above the door or nearby to give blessings to those who enter. Thus, he is also the guardian of the doorways. This is the case in many Vedic temples. As we enter the temple, we first see a deity of Ganesh to whom we pray for blessings and the removal of obstacles in our devotion or the rituals that we do inside the temple.

Ganesh is also considered the Lord of astrology. He is said to know the language of the stars and the destinies of every living being. Thus, astrologers also petition Ganesh to pen such knowledge to them.

Ganesh is also said to be the writer of the scriptures. (*Mahabharata* 1.1.77) He accepted the position of being Vyasadeva's scribe and wrote the *Mahabharata* and *Srimad-Bhagavatam* as it was dictated by Srila Vyasadeva, the compiler of the major portions of the Vedic texts. You can see the cave where this is said to have happened at Mana, near the holy place of Badrinatha (Badarikashrama). For this reason the ancient *Brahmana* texts also describe him as the god of learning.

His other names include Ganesh (related to the word *gana*), Vinayaka (a name familiar in South India, meaning great leader), Vighneshvara (the remover of obstacles), Gajanana (elephant-faced), Gajadhipa (lord of elephants), and Jyeshtha-raja (King of the elders).

Ganesh is said to have two wives, Siddhi (success) and Riddhi (prosperity). Thus, if anyone pleases Lord Ganesh with nice prayers or worship, the person also attains the company or blessings of the wives of Lord Ganesh. However, if used improperly, success and prosperity can be distractions on the path toward the goal of spiritual wisdom.

The most prominent characteristic of Lord Ganesh is that he has the head of an elephant. How Lord Ganesh got an elephant's head is related in several places in the Vedic texts. There may be a few different versions, but the general way in which it is accepted relates as follows: Once when Lord Shiva's wife, Parvati, was going to bathe in the forest, she wanted someone to guard the area. Some references say she was going to bathe in her house. She then rubbed her skin so she was able to gather the substance from which she could form and cause the birth of a son. When he came to life, she ordered him to let no one into the area while she was bathing. However, Lord Shiva came after a long absence and wanted in, but was blocked by Ganesh. Lord Shiva did not recognize the boy as his son, nor did Ganesh realize Shiva was his father, and they began to fight. Ganesh lost the battle with his head being cut off. When Parvati entered the scene and saw what had happened, she was so upset that Shiva, after understanding the situation, devised the means to revive his son. He went to find the nearest living entity he saw, which happened to be an elephant. He took the head and attached it to his son's body, after which he was revived. Thus, Ganesh has the head of an elephant.

Part of the meaning behind this symbolism of the man with an elephant's head is to represent the unity between the small entity, or man, and the large universe, the elephant. In the word "gaja", which means elephant, "ga" means the goal, and "ja" means the origin. In the form of Ganesh, the elephant-headed man represents the culmination of the man, the origin, on the path toward universal consciousness, the goal. Ganesh, therefore, is the representation of man who understands the foundation of the reality upon which the universe rests, as is summarized in the Vedic term, "Thou art That," *tat tvam asi*. (*Taittiriya Aranyaka* 8.1.1)

Here is Lord Ganesh in one of his images, holding some of the items that represent his powers, as described in this chapter. This image is on the outside of one of the shrines to Ganesh near the Sri Padmanabhaswamy Vishnu temple in Trivandrum, India.

Ganesh is also shown in particular ways with certain symbols, which is described in the *Ganapati Upanishad* (11-14). He is seen with one tusk and four hands, two of which hold a noose and a hook. The noose that he holds is to catch delusion, to free one from its affects. The noose also represents attachment that can lead to anger, which hurts us like the goad. The noose or rope is also used to pull his devotees nearer to the Truth and to tie them to the Highest God. The hook or goad indicates his power and helps motivate one towards the goal. Sometimes he is also shown holding an axe, which he uses to cut off the worldly attachments of His devotees, which can thus end the cause of their sorrow.

Of the other two hands, one is positioned in the gestures for giving blessings and assuring fearlessness, and the other is often holding a rice ball. Ganesh's hand that gives blessings shows that he can grant one's desires and assures freedom from fear, and that he is beyond the influence of time and space wherein fear exists. In this way, he blesses all and offers protection from all obstacles on their spiritual path in seeking the Supreme. The rice ball he is often seen holding indicates the reward of the *sadhana* or spiritual practice for his devotees. Ganesh also has a big stomach and large ears. The fat belly of Ganesh indicates that the influence of the material manifestation is within him. His big ears represent that he accepts the truthful and positive vibrations, while throwing out the false and non-virtuous words that men may present to him. On his flag is a mouse, which is also his carrier.

Deities of Ganesh are often covered with red vermillion. The significance of the vermillion is that it represents the reddened complexion of one who is absorbed in work, which causes the intensified circulation of blood to all parts of the body. This also produces the skin's red glow. Ganesh is also the lord of action, so he is often seen smeared with red vermillion. He is also worshiped with red flowers. Since Ganesh works wholeheartedly, he has a strong appetite and is thus offered and enjoys a steady supply of sweets and delicacies.

As Vighneshvara, Lord Ganesh also gives us the gifts that destroy obstacles, restrictions, or hindrances. All obstacles exist in the arena of time and space. Through the access of immortality, or the realization of such, we can overcome the fear that is intrinsic in the arena of temporary time and matter. Thus, Lord Ganesh gives and takes away. He gives us what can take away the hindrances and obstacles that keep us from realizing our true potential. Because of this, Lord Ganesh is often worshiped before starting any new project, or before entering a house or building. This is why he is often placed above doorways through which people enter, or is recognized and afforded respect and worship before accepting a new position, starting a new undertaking, or before beginning a new challenge, like taking a difficult test, so we can reach its completion without hindrance.

In worshiping Ganesh, there are several different mantras from which one can choose that help invoke the energy or mercy of Ganesh. There is also a specific graphic design called a yantra that is also a symbol for Ganesh. The swastika is another graphic design that can be used in representing Ganesh and the good fortune that he can provide. This is also why the swastika is a sign for good fortune.

Locally, you often see Ganesh deities as either individual images or as a bas relief carved from stone or boulders. His trunk is also curved to the right and sometimes to the left. This indicates the ways to get around obstacles to reach the goal. This is an indicator of Ganesh's ability to master adversities, and is also a symbol for the *Om* mantra. His trunk also often holds a *modaka*, a type of sweet. The single tusk he has represents the one Truth, while the broken tusk indicates the imperfections of the ever-changing material world. He lost the broken tusk when Parashurama once arrived at Mount Kailash to see Lord Shiva. However, Shiva was sleeping, so Ganesh did not allow Parashurama to get in. When they started fighting, Ganesh lost one tusk. (*Padma Purana*)

The broken piece of the tusk was later used as a pen to write the *Mahabharata* when it had been dictated by Srila Vyasadeva to Ganesh. How Ganesh wrote the *Mahabharata* from the dictates of Srila Vyasadeva is described as follows: Vyasadeva entered into a state of meditation after the death of the Kaurava and Pandava clans, and after the disappearance of Lord Krishna. While the great story of events between the tribes, along with the episodes of the Kuruksetra war, was still in his mind, he wanted to write the epic in the form of a great poem. He went to Brahma for advice regarding a qualified person who could accept his dictation to write the story, and Brahma mentioned Ganesh. When Vyasa thought about Ganesh, he appeared before the sage. However, Ganesh was not so receptive to the idea, so he stipulated that Vyasa dictate it in such a way that Ganesh would never have to put down his pen before it was completed. Vyasadeva countered with the requirement that Ganesh not write down anything before he completely understood the meaning of it. Ganesh was not meant to write anything he did not understand in order that he realize the depths of the meaning, and how to write it in a way that would make the meaning accessible to all humanity. This was agreed, and the *Mahabharata* was completed within three years. (*Mahabharata*, Adi Parva, Chapter 1, verses 74-80)

Sometimes Ganesh is shown as Balaganapati in his child form, or Tarunaganapati as a young man. During the popular Ganesh Chaturthi festival, Ganesh is worshiped as Varasiddhi Vinayaka. At other times Ganesh is portrayed as Herambaganapati, with a third eye in between his eyebrows, along with five heads and ten arms. These show an extended view of his various powers, which are represented by what he holds in his hands, which include a lotus, pomegranate, water-pot, an axe, a lute, a sugarcane, ears of paddy, a bow and arrow, a thunderbolt, prayer beads, and a book.

The mouse that accompanies Ganesh is his carrier. The mouse is often seen in pictures eating or stealing the sweets that are piled near Ganesh. The mouse is the desire to enjoy material pleasures and the dangers of the ego. Though the mouse is small, this desire for material happiness, and the driver that motivates one into actions to acquire such pleasure, is like a thief that takes away all that people possess. It steals away one's life that could be used to acquire the goal of spiritual perfection toward true happiness and liberation. The mouse also represents the mind, which is always active. It takes much weight to keep the mind from going astray. The weight of an elephant, Ganesh, on the mouse represents controlling the mind. Thus, Ganesh rides on this mouse as the controller of material desire and the effects of illusion.

MURUGAN

Murugan is the son of Shiva and Parvati, but the story is a lengthy one, much of which is in the *Valmiki Ramayana*, *Mahabharata* and *Brahmanda Purana*. So, I will provide only a summary. Murugan was born to kill the demon Tarakasura. Taraka had been troubling the gods to the point where they went to Lord Brahma to ask for advice. He told them that only Shiva could produce a son who could defeat such evil. Shiva was deep in meditation, and though the god of lust, Kama, tried to awaken him, Kama was reduced to ashes by Shiva's third eye. Thus, Parvati practiced long austerities until she was noticed by her husband, Shiva. Once Shiva focused his attention, his seed was so powerful that no one could bare it. It went into the mouth of Agni (fire), and he could not handle the task, so it was then accepted by the Ganga, the Ganges River personified. She could no longer deal with it, so then she threw it into a forest of kusha grass, which is how Murugan got the name Sharavanabhava. This seed gave birth to a child named Kumara, the form of Murugan who remains young and single.

Here Murugan or Subrahmanya is seen riding his peacock carrier and is accompanied by his two wives on each side of him. This image is located on top of the entranceway to his temple at the large Shiva temple in Chidambaram in South India.

Murugan was raised by six celestial mothers from the Krittika (Pleiades) constellation, which is how he got the name "Karttikeya" and "Shanmatura." Murugan is also seen with six faces, said to enable him to suckle the milk from the six mothers, which is how he also got the name of "Shadanana" and "Shanmukha." He was called "Devasenapati" when he became the commander of the gods. And by using his weapon the lance or *shakti* to destroy the demon Tarakasura, he became known as "Shaktidhara" and "Tarakari." Due to his young form he is known as "Kumara." He is known as "Subrahmanya" for favoring the brahmanas, or assisting the development of spiritual aspirants. And for being a strong warrior due to the power that comes from being celibate, he is called "Skanda." Other names Murugan is known to have is "Brahma-Shasta" for knowing the Vedic science better than Lord Brahma, "Gangeya" or "Ganga-putra" as the son of Ganga, "Swami-natha" for being the teacher of his own father, and others, including "Rudra-sunu," the son of Rudra (Shiva).

Most of his temples are found on hilltops, particularly in South India, but there are also many shrines that are included within courtyards or complexes of larger temples, especially those dedicated to Shiva. He is usually portrayed sitting on his carrier, which is a peacock called Paravani, with one head and two arms, or sometimes as Subramaniya with six heads and twelve arms. Dressed in red, he also holds his brilliant lance, which represents wisdom and intelligence, and destroys the darkness of ignorance, symbolized by the demons he kills. His additional hands hold a bow, arrows, a sword, thunderbolt, and ax, all which indicate his powers. His emblem is the fowl or rooster and his fiery banner flames high above his chariot.

The esoteric meaning behind the image of Murugan is that he represents the complete yogic control of preserving the semen. If this control is not attained, then the mind is always stifled by sensual desires, which means that the child, or the power of youth in the form of Kumara, is never born, and, thus, the demons take control over the gods. This signifies that only by allowing the seed (semen) to rise up through the yogic *sushumna* channel into the *vani-mukha* or fire center in the sixth *chakra*, can the yogi become master of his tendencies and impulses. (There is also an old Egyptian saying that only by preserving one's semen can one communicate with the gods.) Only then can Skanda, or the inner strength or power, be born. Such a master can use his sexual powers for mental clarity, discernment, stamina, and spiritual progress. Lasting youth is also connected with the practice of preserving one's seed, which is represented by Murugan's peacock, which is his carrier.

Murugan rides a peacock which also holds a serpent in its claws. As we know, the peacock is an enemy of the serpent and can kill it. The serpent represents the ego and carnal temptations of mankind. It indicates the subtle material attachments that keep the spiritual living being fond of staying in a material body. It is this serpent of the ego that causes man to crawl in the darkness of ignorance, lost from the Supreme Truth and enveloped in his own desires. However, the peacock holds the serpent ego in check, which herein can be channeled to using itself to help uncover the Absolute Truth. The serpent also indicates the aging that comes with time. In this case, the peacock kills time, or represents one's ability through yogic powers to reverse the aging process by holding one's youthful powers.

The six mothers of the Pleiades who raised Murugan, or Kumara, are also associated with the six *chakras* through which Kumara develops his strength and power. When he has six heads, it represents the five senses and the mind, all of which must be controlled for spiritual advancement. In this way, Murugan represents the highest goal or consciousness that a spiritual yogi can reach. He is also the potential for perfection that exists within all of us.

When Murugan is shown with two consorts, these are Valli, the daughter of a chief of a race of humble agriculturalists and woodsmen, and Devasena, the daughter of Indra. This indicates his unbiased nature in distinguishing between the simple and the aristocratic.

Murugan is an ancient deity, with his name on Kushan coins, and was worshiped in northern India by the Guptas. He is described in the *Shiva Purana*, the *Mahabharata*, and the *Kumara-sambhava* poem by Kalidasa. The *Skanda Purana* is said to encompass his teachings. However, it is said that women should not worship him.

AYYAPPAN

Ayyappan is said to be the son of Shiva and the incarnation of Vishnu known as Mohini Murti, Lord Vishnu's form as a most beautiful woman. This is why Ayyappa is also called Hariharaputra, meaning the son of both Hari, or Vishnu, and Hara, Shiva.

The reason for this is described in the *Srimad-Bhagavatam* (Canto Eight, Chapter Twelve). Therein it is related that once when Lord Shiva had heard about the pastimes of the Lord in the form of an attractive woman during the churning of the milk ocean, Shiva went to see the Lord. After offering descriptive prayers, he asked to see this beautiful feminine form of the Lord. Being merciful to His devotee, the Lord expanded His energy and manifested Himself as a most attractive woman, Mohini. Lord Shiva, upon seeing this form, was immediately captivated. Shiva lost his sense and began to follow Her. While chasing Her through the woods for some time, he passed semen. Only after discharging semen did Lord Shiva realize how he had been dragged by the illusory energy, and then he ceased to follow the beautiful form. However, in the version in the *Bhagavatam*, Shiva's semen did not produce the child Ayyappa, but fell on the earth where mines of gold and silver later formed.

Ayyappa is often portrayed with four arms, three eyes, and seated peacefully in the lotus position, *padmasana*, often in meditation. Two of his hands carry a sword and a shield, while the other two exhibit the *mudras* or positions of assurance of fearlessness and giving blessings. Other views of him present an image with only two arms and two eyes. He wears gold ornaments and a crown. Ayyappa is also called Shasta, which means the controller of the world.

The holy place where Ayyappa is worshiped is the hill of Shabarimalai. The story is that after Durga killed the demon Mahishasura, the demon's spouse, Mahishi, undertook the endeavor of intense austerities to gain the favor of Lord Brahma that she would not be killed by Shiva or Vishnu. She became increasingly powerful, much to the consternation of the gods. Then Shiva and Vishnu together formed an idea in which she could be destroyed by creating a person fit for the job. This child was discovered by King Rajashekara who reigned in Panthalam in Kerala. He had no children so he named the child Manikanthan and raised him as a son. The child killed Mahishi when he was only twelve years old. He had also brought female leopards back from the forests since the milk was supposed to cure the queen's headache. The king, however, had realized the divine nature of Manikantham. The king had been told to build a temple to Manikantham at the spot where his arrow landed, after Manikantham disappeared. The arrow found its mark at the top of Shabarimalai hill. This is where the temple was supposed to have been built originally by Lord Visvakarma, the demigod architect. Parashurama is said to have made and installed the image. Now there are millions of pilgrims who make the trip to the hill to see this temple of Lord Ayyappa.

CHAPTER NINE

The Remaining Demigods

Along with the major personalities that have already been described, there is another level of *devas* or Vedic gods that can also be explained. The names of these gods are considered as offices or positions, rather than the actual name of the demigod. For example, we may call the president of the country by his personal name, or simply Mr. President. It is the position itself that allows for him to have particular powers or areas of influence. In the case of the demigods, it is only after accumulating much pious credit that a living being can earn the position of being such a demigod. Then a person may become an Indra, or Vayu, or attain some other position to assume particular powers, or to control various aspects of material energy. Many of the following *devas* are closely associated with the original *Vedas*, such as the *Rig*, *Sama*, *Atharva*, and *Yajur Vedas* wherein many mantras and verses focused on acquiring their blessings.

ADITYAS

The Adityas are the personifications or the embodiment of the universal laws. They regulate the behavior of humans among themselves in conjunction with the natural forces. The Adityas are the twelve sons of Aditi, wife of Kashyapa. Their dynasty is described in the *Bhagavata Purana*, which includes descendants that were great personalities and additional lesser demigods.

There are twelve Adityas listed in the later Vedic literature, such as the *Shatapatha Brahmana*, while the *Rig Veda* lists six, and eight are listed in other *Brahmanas*. The names are: Amsha (one who is munificent), Aryaman (one who eliminates foes), Bhaga (one who bestows), Daksha (one who is skilled in ritual and magic), Mitra (friend), Pushan (one who nurtures), Savitri (one who activates), Shakra (the forceful), Tvashtri (one who designs), Varuna (he who surrounds or

The Remaining Demigods

restrains), Vishnu (the omniscient maintainer) and Vivasvat (or Vivasvan, the brilliant, or the sun, Surya). In the same order, these also refer to the universal principles known as: the share given by the gods, chivalry and honor, that which is inherited, skill in ritual, solidarity in friendship, prosperity, the potency in language, courage, skill in crafts, laws of providence as directed by the gods, universal law, and morality and social order.

The name Aditya also refers to the sun. And the Adityas together are considered the eternal gods of light, or the beings that manifest luminous life throughout the universe. They are also connected to the aspects of the sun divided into the annual twelve months, or the twelve spokes of the wheel of time.

AGNI

Agni is the fire-god, referred in the *Rig Veda*. He is the god who accepts the offerings in the ancient fire *yajnas*, or rituals, and carries them to the appropriate gods. In the early hymns, he is credited as being the creator, sustainer, or omniscient cosmic being. All light are reflections of him, even ordinary fire (Prithvi), lightning (Indra) in the sky or space (Antariksha), as well as the sun (Surya) in the heaven (Dyuloka). He is immortal yet dwells with mortals in the form of fire in their houses. With him, the world sustains itself.

Agni is portrayed as an old man with a red complexion. He has two heads, three eyes and two horns on each, with long braided hair. His belly is big and his six arms holds such items as a rosary, a sphere, spoon, ladle, fan, and one hand is held in the position of offering blessings. He has seven tongues of fire used to lick the offerings given in the Vedic rituals. He also has three legs, and wears a red garment. His two consorts, Svaha and Svadha, accompany him at his sides. The ram is his carrier, while smoke is his flag. At times he is viewed riding a chariot, in which case it is drawn by red horses, and the seven winds are the wheels. He is also called other names according to his qualities, such as: Jvalana (burning), Pavaka (purifier), Vibhavasu (abundant in light), Chitrabhanu (multicolored), Bhuritejas (resplendent), Shikhin (flaming), Plavanga (flickering), and others.

ASVINS

The Asvins are twins who are said to represent a few possibilities, such as earth and space, night and day, or even sun and moon. They may have been kings who became qualified to take the position of gods. They are mostly praised as being the twilight before the dawn, and the early morning moisture and light. It is said that they appear in the night sky before daybreak preparing the way for dawn to arrive by riding in the sky in a golden car pulled by birds or horses.

They are portrayed as handsome and the youngest of the gods. They are almost never separated, but individually they are named Nasatya or Satya (no untruth and truth) and Dasra (the miraculous). They are skillful physicians and surgeons, and because they are expert in the knowledge of plants and herbs, they are masters in the arts of healing and rejuvenation. They are always doing good for others. The *Asvinikumara-samhita* is a medical book attributed to them. They also showed the gods and humanity the use of liquor. They are worshiped for the blessings of excellent health, good children, food, wealth, and freedom from enemies.

The *Mahabharata* recounts how once when Surya's (the sun god's) brilliance was so great that his wife, Samjna, was unable to bear it, she left for the forest to concentrate on religious pursuits. She left Chaya, Surya's other wife, with him. Samjna took the form of a mare to hide herself. But Surya discovered her and, taking the form of a horse, approached her. In this way, she bore him two sons who are called the Ashvini-kumaras (mare's boys), also known as the gods of agriculture. These Asvins are also the fathers of two of the Pandavas, Nakula and Shadeva.

INDRA

Indra is known as the King of Heaven, and, thus, the king of the celestial gods. Along with Agni, he is the main deity of the *Rig Veda* and is described in many exploits. His name is always invoked in the Soma rites of the *Rig Veda*. He is also known for being a magician, a knower of all mystic powers, and a dancer. He has many different names according to his abilities and qualities. However, he is overly attracted to intoxicants and sensual pleasure, which has got him into big trouble at times. Once he seduced Ahalya, the wife of the sage Gautama. The sage cursed Indra and Indra developed a thousand marks on his body that took the form of a woman's organ. Only later were they changed into eyes,

The Remaining Demigods

which gives him the name of Sahasraksha. So, Indra is seen sometimes with a body covered with eyes as a sign of his lechery. However, Indra is representative of the power of virility. He is also known to disturb holy men from their vows by tempting them with the heavenly girls. He fears the power that such sages can develop that could be used to usurp his own position, so he tries to distract them in this way.

He is portrayed with a human form with four long arms and riding on his elephant, Airavata. He is always seen holding the thunderbolt, his weapon, in his right hand. The thunderbolt was made from the bones of the great sage Dadhichi. It is this thunderbolt that removed the head of the demon Vritra. He also carries a hook, noose, his bow (Vijaya), a sword (Paranjaya), and a conch (Deva-datta, the gift of God). Or he is seen on a chariot which travels faster than the mind and drawn by golden horses. It bears a flag that is gold and dark blue. His chariot contains such weapons as swords, spears, and serpents. As it crosses the sky, it scatters the clouds with the sounds of thunder. The *Puranas* also describe Indra as a handsome young man riding a white horse (Uccaihshravas) or elephant (Airavata).

Indra is considered the controller of rain and lightning, and is also worshiped when there is a need for such. Indra is the power of the thunderbolt, and is a friend to Vayu, the wind god. They work together. Also, it is Agni, Indra and Surya who represent the three forms of fire in its earthly state, its electrical charge, and the sun globe.

Indra was born from the sage Kashyapa and his wife Diti. Indra's wife, Indrani or Aindri, also called Sachi, is noted among the goddesses. Indra had three sons, namely Jayanta, Rishabha, and Midhusha. Indra also fathered the great monkey king Valin.

Being the king of heaven, Indra's abode is a great city of beauty and immortality, called Amaravati, that is located near Mount Meru.

KUBERA

Kubera is considered the god of wealth, the treasurer of the demigods. He is also a friend of Lord Shiva. Kubera is the leader of the spirits of darkness, the *yakshas* and *guhyakas*, who assist and protect Kubera and also act as guardians of the precious jewels and ores of the earth. These entities are the wizard-like beings that exist in the subtle realm. They use swords, clubs, and even javelins to guard his city of Alakapuri. They are generally good-natured beings that live in the realm of the earth or its borders. Kubera is also the ruler of the *rakshasas*. They are protective toward Kubera, but are demoniac ghostly creatures who are shape-shifting flesh or man-eaters.

Kubera is associated with Ganesh and is the giver of wealth when he is pleased with someone, especially jewels since those are the treasures of the earth, which is what he keeps. Only through him can men, according to what they deserve, find or attain the treasures of the earth. He also can protect travelers.

Kubera is the son of Pulastya and Idavida. Idavida was the daughter of the great sage Bharadvaja (*Vishnu Purana*) or Trinabindu (*Bhagavata Purana* 1.4.3). On Kubera's demoniac (*asuric*) side, his brothers include the demon Ravana, Kumbhakarna (who were great enemies of Lord Rama) and Vibhishana (who became Rama's ally). The demoness Shurpanakha was their sister. Kubera once lived in the capital of Ceylon, but was banished by Ravana after he acquired it because he wanted the riches of the city for himself.

Bhadra is Kubera's wife, also called Yakshi. They had three sons, Nalakubera, Manigriva, and Mayuraja, and one daughter, Minakshi.

Kubera is usually displayed as a dwarf with a white complexion and big belly. His body, which has three legs, eight teeth and one eye, is decorated with jewels. He holds a mace in his hands. He sits on a throne in his huge hall, and his city is filled with riches, which is located near Mount Kailash, north of the Himalaya.

MARUTS

The Maruts are another class of divine beings of the subtle world. The name *marut* means to not cry or weep. They move through the sky, in the subtle realm. They are a group of war-like men who engage in esoteric practices. They are the friends of Indra and help him in his wars. It is Indra who raised them to the status of god-like beings.

As described in the *Rig Veda*, they live in the north and embody youth and moralistic and chivalrous activities. They roam the skies in golden chariots that are drawn by flaxen stallions. They roar and move with loud noise, directing the storms. They hold bows and arrows, and although they are good-natured, they can be brutal and are feared. They cause rain and can direct or repel violent weather. When they move, the mountains may tremble and shake, and trees can topple.

They are said to be the sons of Rudra, and are called Rudriyas, sons of Rudra, which is also why they are like the Rudras. Yet in the

The Remaining Demigods

Mahabharata and *Bhagavata Purana* they are described as being the sons of Dharma (Yamaraja, the lord of death).

The Maruts are viewed as the chiefs of the vaishyas, or farmers and traders. They are worshiped for supernatural powers or for the results of challenging projects. Their realm is the heaven reached by the vaishyas. Their number is often counted as eleven, the same as the Rudras, whereas other places say they are 21, 27, 49, or even 180 in number.

The story in the *Bhagavata Purana* (Canto Six, Chapter Eighteen) also relates how the Maruts appeared. Diti, the second wife of Kashyapa, had given birth to a number of demons, including Hiranyaksha and Hiranyakashipu. Both of them were killed by Lord Vishnu in His assistance to Lord Indra, which upset their mother greatly. Her goal became to give birth to a son who would kill Indra. Thinking like this, she constantly acted in a way that was most pleasing to her husband until he granted whatever she wanted. So, she asked for a son who could kill Indra. Then Kashyapa gave her an austerity to follow in worship of Lord Vishnu. Once she became pregnant, she followed the vow intently. Indra heard of this and devised a plan. He engaged in the service of his aunt, Diti, who was residing in an ashrama, and waited for a flaw in her execution. Only once, after growing weary, did she fail to execute part of the vow, which gave Indra the chance he was waiting for. Then Indra, the master of yogic powers, became so small that he could enter Diti's womb while she was sleeping. He then took his thunderbolt and cut the growing embryo into seven pieces, in which seven living beings started to cry. He told them not to cry, from which came the name Maruts. Then he again cut each of them into seven, creating 49 living beings.

They called out to him asking why he was trying to kill them when they are his brothers. Indra realized that they were his followers, so assured them that they had nothing more to fear. He understood that they survived his cutting of the embryo because of Diti's great service to Lord Vishnu. Thus, when he later left the area, Indra took the Maruts with him to the heavenly planets.

SOMA

Soma is another of the main deities of the *Rig Veda*, and is also called Indu or Soma-Pavamana. The ninth book of the *Rig Veda* is devoted to the soma ritual. Soma is the deity of the soma plant, the juice of which was used in sacrificial rituals and for a powerful rejuvenating drink. The Soma deity also empowers the soma plant, as does the moon. Thus, Soma also represents the moon.

Soma is known for giving the mortals happiness, freedom from disease, and entrance into the worlds of immortality. He gives power to the mind and speech, and is therefore also called Vachaspati, or lord of speech. It is said that he also rules over mountains and rivers.

In the *Rig* and *Atharva Vedas*, Soma is also related to the moon, Chandra. Soma as the moon is the son of Atri (detachment) and Anasuya (benevolence), according to the *Skanda Purana* (4.1.14) and the *Vishnu Dharmottara* (1.106). Yet, he is also considered the son of Dharma and Prabhakara in other places. In the *Bhavagata Purana* (11:13) and *Mahabharata* (12:208 & 1.18.34) he is described as coming forth from the churning of the ocean of milk after the Goddess Lakshmi appeared.

He is shown as a white complexioned being, dressed in white, wearing gold ornaments. He rides a chariot with three wheels, drawn by ten horses, all as white as jasmine. He has two hands, one holding a mace while the other rests in a posture showing assurance from fear.

The soma plant, according to the *Rig Veda* (3.48.2) comes from the mountains. Its juice may have been mixed with milk and butter or barley. It gives power, strength, good health, yet may cause nausea if too much is drunk. It is also called a celestial dew or rain. It is also difficult to find. Its preparation is ritualistic, as the bulb is pricked with a golden needle to let the juice out into a gold cup. The husk is also pressed to squeeze the fluid out. The one who drinks it must have already undergone purificatory rites in preparation for it.

VARUNA

Varuna is an ancient Vedic deity. He is associated with the rivers and ocean, as well as the clouds and water in general. He is the lord of the oceans and aquatics. He rules over the rivers and their spirit beings, as well as the serpent gods called the nagas. It is considered that those who drown go to him. He also can ward off any bad effects related to water. Varuna is considered to have unlimited power and understanding. He rules over moral principles and punishes those who break them, but with compassion he forgives them if they repent and pray. He is one of the Adityas, and as such participates in the celestial order of things.

It is not so often that you will see images of him in temples, but he is portrayed in a human form, riding on a crocodile, holding in two of his four hands a serpent and noose. At other times he may be seen riding a chariot with an umbrella over him, pulled by seven swans and holding a noose, lotus, a conch, and a cup or pot of gems. Occasionally, he may also be riding on the back of a swan.

VASUS

There are eight Vasus who are, more or less, attendants of Indra, or his thunderbolt, which is also the heavenly form of Agni. They are also considered to be gods of atmospheric or celestial powers. *Vasu* means to dwell, or dwellings, and, thus, represent all realms of space and dimension. The Vasus are also considered extensions of Lord Brahma, who is the lord of extensions or dwellings since he is the origin of the universal planets and space. Thus, the Vasus also have a red complexion representing the passionate nature of creation. They do not have specific functions, yet are invoked in the *Rig Veda* for material aid or blessings.

These eight Vasus are known as: Dhara (the earth, the nourisher or support of all other creatures), Anala or Agni (fire), Anila (or Vayu, wind, the area between the earth and sky, and abode of subtle beings), Ap (water), Dhruva (polestar and the constellations), Prabhasa (dawn or sky, also called Dyaus), Pratyusha (or Surya, the sun and light), and Soma (moon). These are some of the spheres of existence, or dwellings of the living beings in the universe.

VAYU

Vayu is known as the wind-god and is connected with the Prana (the life airs in the body). He is also considered a lord of the sky (*antariksha*). The name *Vayu* comes from the root, *va*, which means to blow. He is seen as riding a chariot, which roars as he travels, announcing his presence. It is pulled by two, or ninety-nine, or even a thousand horses depending on the force with which he arrives. He is shown with a blue complexion, with four hands, two of which hold a fan and a flag, and the other two in the postures (*mudras*) of giving blessings and protection. At other times he is viewed as a powerful man with a white complexion, riding a deer, and holding a bow and arrows. Nonetheless, being the wind, he is invisible. As the life airs in the body, he can provide health and strength. Vayu is also called Vata (the wanderer) and Pavana (purifier).

VISVADEVAS

These deities are protectors of the moral law (*rita*). They protect their devotees from enemies, assist the pious, and provide auspicious results or abodes for the pious. They are always young, pleasant in appearance, and always favorable toward those who respect them.

The word "Visvadevas" means all the gods, as if for all those who do not hold a specific post, or referring to a group of the personifications of the moralistic principles. There are ten in number named, Daksha (skill), Dhriti (forbearance), Kala (time), Kama (lusty desire), Kratu (will), Kuru (the ancestor of Kurus), Madravas (cry of joy), Pururavas (a being that dwells in the atmosphere), Satya (truth), and Vasu (place of dwelling).

YAMA

Yama, or Yamaraja, is the god of death and oversees the spirits of the departed. The word *yama* means to arrest or restrain. He is also called Dharmaraja, or the king of Dharma, the principles of duty and law upon which the world is supported. This law is what gives balance to society. Within the hall of judgment (*kalchi*) he sits on his throne (*vicharabhu*) and gives the judgment of rewards or punishments to all who have died, and sends them to the appropriate abodes for the results of their life's actions. In this purpose he is assisted by Chitragupta, the recorder of everyone's life, and his ministers Chanda (anger) and Mahachanda (terror). His messengers of death, the Yamadutas, also assist in gathering and bringing to him the sinful souls who have left their bodies. Yamaraja also has two fierce dogs, each with four eyes, which guard the path that leads to Yama's abode. The departed are brought to him at his city of Samyamini (place of confinement), which is below the earth. They are taken along a path without food, water or shelter and are forced along regardless of how tired or fearful they may be. Detailed descriptions of the descent into hell are given in the *Puranas*.

The city has four gates and seven arches, within which there are the rivers Pushpodaka (river of flowers) and Vaivasvati (roaring river). Though he is surrounded by many demons, which represent various diseases, he also has numerous sages that come to his court to pay their respects. They are entertained by the heavenly musicians and dancers. The dead must face Yama alone, without friends or family, and accompanied only by their past actions. Then Chitragupta reads the account of the person's history, forcing them to experience a review of their life, and Yamaraja gives the sentence of rewards or punishment for their conduct.

Yama is portrayed as being fearful to see, having a green complexion with red eyes that glow. He wears red garments and a golden crown. He appears differently to various people. To the pious he looks handsome and appears like Vishnu, with four arms, lotus eyes, a lovely face, and a flower garland. Yet, to the devious he looks gruesome with eyes like deep wells under a serious frown. He has extremely long limbs, and he roars like the annihilating ocean. His crown is like flames and his teeth are long.

He rides a powerful, black male buffalo. He also carries a large mace for punishment, a noose to arrest, as well as an axe, sword, and knife in his hands. He is the son of Surya, brother of Manu. He is sometimes seen with three of his wives, namely Sushila (good behavior), Hemamala (garland of gold) and Vijaya (victory). However, he is also said to have married ten of Daksha's daughters, which are particular potencies that arose from the rituals that were performed. Yet, Dhumorna (smoke from the cremation fire) is also described as his wife.

He is also called Pashin (the one who carries the noose), Pitripati (lord of the ancestors), and Shraddhadeva (lord of the rites for the departed).

THE NAVAGRAHAS

The Navagrahas are the nine planets. They are viewed as astrological influences that can be understood and even stifled or amplified with proper rituals, amulets, yantras, gemstones, etc. They are divided into two parts, the auspicious and inauspicious. The first group consists of Ravi or Surya (the sun), Soma or Chandra (moon), Budha (Mercury), Shukra (Venus), Mangala, Kuja or Angaraka (Mars), and Brihashpati or Guru (Jupiter). The inauspicious planets are Shani (Saturn), Rahu (the ascending node of the moon), and Ketu (the descending node of the moon). Planet Earth is called Bhumi.

In many of the Shiva temples in South India there is always a Navagraha shrine or pavilion in which people can perform worship, offer lamps, prayers, or circumambulate all the symbols or deities of the nine planets. There are few temples dedicated only to the nine planets, but you can find some in India, such as at Ujjain and Guwahati.

SURYA

Among all the Navagrahas, Surya the sun-god is the most important. He is always placed in the center of the other planets since he is like the center of creation. He is the nearest and most easily recognized form of divinity, the visible source and cause of life, and is, thus, accepted as a form or representation of the Supreme God. He is also accepted as the all-seeing eye of the Supreme. It is through his rays that he puts life into all beings. However, he also gives death. He perpetually creates, supports, and then destroys all life. He is also called Aditya since he is the source of the world. He has many other names that relate to his abilities and character. A few are Aharpati (lord of the day), Jagatchakshus (eye of the universe), Karmasakshin (witness of actions), Graharajan (king of planets), Sahasrakirana (one with a thousand rays), Dyumani (jewel of the sky), and others.

As one of the Vasus, he is also the physical sun or celestial form of Agni, fire. He is also identified with Aditya, Savitri (the sun before it rises in the morning) and Pushan (the strength-giving and healthful aspect of the daytime sun). The early rendition of the Gayatri mantra is dedicated to this Savitri.

Surya, the son of Kashyapa and Aditi, is portrayed as being an extremely brilliant deity, riding in a wonderful chariot with one wheel pulled by seven horses, representing the orbits of the other seven planets. He is of dwarfish stature, with a shiny copperish complexion and burning eyes. Aruna (the deity of the dawn, the elder brother of Garuda and son of Kashyapa) is his charioteer. Surya's brilliance is what gives light that produces the day, the absence of which naturally causes night. It is his light which activates the living beings and gives them strength and health. He looks at all with equality, and is very generous and protective. He is seen with two hands, holding a lotus in each.

He has four wives: Samjna (knowledge), Rajni (Queen), Prabha (light), and Chaya (shade), as described in the *Kurma Purana*. In the same *Purana* it is related that Surya's children are Vaivasvata Manu (father of Iksvaku), Yama, and Yamuna, all born of Samjna; Revanta was born of Rajni; Prabhata (dawn) born of Prabha; and Savarni to Chaya. However, Savarni, Revanta and Sani (Saturn) are born to Chaya in the *Markandeya Purana*. These relations can change with different *kalpas*, or days of Brahma when the creation is again manifest in slightly varying orders. These are the differences between the descriptions in the Puranic literature, they describe the history of events in different *kalpas*.

It is also described how Surya had a son with Kunti named Karna. Surya was also the father of Sugriva, the chief of monkeys in the *Ramayana*.

There are rarely any temples dedicated solely to Surya, but there are a few. However, the most prominent, such as at Konarka in Orissa and Modhera in Gujarat, are no longer functioning as active temples. But they are very beautiful and amazing temples to see. An active Surya temple is found in Ranakpur, across from the main Jain temple. Otherwise, smaller shrines to Surya can be found in the larger temple complexes or with the Navagraha deities.

HANUMAN

Hanuman holds a most special place in the hearts of many followers of the Vedic tradition. He is most known as the son of Vayu the wind-god, and his mother Anjana, though there are different versions of how this happened. He is also considered a partial expansion and son of Shiva, or the 11th *avatar* of Shiva. He is part of the special race of monkeys who were dedicated to Lord Rama, of whose activities are found described in the *Ramayana*. Hanuman in particular is the most dedicated devotee, and risked life and limb in his escapades to serve Lord Rama.

He is often shown in a humble position when pictured with Sita-Rama and Lakshmana, kneeling at the feet of Lord Rama, hands folded in devotion. Otherwise, he is also shown holding his mace in his left hand and carrying the Sanjivini Mountain in his right. This displays the time when he got the mountain for its herbs to help bring back to life Rama and his brother Lakshmana after an exhausting battle. In shrines or temples for Hanuman, he is usually posed in a heroic stance, carrying his mace.

Hanuman has super-human strength, and being the son of the wind-god, Vayu, he can leap great distances. He is highly erudite and just as wise. Devotees worship him for acquiring the devotion to Lord Rama that Hanuman has and can bestow on others. By meditating on Hanuman, one reaches Lord Rama where he will always be a devotee of the Lord, and, thus, eliminate the sufferings of many lifetimes.

CONCLUSION

All of the divine personalities that have been described herein are the main deities of the Vedic pantheon. Besides these *devas*, there are numerous other beings that are recognized for having a god-like status, or are the presiding personalities over areas of power, the directions, planets, or are special types of living beings. Others are those who live in higher dimensions or subtle realms. A few of these include beings like the *gandharvas* (angels), *apsaras* (heavenly dancing girls), *prajapatis* (progenitors), *siddhas* (the perfected beings expert in the mystic sciences), *vidyadharas* (wisdom bearing spirits), the *pretas* and *bhutas* (ghostly beings), *upanayikas* (fairies), and many other minor local village gods and goddesses that are emphasized according to the orientation and traditions of the people. So, what we have covered in this book are the main Divinities that are the most important to understand.

By reviewing the information that has been presented, we can begin to see that it is not so difficult to comprehend how each of the various Divinities of the Vedic culture have particular characteristics and blessings that they can offer to those who show respect or worship them. They all have specific purposes. Furthermore, they are not merely different representations of some vague power or amalgamated Absolute Truth. They all have their particular pastimes, positions and jurisdictions, or oversee certain universal powers of nature. Some of them also lead a person to deeper aspects of spiritual knowledge and truths, or can bless an individual with more insights and higher realizations. Thus, they all have a function and benefit that they can provide to someone for whatever is most needed by that person. And, ultimately, there is indeed, one Supreme Being that oversees everything and is the source of all.

The Vedic spiritual knowledge is not for a particular group, country, race, or people. It is for everyone. That is why it is also called Sanatana-dharma, it is a way of life. But it also means the eternal (Sanatana) nature (dharma) of us all as spiritual beings, which means that our eternal duty in whatever situation we find ourselves is to regain that spiritual knowledge of our real identity, and then realize that by actual perception and then act accordingly. That is real Sanatana-dharma. That is beyond mere religiosity or moral standards. It is the highest level of spiritual understanding and perception. And becoming acquainted with the Vedic Divinities is only a part of that, for they are only there to assist us in various ways that we may need, both materially and spiritually.

APPENDIX ONE

Sri Caitanya Mahaprabhu
The Most Recent Avatar

Sri Caitanya Mahaprabhu [pronounced Chaitanya] (February 27,1486 to 1534 CE) was born in Navadvipa, Bengal, on a full moon night during a lunar eclipse. It is typical for people to bathe in the Ganga River during an eclipse and chant the Lord's holy names for spiritual purification. So, everyone in the area was chanting the holy names when He was born. His parents, Jagannatha Misra and Sachidevi, gave Him the name of Vishvambhara, meaning the support of the universe, because astrologers had predicted His super human qualities and that He would deliver the people of the world. He was also nicknamed Nimai because He had been born under a *nima* tree.

During His childhood He exhibited extraordinary qualities, even having philosophical discussions with His mother. While growing, His brilliant intelligence began to become apparent. While still a child, He mastered Sanskrit and logic to the point of defeating local pundits, and established the truth of His spiritual wisdom and the Vedic philosophy. He became so well known that many logicians of various religious and philosophical persuasions began to fear His presence and refused to debate with Him. Thus, Sri Caitanya established the authority of the Vaishnava tradition through the process of debate and logic.

Then, when Sri Caitanya went to Gaya on the pretext to perform ceremonies for the anniversary of His father's death, He received Vaishnava initiation from Ishvara Puri. Thereafter, He lost all interest in debate and simply absorbed Himself in chanting and singing the names of Lord Krishna in devotional ecstasy. Upon returning to Navadvipa, He gathered a following with whom He would engage in congregational singing of the Lord's holy names. Thus, He started the first *sankirtana* (congregational devotional singing) movement, and established the importance of chanting the names of God in this age as the most elevated of spiritual processes, and the prime means for liberation from material attachments.

At first, His chanting with people was for the few participants who were a part of His group, but then Sri Caitanya ordered that the ecstasy of love of God be distributed to all people of the area. He gave no recognition for the privileges of caste, or for position, or type of philosophy a person had, or yogic asceticism. He only emphasized the devotional chanting of the Lord's holy names, using the Hare Krishna mantra (Hare Krishna, Hare Krishna, Krishna Krishna, Hare Hare / Hare Rama, Hare Rama, Rama Rama, Hare Hare) which can bring out the natural loving sentiments for God.

It was at the age of 24 when He shaved His head and took the order of *sannyasa*, the renounced stage of life, when He accepted the name of Krishna Caitanya from Keshava Bharati during the initiation. He then spent four years traveling through South India, and also visited Vrindavana and Varanasi. During this time he also gave special instructions to Rupa and Sanatana Gosvamis, who then also spread the glories of the Divine Love for Radha and Krishna. They settled in Vrindavana where they spent their years in writing many books elaborating the instructions of Lord Caitanya and the glories of *bhakti* pr devotion for Radha and Krishna. They also revealed the places where Radha and Krishna performed many varied pastimes in that land of Vrindavana, which have remained special locations where devotees can become absorbed in the bliss of love of Radha and Krishna.

Lord Caitanya spent His remaining years in Jagannatha Puri. During this time He was absorbed in ecstatic devotion to Krishna in the loving mood of Radharani, in which He would lose all external consciousness. He freely distributed the divine nectar of this love for Krishna to everyone and anyone, day and night. Even His presence or mere touch could transform everyone that came near Him into the same devotional mood. He remained like this until He finally left our vision at the age of 48.

Lord Caitanya is considered and was established by Vedic scripture as the most recent *avatar* of God. The Lord always descends to establish the codes of religion. This is confirmed in *Bhagavad-gita* (4.6-8) where Lord Krishna explains that although He is unborn and the Lord of all living beings, He still descends in His spiritual form in order to re-establish the proper religious principles and annihilate the miscreants whenever there is a decline of religion and a rise in irreligious activity.

Though there are many *avatars* and incarnations of God, all incarnations are known and predicted in the Vedic literature. Each one performs many wonderful pastimes. But in Kali-yuga, the Lord descends in the form of His own devotee as Sri Caitanya in order to show the perfect example of how devotional service should be performed, and to stress the chanting of the Hare Krishna mantra for this age by inaugurating the process of the *sankirtana* movement (congregational chanting).

Predictions of the appearance of Lord Caitanya can be found in many Vedic texts. One of the oldest prophecies concerning Sri Caitanya's appearance in this world is found in the *Atharva-veda* verse, starting as: *ito 'ham krita-sannyaso 'vatarisyami*. In this verse, the Supreme states: "I will descend as a sannyasi, a tall, fair, and saintly brahmana devotee, after four to five thousand years of Kali-yuga have passed. I will appear on earth near the Ganges shore and with all the signs of an exalted person, free from material desires. I will always chant the holy names of the Lord, and, thus, taste the sweetness of My own devotional service. Only other advanced devotees will understand Me."

Also, in a verse from the *Sama Veda*, starting as: *tathaham krita-sannyaso bhu-girbanah avatarisye*, the Supreme Being says that He will descend to earth as a brahmana-sannyasi at a place on the shore of the Ganges. Again and again He will chant the names of the Lord in the company of His associates to rescue the people who are devoured by sins in the age of Kali.

The *Mundaka Upanishad* (3.3) also relates the prophecy of Sri Caitanya in a different way. It states, "When one realizes the golden form of Lord Gauranga, who is the ultimate actor and the source of the Supreme Brahman, he attains the highest knowledge. He transcends both pious and impious activities, becomes free from worldly bondage, and enters the divine abode of the Lord."

Another prophecy of the appearance of Sri Caitanya is found in two verses in the *Bhavishya Purana*. It states:

ajayadhvamaja yadhvam na sansayah
kalau sankirtana rambhe bhavisyami saci sutah

"The Supreme Lord said: 'In Kali-yuga, I will appear as the son of Sachi, and inaugurate the *sankirtana* movement. There is no doubt about this.'"

anandasru-kala-roma-harsa-purnam tapo-dhana
sarve mam eva draksyanti kalau sannyasa-rupinam

"O sage whose wealth is austerity, in the Kali-yuga everyone will see My form as a sannyasi, a form filled with tears of bliss and bodily hairs standing erect in ecstasy."

Another is from the *Svetasvatara Upanishad* (3.12): "Mahaprabhu [the great master], the Supreme Being, is brilliantly effulgent and imperishable like molten gold, and [through *sankirtana*] bestows spiritual intelligence on the living beings. In the guise of a *sannyasi*, He is the source of spiritual purity and liberation."

It is also found in the *Vayu Purana*: "In the age of Kali I shall descend as the son of Sachidevi to inaugurate the *sankirtana* movement." This is also confirmed in the *Srimad-Bhagavatam* (11.5.32) where it states: "In the age of Kali, intelligent persons perform congregational chanting to worship the incarnation of Godhead who constantly sings the names of Krishna. Although His complexion is not blackish [like that of Lord Krishna], He is Krishna Himself. He is accompanied by His associates, servants, weapons, and confidential companions."

The great classic *Mahabharata* (*Vishnu-sahasra-nama-stotra*, 127.92.75) confirms that Sri Caitanya Mahaprabhu is not different from Lord Sri Krishna: "The Supreme Lord has a golden complexion [when He appears as Lord Caitanya]. Indeed, His entire body, which is very nicely constituted, is like molten gold. Sandalwood pulp is smeared all over His body. He will take the fourth order of life [sannyasa] and will be very self-controlled. He will be distinguished from Mayavadi sannyasis in that He will be fixed in devotional service and will propagate the *sankirtana* movement."

The *Caitanya-caritamrita* (Adi-lila, 3.19-20) also explains how the Supreme Lord Himself describes how He will appear as His own devotee to perform and teach devotional service by inaugurating the *sankirtana* movement, which is the religion for this age.

How He is the "great master" (Mahaprabhu) or will "bestow spiritual intelligence" is described in another *Upanishad*. This is one of the lesser *Upanishads* known as the *Chaitanyopanishad*, or *Sri Caitanya Upanishad*. This comes from the ancient *Atharva Veda*. In this description there is not only the prediction of His appearance but a description of His life and purpose, and the reasons why His process of spiritual enlightenment is so powerful and effective in this age of Kali. The *Chaitanyopanishad* is a short text with only nineteen verses. All of them are very significant.

The *Sri Caitanya Upanishad* (texts 5-11) explains that one day when Pippalada asked his father, Lord Brahma, how the sinful living entities will be delivered in Kali-yuga and who should be the object of their worship and what mantra should they chant to be delivered, Brahma told him to listen carefully and he would describe what will take place in the age of Kali. Brahma said that the Supreme Lord Govinda, Krishna, will appear again in Kali-yuga as His own devotee in a two-armed form with a golden complexion in the area of Navadvipa along the Ganges. He will spread the system of devotional service and the chanting of the names of Krishna, especially in the form of the Hare Krishna *maha-mantra*; Hare Krishna, Hare Krishna, Krishna Krishna, Hare Hare/Hare Rama, Hare Rama, Rama Rama, Hare Hare.

Another interesting story about the prediction of the appearance of Lord Caitanya in Kali-yuga is related in a lengthy conversation between Murari Gupta and Damodara Pandita, two contemporaries of Sri Caitanya. It is found in the *Sri Caitanya Mangala*, a biography of Sri Caitanya by Srila Locana Dasa Thakura. Among the many things they discuss are the symptoms and difficulties found in the age of Kali, how Lord Krishna appears on earth in this age, His confidential reasons for doing so, and how He revealed to Narada Muni His form as Lord Gauranga that He would accept while appearing on earth in this age. In this form He would distribute love of God to everyone He met by chanting the holy names. This conversation is very enlightening.

Within this conversation they further relate an incident recorded as the *Vishnu-Katyayani Samvada* of the *Padma Purana*. This is a conversation between Lord Vishnu and Katyayani (Parvati), Lord Shiva's wife. The story is that one time the great sage Narada Muni acquired the *maha-prasada*, personal food remnants, of Lord Narayana, Vishnu, and gave a morsel to his friend Lord Shiva. Shiva tasted it and he began to dance in ecstasy, to the point of disturbing the earth. When he was approached by Parvati about why he was dancing so, he explained what happened. However, she was unhappy and angry that he did not share any with her. Being devoted to Lord Vishnu and concerned for the spiritual well-being of all conditioned souls, she then vowed that if she should get the blessings of Lord Vishnu, she would see to it that the Lord's *maha-prasada* was distributed to everyone. Just then Lord Vishnu Himself appeared and conversed with her. He assured her that He would appear in the world as Sri Caitanya Mahaprabhu in the age of Kali and would keep her promise and spread His mercy in the form of *maha-prasada*, food that has been offered to Him, and the chanting of His holy names to everyone, distributing His mercy everywhere.

Another book is the *Sri Hari-bhakti-vilasa* by Sanatana Gosvami. Sanatana lived about 500 years ago in Vrindavana, India and was a great scholar of the Vedic scripture. A portion of the book contains an anthology of an amazing assortment of verses from the Vedic texts which predict the appearance of Lord Caitanya. Besides some of the quotes we have already cited, he includes verses from such texts as the *Chandogya Upanishad, Krishna Upanishad, Narada Purana, Kurma Purana, Garuda Purana, Devi Purana, Nrisimha Purana, Padma Purana, Brahma Purana, Agni Purana, Saura Purana, Matsya Purana, Vayu Purana, Markandeya Purana, Varaha Purana, Vamana Purana, Vishnu Purana, Skanda Purana, Upapuranas, Narayana-Samhita, Krishna-yamala, Brahma-yamala, Vishnu-yamala, Yoga-vasistha,* and the *Tantras,* such as *Urdhvamnaya-tantra, Kapila Tantra, Visvasara Tantra, Kularnava Tantra,* and others.

These and other predictions confirm the fact that Sri Caitanya Mahaprabhu would appear to specifically propagate the chanting of the holy names. Furthermore, in the Fourth Chapter of the *Antya-lila* of the *Caitanya Bhagavata*, which is a biography of Sri Caitanya Mahaprabhu written by Sri Vrindavan dasa Thakura who is said to be a later incarnation of Srila Vyasadeva, Lord Caitanya explains: "I have appeared on earth to propagate the congregational chanting of the holy names of God. In this way, I will deliver the sinful material world. Those demons who never before accepted My authority and lordship will weep in joy by chanting My names. I will vigorously distribute devotional service, *bhakti*, which is sought after even by demigods, sages, and perfected beings, so that even the most abominable sinners will receive it. But those who, intoxicated with education, wealth, family background, and knowledge, criticize and offend My devotees, will be deprived of everything and will never know My true identity." Then Sri Caitanya specifically states (*Antya-lila* 4.126): "I declare that My name will be preached in every town and village on this earth."

This verifies the fact that the chanting of the *maha-mantra* is the rare and special opportunity given by God for all to be relieved from the problems of the age of Kali and of material life in general. As confirmed in the *Caitanya-caritamrita* (Adi-lila, 3.77-78), it is Sri Krishna Caitanya who inaugurates the congregational chanting of the holy names, which is the most sublime of all spiritual sacrifices. Intelligent people will worship Him through this means, while other foolish people will continue in the cycle of repeated birth and death in this material world.

In another place of the *Caitanya-caritamrita* (Antya-lila, 20.8-9), Sri Caitanya specifically tells Svarupa Damodara and Ramananda Raya that chanting the holy names is the most practical way to attain salvation from material existence in this age, and anyone who is intelligent and takes up this process of worshiping Krishna will attain the direct shelter of Krishna.

He also strongly opposed the impersonalist philosophy of

Shankaracharya and established the principle of *acintya-bhedabheda-tattva*. This specified that the Supreme and the individual soul are inconceivably and simultaneously one and different. This means that the Supreme and the *jiva* souls are the same in quality, being eternally spiritual, but always separate individually. The *jivas* are small and subject to being influenced by the material energy, while the Supreme is infinite and always above and beyond the material manifestation.

Sri Caitanya taught that the direct meaning of the Vedic *shastras* is that the living entities are to engage in devotional service, *bhakti*, to the Supreme, Bhagavan Sri Krishna. Through this practice there can develop a level of communication between God and the individual by which God will lovingly reveal Himself to those who become qualified. In this understanding, the theistic philosophy of Vaishnavism reached its climax.

As previously explained, there is a system of self-realization especially recommended for each age. In the age of Kali, people are not attracted to spiritual pursuits and are often rebellious against anything that seems to restrict or stifle their freedom to do anything they want. Since in this age we are so easily distracted by so many things and our mind is always in a whirl, we need an easy path. Therefore, the Vedic *shastra* explains that God has given us an easy way to return to Him in this age. It is almost as if He has said, "Since you are My worst son, I give you the easiest process." The *Caitanya-caritamrita* (Adi-lila, 3.40) confirms this and says that the Supreme Being descends as Sri Caitanya, with a golden complexion, to simply spread the glories of chanting the holy names, which is the only religious principle in this age of Kali. In this way, God Himself has given the method of chanting His holy names as the most effective means to reach His spiritual abode.

Sri Caitanya Mahaprabhu did not become much involved in writing. In fact, He only wrote eight verses known as *Shikshastaka*, but His followers compiled extensive Sanskrit literature that documented His life and fully explained His teachings. Thus, other books are available that give a much more elaborate biography of Sri Caitanya Mahaprabhu.

APPENDIX TWO

The Significance of Deities and Deity Worship

Deities and images of the Supreme, His *avatars,* and the demigods have been shown many times in this volume, but what is the significance of deities and deity worship? One thing to understand is that all the images of the deities in the Vedic pantheon, as found in the temples, are made according to explicit details and instructions found in the Vedic texts. Then they are installed in the temple in an elaborate ceremony wherein the personalities are called to appear in the form of that deity. Some of the deities are demigods, while others, such as Krishna, Vishnu, Ramachandra, are of the Supreme Being.

Some people, however, do not believe that God has a form. But many verses in the *Puranas* and, particularly, the *Brahma-samhita* establish that the Supreme Being does have a specific form. These texts also describe His variegated features, which include His spiritual shape, characteristics, beauty, strength, intelligence, activities, etc. Therefore, it is considered that the authorized deities of the Supreme that are shaped according to these descriptions provide a view of the personal form of God.

Those who have no knowledge of God or His form will certainly consider the temple deities as idols. But this is the effect of their foolishness or lack of knowledge. They think that the deities are simply the products of someone's imagination. Of course, there are those who say that God has no form, spiritual or material, or that there is no Supreme Being. Others think that since God must be formless, they can imagine or worship any material form as God, or they regard any image as merely an external manifestation of the Supreme. But images of the demigods are not additional forms of an impersonal God, nor are they equal to God. All such people who think in the above mentioned ways have resorted to their own imagination to reach such conclusions and are, therefore, idolaters. The imaginary images and opinions of God that are formed by those who have not properly learned about, seen, or realized God are indeed idols, and those who accept such images or opinions are

The Significance of Deities

certainly idolaters. This is because their images or opinions are based on ignorance and are not a likeness of His form.

Nonetheless, God is described in the Vedic literature, which explains that God is *sat-chit-ananda vigraha*, or the form of complete spiritual essence, full of eternity, knowledge, and bliss, and is not material in any way. His body, soul, form, qualities, names, pastimes, etc., are all nondifferent and are of the same spiritual quality. This form of God is not an idol designed from someone's imagination, but is the true form, even if He should descend into this material creation. And since the spiritual nature of God is absolute, He is nondifferent from His name. Thus, the name *Krishna* is an *avatara* or incarnation of Krishna in the form of sound. Similarly, His form in the temple is not merely a representation, but is also qualitatively the same as Krishna as the *archa-vigraha*, or the worshipable form as the deity. We simply have to raise or spiritualize our consciousness enough to perceive this.

Some people may question that if the deity is made from material elements, such as stone, marble, metal, wood, or paint, how can it be the spiritual form of God? The answer is given that since God is the source of all material and spiritual energies, material elements are also a form of God. Therefore, God can manifest as the deity in the temple, though made of stone or other elements, since He can transform what is spiritual into material energy, and material energy back into spiritual energy. Thus, the deity can easily be accepted as the Supreme since He can appear in any element as He chooses. In this way, even though we may be unqualified to see God, who is beyond the perceptibility of our material senses, the living beings in this material creation are allowed to see and approach the Supreme through His *archa-vigraha* form as the worshipable deity in the temple. This is considered His causeless mercy on the materially conditioned living beings.

In this manner, the Supreme Being gives Himself to His devotees so they can become absorbed in serving, remembering and meditating on Him. Thus, the Supreme comes to dwell in the temple, and the temple becomes the spiritual abode on earth. In time, the body, mind and senses of the devotee become spiritualized by serving the deity, and the Supreme becomes fully manifest to him or her. Worshiping the deity of the Supreme and using one's senses in the process of bhakti-yoga, devotional service to the Supreme, provides a means for one's true essential spiritual nature to unfold. The devotee becomes spiritually realized and the deity reveals His spiritual nature to the sincere souls according to their evolutionary spiritual development. This can continue to the level in which the Supreme Being in the form of the deity engages in a personal relationship and performs reciprocal, loving pastimes with the devotee, as has previously taken place with other advanced individuals.

At this stage, what is called *darshan* is not simply a matter of viewing the deity in the temple, but to one who is spiritually realized it is a matter of experiencing the deity and entering into a personal, reciprocal exchange with the Supreme Personality in the form of the deity. At that stage, you may view the deity, but the deity also gazes at you, and then there is a spiritual exchange wherein the deity begins to reveal His personality to you. This is what separates those who are experienced from those who are not, or those who can delve into this spiritual exchange and those who may still be trying to figure it out. For those who have experienced such an exchange with the Supreme or His deity, at this stage the worship of the Supreme Being in the deity form moves up to a whole different level, with no limits as to the spiritual love that can be shared and experienced between the devotee and the deity.

APPENDIX THREE

Deity Worship From Thousands of Years Ago

When it comes to understanding the Vedic gods and goddesses, and to the topic of worshiping deities, some question that it was not really a Vedic custom, but was only a recent invention. Thus, they try to push the idea that it is not an authorized Vedic process.

However, if we look into this we can see that there certainly are various references in assorted Vedic texts that do recommend it. Furthermore, there are several famous temples in holy places of India where it is known that the deities were installed or established by Vajranabha, Lord Krishna's great-grandson as far back as nearly 3000 BCE. A few of these can be described as follows:

For example, in the land near Mathura, several kilometers farther south of Gokul is the Dauji temple. Dauji is the deity of Lord Balarama that was one such deity originally installed 5,000 years ago by King Vajranabha, Krishna's great-grandson. In fact, he established a number of other Krishna deities in the area. The present temple was built 200 years ago by Shyama Das of Delhi. Many people attend this temple to get *darshan* of the single deity of Lord Balarama that stands 6 feet tall. From the other side of the temple you can see the deity of Revati, Lord Balarama's wife. Nearby is the Balabhadra Kund or Kshira (milk) Sagara (sea) where the deity of Lord Balarama had been hidden during the Moghul invasion. Near this kund is a temple to Harideva and in the bazaar is another temple to Banke Bihari.

In Vrindavan is the Radha-Govindaji temple that is another of the seven major temples of Vrindavan. It is across the road and a little farther down the street from the Rangaji temple. It was established by Rupa Gosvami where he discovered the Gopala deity. The beautiful temple is made out of red sandstone and was completed in 1590. The temple is now only two storeys tall but once reached up to seven storeys. The Muslim fanatic Aurangzeb, doing his dirty work once again, dismantled the upper five storeys of the temple due to his envy. While his men were destroying the temple, there was a loud thunderous noise that shook the ground. This put fear into the hearts of the men and they immediately stopped and ran away. Due to fear of the Moghuls, before they arrived the devotees moved the original deities to Jaipur where today many pilgrims go to see them. So, the Vrindavana temple now has *pratibhuh* deities, or representative expansions, of the original Radha-Govindaji that are worshiped. The original Govindaji deity is said to have been installed thousands of years ago by Vajranabha.

Also in Vrindavan, farther into the eastern part of town are many other temples; including the large and ornate Lala Babu Mandir with Radha, Krishna, and Lalita deities. Then at the corner where we turn off from Loi Bazaar to go toward the Banke Bihari Mandir, we find the Gopishwara Mahadeva Shiva temple with a Shiva *linga*, said to have been originally installed by Krishna's great-grandson, Vajranabha, and is the place where Lord Shiva did austerities in hopes of entering the *rasa-lila* dance as a *gopi* (cow-herd girl). In the morning devotees wash the *linga* with milk and other items, and then later the *pujaris* dress the *linga* in bright colored clothes.

A few miles from Barsana is Nandagram, another place where Krishna performed many childhood pastimes described in the *Bhagavatam*. On top of the hill is the main temple that has deities of Krishna, Balarama, Nanda Maharaja (Krishna's father), Mother Yashoda, Srimati Radharani, and two of Krishna's friends. There is also a Shiva *lingam* in a small shrine across from the temple called Nandisvara, said to have been installed by Vajranabha many hundreds of years ago. It is considered that this hill is an incarnation of Lord Shiva. From the top of the walls that surround the temple we can get good views of the area, and someone who is familiar with it can point out other nearby places connected with Krishna's pastimes that we may want to visit.

In the foothills of Girnar Hill is the Radha-Damodara temple with beautiful deities of Krishna's four-armed form. As Lakshmi-Narayana, the deities are formed of the typical black and brown stone, and are described in the *Skanda Purana* as being self-manifested over 12,000 years ago. Next to the main temple is another for Lord Balarama and Revati, His consort. The original temple at this site is said to have been built 4500 years ago by Vajranath, Lord Krishna's great-grandson. Not far away is a place where lived Vallabha, the 16th century Vaishnava *acharya*.

Another interesting story is in regard to Guruvayoor in south India, which has the deity of a four-armed standing Vishnu with a chakra in the right hand, conchshell in the left, and mace and lotus flower in the other two. Sri Krishna showed this form of His only twice during His appearance on earth: once to Arjuna just before the battle of Kurukshetra while speaking the *Bhagavad-gita*, and once to His parents, Vasudeva and Devaki, at the time of His birth. This deity is said to have been worshiped by Lord Krishna Himself at Dwaraka thousands of years ago. The legend is that when Krishna left this world, He gave the deity to His devotee Uddhava to look after it. He then ordered Brihaspati, the guru or spiritual teacher of the demigods, and Vayu, demigod of the wind, to take care of this Vishnu deity and to install it somewhere for the benefit of humanity. When they arrived at Dwaraka to get the deity, the city of Dwaraka had already sunk into the sea. After searching in the water, they found the deity and went south. Not knowing where to go, they sat down by the side of a lake and began to meditate. Soon, Shiva appeared and after some discussion they decided to start a new temple for the deity of Vishnu near the Rudratirtha Lake. Since that time 5,000 years ago, the place has been known as Guruvayoor (*guru* for Brihaspati and *vayoor* for Vayu).

Other examples could be given of the stories and legends of deities that are found in various temples throughout India, or holy places where temples have been established thousands of years ago. (My book *Seeing Spiritual India* goes into many of these.) But there are additional references we can use as well.

For example, even in the *Puranas* there are stories that include the importance of worshiping deities. In the *Bhagavata Purana* (4th Canto, 8th Chapter) there is the popular story of the great sage Narada Muni teaching Dhruva Maharaja the best way to become spiritual realized and explains the form of the Lord upon which to meditate and how to worship the deity of the Lord. The interesting thing here is that the *Bhagavata Purana* was composed by Srila Vyasadeva about 5,000 years ago, and the incident of Dhruva Maharaja is known to have taken place thousands of years before that. So, this gives some indication of how long deity worship has been going on. Also, in the 11th Canto, Chapter 27 of the *Bhagavata Purana*, Lord Krishna explains to Uddhava the details of deity worship, how it is important, the benefits of someone installing a deity in the temple, maintaining it, or the harm that comes to one for dishonoring the deity or the temples. So, this has been a serious aspect of the Vedic process for spiritual development for many thousands of years.

REFERENCES

The following is a list of all the authentic Vedic and religious texts that were used, researched, referred to or directly quoted to explain or verify all the knowledge and information presented in this book.

Agni Purana, translated by N. Gangadharan, Motilal Banarsidass, Delhi, 1984

Atharva-veda, translated by Devi Chand, Munshiram Manoharlal, Delhi, 1980

Bhagavad-gita As It Is, translated by A. C. Bhaktivedanta Swami, Bhaktivedanta Book Trust, New York/Los Angeles, 1972

Bhagavad-gita, translated by Swami Chidbhavananda, Sri Ramakrishna Tapovanam, Tiruchirappalli, India, 1991

The Song of God, Bhagavad-gita, translated by Swami Prabhavananda and Christopher Isherwood, New America Library, New York, 1972,

Bhagavad-gita, translated by Winthrop Sargeant, State University of New York Press, Albany, 1984

Bhakti-rasamrita-sindhu, (Nectar of Devotion), translated by A. C. Bhaktivedanta Swami, Bhaktivedanta Book Trust, New York/Los Angeles, 1970

Bhakti-sandarbha sankhya

Brahma Purana, edited by J.L.Shastri, Motilal Banarsidass, Delhi 1985

Brahmanda Purana, edited by J.L.Shastri, Motilal Banarsidass, 1983

Brahma-samhita, translated by Bhaktisiddhanta Sarasvati Gosvami Thakur, Bhaktivedanta Book Trust, New York/Los Angeles,

Brahma-Sutras, translated by Swami Vireswarananda and Adidevananda, Advaita Ashram, Calcutta, 1978

Brahma-vaivarta Purana

Brihad-vishnu Purana

Brihan-naradiya Purana

Brihadaranyaka Upanishad

Caitanya-caritamrita, translated by A. C. Bhaktivedanta Swami, Bhaktivedanta Book Trust, Los Angeles, 1974

Caitanya Upanisad, translated by Kusakratha dasa, Bala Books, New York, 1970

Chandogya Upanishad

Garbha Upanishad

References

Garuda Purana, edited by J. L. Shastri, Motilal Barnasidass, Delhi, 1985
Gautamiya Tantra
Gitabhasya of Ramanuja, translated by M. R. Sampatkumaran, M.A., Ananthacharya Indological Research Institute, Bombay, 1985
Hari-bhakti-vilasa
Jiva Gosvami's Tattvasandarbha, Stuart Mark Elkman, Motilal Banarsidass, Delhi, 1986
Kali-santarana Upanishad
Katha Upanishad
Kaushitaki Upanishad
Kurma Purana, edited by J. L. Shastri, Motilal Banarsidass, Delhi, 1981
Linga Purana, edited by J. L. Shastri, Motilal Banarsidass, Delhi, 1973
Mahabharata, translated by C. Rajagopalachari, Bharatiya Vidya Bhavan, New Delhi, 1972
Mahabharata, Kamala Subramaniam, Bharatiya Vidya Bhavan, Bombay, 1982
Matsya Purana
The Law of Manu, [*Manu-samhita*], translated by Georg Buhlerg, Motilal Banarsidass, Delhi, 1970
Minor Upanishads, translated by Swami Madhavananda, Advaita Ashram, Calcutta, 1980; contains Paramahamsopanishad, Atmopanishad, Amritabindupanishad, Tejabindupanishad, Sarvopanishad, Brahmopanisad, Aruneyi Upanishad, Kaivalyopanishad.
Mukunda-mala-stotra
Mundaka Upanishad
Narada-pancaratra
Narada Purana, tr. by Ganesh Vasudeo Tagare, Banarsidass, Delhi, 1980
Narada Sutras, translated by Hari Prasad Shastri, Shanti Sadan, London, 1963
Narada-Bhakti-Sutra, A. C. Bhaktivedanta Swami, Bhaktivedanta Book Trust, Los Angeles, 1991
Padma Purana, tr. by S. Venkitasubramonia Iyer, Banarsidass, Delhi, 1988
Ramayana of Valmiki, tr. by Makhan Lal Sen, Oriental Publishing Co., Calcutta
Hymns of the Rig-veda, tr. by Griffith, Motilal Banarsidass, Delhi, 1973
Rig-veda Brahmanas: The Aitareya and Kausitaki Brahmanas of the Rigveda, translated by Arthur Keith, Motilal Banarsidass, Delhi, 1971
Samnyasa Upanisads, translated by Prof. A. A. Ramanathan, Adyar

Library, Madras, India, 1978; contains Avadhutopanisad, Arunyupanisad, Katharudropanisad, Kundikopanisad, Jabalopanisad, Turiyatitopanisad, Narada-parivrajakopanisad, Nirvanopanisad, Parabrahmopanisad, Paramahamsa-parivrajakopanisad, Paramahamsopanisad, Brahmopanisad, Bhiksukopanisad, Maitreyopanisad, Yajnavalkyopanisad, Satyayaniyopanisad, and Samnyasopanisad.

Shiva Purana, edited by Professor J. L. Shastri, Banarsidass, Delhi, 1970

Siksastaka, of Sri Caitanya Mahaprabhu.

Sixty Upanisads of the Vedas, by Paul Deussen, translated from German by V. M. Bedekar and G. B. Palsule, Motilal Banarsidass, Delhi, 1980; contains Upanishads of the Rigveda: Aitareya and Kausitaki. Upanisads of the Samaveda: Chandogya and Kena. Upanisads of the Black Yajurveda: Taittiriya, Mahanarayan, Kathaka, Svetasvatara, and Maitrayana. Upanisads of the White Yajurveda: Brihadaranyaka and Isa. Upanisads of the Atharvaveda: Mundaka, Prasna, Mandukya, Garbha, Pranagnihotra, Pinda, Atma, Sarva, Garuda; (Yoga Upanisads): Brahmavidya, Ksurika, Culik, Nadabindu, Brahmabindu, Amrtabindu, Dhyanabindu, Tejobindu, Yoga-sikha, Yogatattva, Hamsa; (Samnyasa Upanisads): Brahma, Samnyasa, Aruneya, Kantha-sruti, Paramahamsa, Jabala, Asrama; (Shiva Upanisads): Atharvasira, Atharva-sikha, Nilarudra, Kalagnirudra, Kaivalya; (Vishnu Upanisads): Maha, Narayana, Atmabodha, Nrisimhapurvatapaniya, Nrisimhottara-tapaniya, Ramapurvatapaniya, Ramottaratapaniya. (Supplemental Upanisads): Purusasuktam, Tadeva, Shiva-samkalpa, Baskala, Chagaleya, Paingala, Mrtyulangala, Arseya, Pranava, and Saunaka Upanisad.

Skanda Purana

Sri Bhakti-ratnakara, by Sri Narahari Cakravarti Thakura

Sri Brihat Bhagavatamritam, by Sri Srila Sanatana Gosvami, Sree Gaudiya Math, Madras, India, 1987

Sri Caitanya Bhagavat, by Sri Vrindavan dasa Thakura

Sri Isopanisad, translated by A. C. Bhaktivedanta Swami, Bhaktivedanta Book Trust, New York/Los Angeles, 1969

Srimad-Bhagavatam, translated by A. C. Bhaktivedanta Swami, Bhaktivedanta Book trust, New York/Los Angeles, 1972

Srimad-Bhagavatam, translated by N. Raghunathan, Vighneswar Publishing House, Madras, 1976

Srimad-Bhagavatam MahaPurana, translated by C. L. Goswami, M. A., Sastri, Motilal Jalan at Gita Press, Gorkhapur, India, 1982

Svetasvatara Upanishad

References

Taittiriya Upanishad
Twelve Essential Upanishads, Tridandi Sri Bhakti Prajnan Yati, Sree Gaudiya Math, Madras, 1982. Includes the *Isha, Kena, Katha, Prashna, Mundaka, Mandukya, Taittiriya, Aitareya, Chandogya, Brihadaranyaka, Svetasvatara,*and *Gopalatapani Upanishad* of the Pippalada section of the *Atharva-veda.*
Upadesamrta (Nectar of Instruction), translated by A. C. Bhaktivedanta Swami, Bhaktivedanta Book Trust, New York/Los Angeles, 1975
The Upanishads, translated by Swami Prabhavananda and Frederick Manchester, New American Library, New York, 1957; contains Katha, Isha, Kena, Prasna, Mundaka, Mandukya, Taittiriya, Aitareya, Chandogya, Brihadaranyaka, Kaivalya, and Svetasvatara Upanishads.
The Upanisads, translated by F. Max Muller, Dover Publications; contains Chandogya, Kena, Aitareya, Kausitaki, Vajasaneyi (Isa), Katha, Mundaka, Taittiriya, Brihadaranyaka, Svetasvatara, Prasna, and Maitrayani Upanisads.
Varaha Purana, tr. by S.Venkitasubramonia Iyer, Banarsidass, Delhi, 1985
Vayu Purana, translated by G. V. Tagare, Banarsidass, Delhi, India, 1987
Veda of the Black Yajus School: Taitiriya Sanhita, translated by Arthur Keith, Motilal Banarsidass, Delhi, 1914
Vishnu Purana, translated by H. H. Wilson, Nag Publishers, Delhi
Vishnu-smriti
Vedanta-Sutras of Badarayana with Commentary of Baladeva Vidyabhusana, translated by Rai Bahadur Srisa Chandra Vasu, Munshiram Manoharlal, New Delhi, 1979
White Yajurveda, translated by Griffith, The Chowkhamba Sanskrit Series Office, Varanasi, 1976
Yajurveda, translated by Devi Chand, Munshiram Manoharlal, Delhi, 1980
Yoga Sutras of Patanjali

Other references that were helpful are listed as follows:
Dictionary of Philosophy and Religion, Reese, Humanities Press, Atlantic Highlands, New Jersey, 1980
Elements of Hindu Iconography, by T. A. Gopinatha Rao, Motilal Banarsidass, Delhi, 1985
The Gods of India, by Alain Danielou, Inner Traditions, New York, 1985
Harper's Dictionary of Hinduism, by Margaret and James Stutley, Harper & Row, San Francisco, 1917

Hindu Gods and Goddesses, Swami Harshananda, Sri Ramakrsihna Math, 16, Ramakrishna Math Road, Mylapore, India

Puranic Encyclopaedia, Vettam Mani, Motilal Banarsidass, Delhi, 1964

Vedanta: Its Morphology and Ontology, by Bhakti Siddhanta Sarasvati Gosvami, Sree Chaitanya Gaudiya Math, Vrindaban, India, 1998

GLOSSARY

Acharya--the spiritual master who sets the proper standard by his own example.

Acintya-bhedabheda-tattva--simultaneously one and different. The doctrine Lord Sri Caitanya taught referring to the Absolute as being both personal and impersonal.

Advaita--nondual, meaning that the Absolute is one with the infinitesimal souls with no individuality between them. The philosophy of Sankaracharya.

Agni--fire, or Agni the demigod of fire.

Agnihotra--the Vedic sacrifice in which offerings were made to the fire, such as ghee, milk, sesame seeds, grains, etc. The demigod Agni would deliver the offerings to the demigods that were referred to in the ritual.

Ahankara--false ego, identification with matter.

Ananda--spiritual bliss.

Ananta--unlimited.

Aranyaka--sacred writings that are supposed to frame the essence of the *Upanishads*.

Arati--the ceremony of worship when incense and ghee lamps are offered to the Deities.

Arca-vigraha--the worshipable Deity form of the Lord made of stone, wood, etc. Aryan--a noble person, one who is on the path of spiritual advancement.

Asana--postures for meditation, or exercises for developing the body into a fit instrument for spiritual advancement.

Asat--that which is temporary.

Ashrama--one of the four orders of spiritual life, such as *brahmachari* (celibate student), *grihastha* (married householder), *vanaprastha* (retired stage), and *sannyasa* (renunciate); or the abode of a spiritual teacher or *sadhu*.

Asura--one who is ungodly or a demon.

Atma--the self or soul. Sometimes means the body, mind, and senses.

Atman--usually referred to as the Supreme Self.

Avatara--an incarnation of the Lord who descends from the spiritual world.

Avidya--ignorance or nescience.

Aum--*om* or *pranava*

Ayurveda--the original holistic form of medicine as described in the Vedic literature.

Bhajan--song of worship.

Bhakta--a devotee of the Lord who is engaged in *bhakti-yoga*.

Bhakti--love and devotion for God.

Bhakti-yoga--the path of offering pure devotional service to the Supreme.

Bhava--preliminary stage of love of God.

Brahma--the demigod of creation who was born from Lord Vishnu, the first created living being and the engineer of the secondary stage of creation of the universe when all the living entities were manifested.

Brahmachari--a celebate student who is trained by the spiritual master. One of the four divisions or ashramas of spiritual life.

Brahmajyoti--the great white light or effulgence which emanates from the body of the Lord.

Brahmaloka--the highest planet or plane of existence in the universe; the planet where Lord Brahma lives.

Brahman--the spiritual energy; the all-pervading impersonal aspect of the Lord; or the Supreme Lord Himself.

Brahmana or brahmin--one of the four orders of society; the intellectual class of men who have been trained in the knowledge of the *Vedas* and initiated by a spiritual master.

Brahmana--the supplemental books of the four primary *Vedas*. They usually contained instructions for performing Vedic *agnihotras*, chanting the *mantras*, the purpose of the rituals, etc. The *Aitareya* and *Kaushitaki Brahmanas* belong to the *Rig-veda*, the *Satapatha Brahmana* belongs to the *White Yajur-veda*, and the *Taittiriya Brahmana* belongs to the *Black Yajur-veda*. The *Praudha* and *Shadvinsa Brahmanas* are two of the eight *Brahmanas* belonging to the *Atharva-veda*.

Brahmastra--a nuclear weapon that is produced and controlled by *mantra*.

Caitanya-caritamrita--the scripture by Krishnadasa Kaviraja which explains the teachings and pastimes of Lord Caitanya Mahaprabhu.

Caitanya Mahaprabhu--the most recent incarnation of the Lord who appeared in the 15th century in Bengal and who originally started the *sankirtana* movement, based on congregational chanting of the holy names.

Causal Ocean or Karana Ocean--is the corner of the spiritual sky where Maha-Vishnu lies down to create the material manifestation.

Cit--eternal knowledge.

Glossary

Chakra--a wheel, disk, or psychic energy center situated along the spinal column in the subtle body of the physical shell.

Chhandas--sacred hymns of the *Atharva-veda*.

Darshan--the devotional act of seeing and being seen by the Deity in the temple.

Deity--the *arca-vigraha*, or worshipful form of the Supreme in the temple, or deity as the worshipful image of the demigod. A capital D is used in referring to Krishna or one of His expansions, while a small d is used when referring to a demigod or lesser personality.

Devas--demigods or heavenly beings from higher levels of material existence, or a godly person.

Devaloka--the higher planets or planes of existence of the devas.

Dham--a holy place.

Dharma--the essential nature or duty of the living being.

Dualism--as related in this book refers to the Supreme as both an impersonal force as well as a person.

Durga--the form of Parvati, Shiva's wife, as a warrior goddess known by many names according to her deeds, such as Simhavahini when riding her lion, Mahishasuramardini for killing the demon Mahishasura, Jagaddhatri as the mother of the universe, Kali when she killed the demon Raktavija, Tara when killing Shumba, etc.

Dvapara-yuga--the third age which lasts 864,000 years.

Dwaita--dualism, the principle that the Absolute Truth consists of the infinite Supreme Being and the infinitesimal individual souls.

Gandharvas--the celestial angel-like beings who have beautiful forms and voices, and are expert in dance and music, capable of becoming invisible and can help souls on the earthly plane.

Ganesh--a son of Shiva, said to destroy obstacles (as Vinayaka) and offer good luck to those who petition him.

Ganges--the sacred and spiritual river which, according to the *Vedas*, runs throughout the universe, a portion of which is seen in India. The reason the river is considered holy is that it is said to be a drop of the Karana Ocean that leaked in when Lord Vishnu, in His incarnation as Vamanadeva, kicked a small hole in the universal shell with His toe. Thus, the water is spiritual as well as being purified by the touch of Lord Vishnu.

Gangapuja--the arati ceremony for worshiping the Ganges.

Gangotri--the source of the Ganges River in the Himalayas.

Garbhodakasayi Vishnu--the expansion of Lord Vishnu who enters into each universe.

Gaudiya--a part of India sometimes called Aryavarta or land of the Aryans, located south of the Himalayas and north of the Vindhya Hills.

Gayatri--the spiritual vibration or *mantra* from which the other *Vedas* were expanded and which is chanted by those who are initiated as *brahmanas* and given the spiritual understanding of Vedic philosophy.

Goloka Vrindavana--the name of Lord Krishna's spiritual planet.

Gosvami--one who is master of the senses.

Govinda--a name of Krishna which means one who gives pleasure to the cows and senses.

Gunas--the modes of material nature of which there is *sattva* (goodness), *rajas*(passion), and *tamas* (ignorance).

Guru--a spiritual master.

Hare--the Lord's pleasure potency, Radharani, who is approached for accessibility to the Lord.

Hari--a name of Krishna as the one who takes away one's obstacles on the spiritual path.

Haribol--a word that means to chant the name of the Lord, Hari.

Harinam--refers to the name of the Lord, Hari.

Hiranyagarbha--another name of Brahma who was born of Vishnu in the primordial waters within the egg of the universe.

Hrishikesa--a name for Krishna which means the master of the senses.

Impersonalism--the view that God has no personality or form, but is only an impersonal force.

Impersonalist--those who believe God has no personality or form.

Incarnation--the taking on of a body or form.

Indra--the King of heaven and controller of rain, who by his great power conquers the forces of darkness.

Jiva--the individual soul or living being.

Jivanmukta--a liberated soul, though still in the material body and universe.

Jiva-shakti--the living force.

Jnana-kanda--the portion of the *Vedas* which stresses empirical speculation for understanding truth.

Jnana-yoga--the process of linking with the Supreme through empirical knowledge and mental speculation.

Kala--eternal time.

Kali--the demigoddess who is the fierce form of the wife of Lord Shiva. The word *kali* comes from *kala*, the Sanskrit word for time: the power that dissolves or destroys everything.

Glossary

Kali-yuga--the fourth and present age, the age of quarrel and confusion, which lasts 432,000 years and began 5,000 years ago.
Kalpa--a day in the life of Lord Brahma which lasts a thousand cycles of the four *yugas*.
Kapila--an incarnation of Lord Krishna who propagated the Sankhya philosophy.
Karanodakasayi Vishnu (Maha-Vishnu)--the expansion of Lord Krishna who created all the material universes.
Karma--material actions performed in regard to developing one's position or for future results which produce *karmic* reactions. It is also the reactions one endures from such fruitive activities.
Karma-kanda--the portion of the *Vedas* which primarily deals with recommended fruitive activities for various results.
Karma-yoga--the system of yoga for dovetailing one's activities for spiritual advancement.
Kirtana--chanting or singing the glories of the Lord.
Krishna--the name of the original Supreme Personality of Godhead which means the most attractive and greatest pleasure. He is the source of all other incarnations, such as Vishnu, Rama, Narasimha, Narayana, Buddha, Parashurama, Vamanadeva, Kalki at the end of Kali-yuga, etc.
Krishnaloka--the spiritual planet where Lord Krishna resides.
Kshatriya--the second class of *varna* of society, or occupation of administrative or protective service, such as warrior or military personel.
Ksirodakasayi Vishnu--the Supersoul expansion of the Lord who enters into each atom and the heart of each individual.
Kumbha Mela--the holy festival in which millions of pilgrims and sages gather to bathe in the holy and purifying rivers for liberation at particular auspicious times that are calculated astrologically. The Kumbha Mela festivals take place every three years alternating between Allahabad, Ujjain, Nasik, and Haridwar.
Kurukshetra--the place of battle 5,000 years ago between the Pandavas and the Kauravas ninety miles north of New Delhi, where Krishna spoke the *Bhagavad-gita*.
Lakshmi--the goddess of fortune and wife of Lord Vishnu.
Lila--pastimes.
Lilavataras--the many incarnations of God who appear to display various spiritual pastimes to attract the conditioned souls in the material world.
Linga--the shapeless form of Lord Shiva.

Mahabharata--the great epic of the Pandavas, which includes the *Bhagavad-gita*, by Vyasadeva.

Maha-mantra--the best mantra for self-realization in this age, called the Hare Krishna mantra.

Mahat-tattva--the total material energy.

Maha-Vishnu or Karanodakasayi Vishnu--the Vishnu expansion of Lord Krishna from whom all the material universes emanate.

Mandir--a temple.

Mantra--a sound vibration which prepares the mind for spiritual realization and delivers the mind from material inclinations. In some cases a mantra is chanted for specific material benefits.

Manu--the demigod sons of Brahma. Manu is the forefather and lawgiver of the human race. A succession of 14 Manus exist during each day of Brahma, called the manvantaras.

Manvantara--the series of incarnations of Manus.

Maya--illusion, or anything that appears to not be connected with the eternal Absolute Truth.

Mayavadi--the impersonalist or voidist who believes that the Supreme has no form.

Mitra--the deity controlling the sun, and who gives life to earth.

Moksha--liberation from material existence.

Murti--a Deity of the Lord or spiritual master that is worshiped.

Murugan--means the divine child, the Tamil name for Subramaniya, one of the sons of Shiva and Parvati, especially worshiped in South India.

Narayana--the four-handed form of the Supreme Lord.

Om or *Omkara*--*pranava*, the transcendental *om mantra*, generally referring to the attributeless or impersonal aspects of the Absolute.

Paramahamsa--the highest level of self-realized devotees of the Lord.

Paramatma--the Supersoul, or localized expansion of the Lord.

Parampara--the system of disciplic succession through which transcendental knowledge descends.

Parvati--Lord Shiva's spouse, daughter of Parvata. Parvata is the personification of the Himalayas. She is also called Gauri for her golden complexion, Candi, Bhairavi (as the wife of Bhairava, Shiva), Durga, Ambika, and Shakti.

Patanjali--the authority on the *astanga-yoga* system.

Pradhana--the total material energy in its unmanifest state.

Prajapati--deity presiding over procreation.

Prakriti--matter in its primordial state, the material nature.

Prana--the life air or cosmic energy.

Pranayama--control of the breathing process as in astanga or raja-yoga.

Glossary

Pranava--same as *omkara*.

Prasada--food or other articles that have been offered to the Deity in the temple and then distributed amongst people as the blessings or mercy of the Deity.

Prema--matured love for Krishna.

Puja--the worship offered to the Deity.

Pujari--the priest who performs worship, *puja*, to the Deity.

Purusha or *Purusham*--the supreme enjoyer.

Raja-yoga--the eightfold yoga system.

Rajo-guna--the material mode of passion.

Ramachandra--an incarnation of Krishna as He appeared as the greatest of kings.

Ramayana--the great epic of the incarnation of Lord Ramachandra.

Rasa--an enjoyable taste or feeling, a relationship with God.

Shabda-brahma--the original spiritual vibration or energy of which the *Vedas* are composed.

Sac-cid-ananda-vigraha--the transcendental form of the Lord or of the living entity which is eternal, full of knowledge and bliss.

Sadhana--a specific practice or discipline for attaining God realization.

Sadhu--Indian holy man or devotee.

Saguna Brahman--the aspect of the Absolute with form and qualities.

Samadhi--trance, the perfection of being absorbed in the Absolute.

Samsara--rounds of life; cycles of birth and death; reincarnation.

Sanatana-dharma--the eternal nature of the living being, to love and render service to the supreme lovable object, the Lord.

Sankirtana-yajna--the prescribed sacrifice for this age: congregational chanting of the holy names of God.

Sannyasa--the renounced order of life, the highest of the four *ashramas* on the spiritual path.

Sarasvati--the goddess of knowledge and intelligence.

Sattva-guna--the material mode of goodness.

Satya-yuga--the first of the four ages which lasts 1,728,000 years.

Shaivites--worshipers of Lord Shiva.

Shakti--energy, potency or power, the active principle in creation. Also the active power or wife of a deity, such as Shiva/Shakti.

Shastra--the authentic revealed scripture.

Shiva--the benevolent one, the demigod who is in charge of the material mode of ignorance and the destruction of the universe. Part of the triad of Brahma, Vishnu, and Shiva who continually create, maintain, and destroy the universe. He is known as Rudra when displaying his destructive aspect.

Smriti--the traditional Vedic knowledge "that is remembered" from what was directly heard by or revealed to the *rishis*.

Sravanam--hearing about the Lord.

Srimad-Bhagavatam--the most ripened fruit of the tree of Vedic knowledge compiled by Vyasadeva.

Sruti--scriptures that were received directly from God and transmitted orally by brahmanas or *rishis* down through succeeding generations. Traditionally, it is considered the four primary *Vedas*.

Sudra--the working class of society, the fourth of the *varnas*.

Svami--one who can control his mind and senses.

Tamo-guna--the material mode of ignorance.

Tapasya--voluntary austerity for spiritual advancement.

Tilok--the clay markings that signify a person's body as a temple, and the sect or school of thought of the person.

Tirtha--a holy place of pilgrimage.

Upanishads--the portions of the *Vedas* which primarily explain philosophically the Absolute Truth. It is knowledge of Brahman which releases one from the world and allows one to attain self-realization when received from a qualified teacher. Except for the *Isa Upanishad*, which is the 40th chapter of the *Vajasaneyi Samhita* of the *Sukla (White) Yajur-veda*, the *Upanishads* are connected to the four primary *Vedas*, generally found in the *Brahmanas*.

Vaikunthas--the planets located in the spiritual sky.

Vaishnava--a worshiper of the Supreme Lord Vishnu or Krishna and His expansions or incarnations.

Vedanta-sutras--the philosophical conclusion of the four *Vedas*.

Vedas--generally means the four primary *samhitas;* the *Rig, Yajur, Sama,* and *Atharva*.

Virajanadi or Viraja River--the space that separates the material creation from the spiritual sky.

Vishnu--the expansion of Lord Krishna who enters into the material energy to create and maintain the cosmic world.

Vrindavana--the place where Lord Krishna displayed His village pastimes 5,000 years ago, and is considered to be part of the spiritual abode.

Vyasadeva--the incarnation of God who appeared as the greatest philosopher who compiled all the *Vedas* into written form.

Yajna--a ritual or austerity that is done as a sacrifice for spiritual merit, or ritual worship of a demigod for good *karmic* reactions.

Yamaraja--the demigod and lord of death who directs the living entities to various punishments according to their activities.

Glossary

Yantra--a machine, instrument, or mystical diagram used in ritual worship.

Yuga-avataras--the incarnations of God who appear in each of the four *yugas* to explain the authorized system of self-realization in that age.

INDEX

Adityas. 4, 160
Agamas. 125
Agni................................ 161
Agni 5
Agni Purana. 83
Ambika........................... 115
Amsha. 160
Ananta. 65
Aryaman........................ 160
Asvinikumara-samhita. ... 162
Asvins. 162
Aurangzeb. 183
Avataras,. 49
Ayyappan. 158
Balarama. 67, 68
   expands into Ananta or
      Seshanaga............. 70
Balarama,. 54
Banasura........................... 99
Basava. 106
Bhaga. 160
Bhagavan.......................... 20
Bhagavat Purana. 53
Bhava. 146
Brahma. 4, 96
Brahma Vaivarta Purana. 119
Brahma,...................... 78, 80
   a devotee incarnation
      who carries out orders
      of the Supreme. 83
   creates the functional
      universe. 82
   engaged in bhakti-yoga.85
   his day is equal to one
      thousand cycles of the
      four yugas.............. 87
   his other names. 79
   represents mode of rajas,
      passion................... 78
   when first generated in
      the lotus. 83
   when he sleeps. 87
   when no such being is
      suitable for the post.82
   worshiped Krishna, the
      essence of all Vedic
      knowledge. 85
Brahma,
   lives for 100 years,
      composed of 365 of
      such days in a year .56
   the length of his day ... 56
Brahma-samhita. 84
Brahmaloka,
   or Satyaloka................. 82
Brahman realization. 39
Caitanya Mahaprabhu. 173
   inaugurates the
      congregational
      chanting of the holy
      names 178
   Predictions of His
      appearance........... 176
   started the first sankirtana
      movement............ 173
Chakras. 5
Chanchala...................... 140
Chandra, the moon. 169
Chitragupta..................... 168
Creation, the dawn of. 83

Index

Daksha............................ 160
Dakshinachara................. 123
   Vamachara. 123
Dattatreya,......................... 51
Deities. 180
Demigods
   agents of the Supreme
      Will. 4
   dependent agents of the
      Supreme. 105
Devibhagavat. 114
Dhanvantari....................... 52
Dharmaraja....................... 168
Durga..
   89, 90, 98, 105, 117, 142
   as the maidservant of
      Krishna................. 117
   as Vaishnavishakti. ... 116
   Goddess of universe.. 112
   has many names. 112, 116
   her many names. 112
   means a prison house. 117
   the universal mother.. 127
Durga,
   considered an expansion
      of Radharani......... 118
   has many names. 112
   known as the universal
      mother. 127
Durgasaptashati................ 114
Dusserha.......................... 143
Dvapara-yuga, ... 57
Earth,
   the age of the planet. ... 56
False ego,. 80
Festivals. 142
Gajalakshmi. 139
Ganapati. 150

Ganesh..................... 105, 150
   as Vighneshvara. 153
   his other names. 151
Ganesh Chaturthi. 155
Ganesha............................ 117
Ganga River. 93
Garbhodaka Ocean,........... 83
   the creation of. 81
Garbhodakashayi Vishnu
   .... 68, 72, 81
Garbhodakashayi Vishnu,
   .... 47, 81
   or Hiranyagarbha and
      Antaryami.............. 81
Garuda.............................. 66
Gayatri............................. 143
Gayatri mantra,................... 84
   imparted to Brahma from
      the sound of Sri
      Krishnas flute. 84
God, has a form............... 180
Goloka Vrinadavana,. 118
Goloka Vrindavana. 44
Goloka,
   the transcendental land. 84
Goraknatha....................... 106
Guhyakas........................ 163
Hare Krishna mantra. 147
Hladini-shakti................... 146
Hladini-shakti,................. 119
   pleasure potency of Lord
      Krishna................ 118
Incarnations,
   Buddha, twenty-first.... 54
   Hayagriva, ... 51
   Kalki, twenty-second. . 55
   Kapila, the fifth
      incarnation............. 51

Kumaras, the first
  incarnations. 50
Kurma, the eleventh
  incarnation............. 52
Manus 56
Narada Muni. 50
Parashurama, the
  sixteenth. 53
Prithu, ninth incarnation.52
Rama, the eighteenth... 54
Rohini, the thirteenth
  incarnation............. 52
shaktyavesha-avataras. 58
Vamana, the fifteenth
  incarnation............. 53
Varaha. 50
Vyasadeva, the
  seventeenth............ 53
Yajna. 51
Indra. 4, 105
  the King of Heaven. .. 162
Indralakshmi.................. 139
Jagannatha Misra
  father of Caitanya. 173
Jivatmas. 69
Kalamukhas................... 106
Kali............................ 90, 115
  as Kala, time.............. 117
  became known as
    Chamunda. 115
  has many names. 116
Kali-yuga
  when the age began. 29
Kali-yuga,.......................... 57
Kalki,............................ 55
Kama-bija mantra............. 84
Kama-bija mantra,............. 84
Kama-gayatri.................... 85

Kamsa. 98
Kanphata yogis............... 106
Kapalikas....................... 106
Karana Ocean................... 67
Karanadakashayi Vishnu... 67
Karma-kanda...................... 2
Kartikeya....................... 117
Kaundinya....................... 104
Kaushika Durga............... 115
Kaustubha. 64
Krishna
  better than Brahman
    realization............. 39
  cause of all causes. 37
  descends into world..... 27
  explanation of the name.32
  failing to know Him. ... 42
  His appearance on this
    planet..................... 29
  His beauty. 35
  His eternal abode......... 44
  how to understand Him.38
  never manifest to the
    foolish. 40
  not a representation. 20
  pastimes full of meaning
    and purpose. 33
  perceived by different
    people in different
    ways. 34
  quadruple expansions.. 68
  source of all other
    incarnations of God.25
  source of all spiritual and
    material worlds...... 21
  who is He?. 12
Krishna,....... 54, 84, 119, 128
  battling with Banasura. 99

Index

descends to this world
  once in a day of
  Brahma. 48
has six kinds of
  incarnations. 48
is the primeval Lord. ... 48
Lord of Gokula. 128
pastimes manifest at
  every moment in one
  universe or another. 50
sends His pure
  representative and
  instructions. 47
sends His pure
  representative and
  instructions to guide
  people. 47
Shiva's brother-in-law. 98
He appears on earth. 57
Krishnaloka 44
Kshirodakashayi Vishnu
  .... 68, 72
Kubera. 163
Kumaras, are considered
  empowered
  incarnations. 50
Kundalini. 107, 125
Kurma, ... 52
Lakshmi. 138, 142
  her other names. 139
Lakulisha Pasupatas. 106
Lingam. 108
Lingayatas. 106
Maha-Vishnu. 68, 72, 81
  source of thousands of
  avataras. 69
Maha-Vishnu,
  sends His glance over the
  material energy. ... 128
Mahabharata
  how it was written. 154
Mahadeva Gopisvara. 98
Mahakali. 116
Mahalakshmi. 116, 139
Mahamaya, ... 118, 119
Mahasarasvati. 116
Mahat-tattva. 72, 80, 81
Maheshvara. 128
Mahishasura. 115
Mahishasuramardini. 115
Manvantara. 56
Marginal potency,
  is the living beings. ... 121
Markandeya. 97
Markandeya Purana. 114
Maruts. 164
Matsya, ... 52
Maya, ... 120, 121, 127, 130
  covers living beings with
  material energy. 121
  is the external energy. 120
  secondary cause of
  creation. 120
Mitra. 160
Mohini Murti. 158
Mother Nature, ... 127
  as Durga. 127
Murugan. 150, 155
Nandagram. 184
Nara and Narayana. 51
Narada Muni. 50
Narada Purana. 120
  lists many names of
  Durga. 112
Narada-Pancharatra. 126
Narashimhadeva. 53

Narayana. 9
   is the Supreme
      Personality............ 105
   means the shelter or
      ultimate goal of all
      living beings............ 61
Nataraja. 92
Navagrahas. 169
Navaratri. 142
Nayanmar. 106
Nigamas. 125
Nirvikalpa samadhi. 107
Om tat sat. 6
Pancarthabhasya. 105
Panchamakara. 123
Parashurama. 53
Parvati
   mother of Ganesh. 151
   wife of Lord Shiva. 112
Pasupatas. 104
Pasupatasutra. 105
Pasupati. 105
Pracinibarhi. 94
Pradhana. 67, 120
Prakrita-Sarga
   primary creation. 80
Prakrita-Sarga,
   creation that is due to
      interaction of the
      modes. 80
Prakriti. 120
Pratyabhijna. 106
Pratyabhijnabridaya. 106
Prithu,. 52
Puranas
   different descriptions of
      the creation. 79
Pushan. 160

Radharani
   Her other names. 145
   the Supreme Goddess. 144
   the quintessence of
      spiritual energy.... 118
Rakshasas. 163
Rama. 54
   killed Ravana. 143
Ramadevi,
   the spiritual identity of
      Durga. 129
Ramayana. 54
Ravana. 143
Ravi
   the sun. 169
Rishabha, ... 51
Rudra. 4
   eleven other names. 103
Rudra-sampradaya
   also Vallabha-
      sampradaya............ 90
Sachidevi
   mother of Caitanya. ... 173
Sadashiva. 128
Sadashiva,. 129
Samanyalakshmi. 139
Sanatkumara-samhita. 133
Sankarshana. 67, 68
Sankirtana
   started by Lord Caitanya
      173
   religion for this age. ... 176
Sarasvati. 140, 142
Saravati. 140
   other names. 141
Satya-yuga,. 57
Savitri. 160
Seshanaga,. 85

Index

Shadeva. 162
Shaiva Siddhantas. 106
Shaivism. 104, 106
Shaivites
   those who accept Shiva
      as supreme deity.. 104
Shakra. 160
Shakta. 122
Shakti. 105, 122
Shaktis. 120
Shaktyavesha-avataras,. 50
Shambhu. 71, 128
Shambhu,. 128
   is created from in
      between the two
      eyebrows of Maha-
      Vishnu. 128
Sheshanaga. 65, 68
   expansion of Balarama. 70
Shiva. 71, 89
   as Eshwara or Sadashiva.89
   as Nataraja. 92
   as Rudra. 89
   born from Brahma. 97
   considered an expansion
      of Vishnu. 130
   his Tandava dance of
      destruction. 130
   how he appeared in this
      world. 102
   is not lord of the spiritual
      domain. 130
   Krishnas brother-in-law98
   other names. 103
   ultimate spiritual advice
      133
   worships Lord Krishna.97
Shiva Purana. 104

Shiva,
   a devotee incarnation
      who carries out orders
      of the Supreme. 83
   an associate of the
      external energy. 83
   an expansion of
      Sadashiva. 128
   as Shambhu. 128
   is an assumed form of
      Vishnu. 83
   Maheshvara. 128
Shiva,
   controller of tama-guna.90
   is an expansion of the
      Supreme Lord,
      Krishna. 129
   is called Hara as an
      expansion of Krishna
      130
   worships Lord Krishna130
Shiva-lingam. 108
Shivaratri. 108
Shivasutra. 106
Shuddha-sattva. 68, 118
Soma. 5, 165
Spandakarika. 106
Srimad-Bhagavatam
   gives a participants
      perspective. 16
   Krishna had enlightened
      Brahma with it. 86
Srivatsa. 64
Subhadra. 118
Subhadra,. 118
Sudarshan. 63
Supreme Being, may expand
      to become Brahma. 82

Surya. 105, 161
Suta Gosvami. 97
Svetadvipa. 74
Tantra. 123
    Vaishnava Tantras. 126
Tantras. 125
Thirty-three million gods. ... 4
Treta-yuga,. 57
Trika Shaivites. 106
Tvashtri. 160
Uma. 112
Vaikrita-Sarga
    secondary creation. 80
Vaikrita-Sarga,
    creation from Lord
    Brahma. 80
Vaikuntha. 68
Vaikuntha planets. 118
Vaishnava Tantras. 126
Vaishnavishakti
    creative power from Lord
    Vishnu. 116
Vamanadeva. 61
Varaha,
    the second incarnation. 50
Varuna. 160, 166
Vasudeva. 98
Vasugupta. 106
Vasus. 4, 167
Vayu. 5, 167
    the King of Heaven. ... 163
Vayu Purana. 128
Vedanta-sutras
    point out contradictions
    in the Pasupatas and
    Shaivites. 105

Vedas
    represent a highly
    developed religious
    system. 2
Vedic gods. 4
Viraja River. 70
Virasaiva. 106
Vishnu. 9, 61, 75, 161
    also called Narayana. ... 61
    an expansion of Lord
    Krishna. 66
    holds four items. 63
    some other names. 65
Vishnu Purana. 83
Vishnu,. 85
    gives Brahma instructions
    about the recreation 87
    maintains the universe. 82
    opulences not quite equal
    to Krishna's. 83
Vishnu-sahasranam. 65
Visvadevas. 168
Vivasvat. 161
Vivsvan. 161
Vyasadeva
    dictated the Mahabharata
    to Ganesh. 154
Yajna,
    seventh incarnation. 51
Yakshas. 163
Yamadutas. 168
Yamaraja. 168
Yogamaya. 118
Yogamaya,. 118
Yugavataras,. 57

ABOUT THE AUTHOR

Stephen Knapp grew up in a Christian family, during which time he seriously studied the Bible to understand its teachings. In his late teenage years, however, he sought answers to questions not easily explained in Christian theology. So he began to search through other religions and philosophies from around the world and started to find the answers for which he was looking. He also studied a variety of occult sciences, ancient mythology, mysticism, yoga, and the spiritual teachings of the East. After his first reading of the *Bhagavad-gita*, he felt he had found the last piece of the puzzle he had been putting together through all of his research. Therefore, he continued to study all of the major Vedic texts of India to gain a better understanding of the Vedic science.

It is known amongst all Eastern mystics that anyone, regardless of qualifications, academic or otherwise, who does not engage in the spiritual practices described in the Vedic texts cannot actually enter into understanding the depths of the Vedic spiritual science, nor acquire the realizations that should accompany it. So, rather than pursuing his research in an academic atmosphere at a university, Stephen directly engaged in the spiritual disciplines that have been recommended for hundreds of years. He continued his study of Vedic knowledge and spiritual practice under the guidance of a spiritual master. Through this process, and with the sanction of His Divine Grace A. C. Bhaktivedanta Swami Prabhupada, he became initiated into the genuine and authorized spiritual line of the Brahma-Madhava-Gaudiya *sampradaya*, which is a disciplic succession that descends back through Sri Caitanya Mahaprabhu and Sri Vyasadeva, the compiler of Vedic literature, and further back to Sri Krishna. Through this initiation he has taken the spiritual name of Sri Nandanandana dasa. Besides being *brahminically* initiated, Stephen has also been to India numerous times and traveled extensively throughout the country, visiting all but three small states, and most of the major holy places, thus gaining a wide variety of spiritual experiences that only such places can give.

Stephen has written numerous articles, as well as books such as *The Eastern Answers to the Mysteries of Life* series, which includes *The Secret Teachings of the Vedas, The Universal Path to Enlightenment, The Vedic Prophecies*, and *How the Universe was Created and Our Purpose In It*. He has also written *Toward World Peace: Seeing the Unity Between Us All, Facing Death: Welcoming the Afterlife, The Key to Real Happiness*, and *Proof of Vedic Culture's Global Existence.*, as well as *Reincarnation and Karma: How They Really Affect Us, The Heart of Hinduism, Vedic Culture: The Difference it can Make in Your*

Life, The Power of the Dharma: A Short Introduction to Hinduism and Vedic Culture, and *Seeing Spiritual India: A Guidebook to Temple, Holy sites, Festivals and Traditions,* as well as *Crimes Against India: 1000 Years of Attacks Against Hinduism and What to do About It,* and *Yoga and Meditation: Their Real Purpose and How to Get Started.*

Furthermore, he has authored a novel, *Destined for Infinity,* for those who prefer lighter reading, or learning spiritual knowledge in the context of an exciting, spiritual adventure. Stephen has put the culmination of over forty years of continuous research and travel experience into his books in an effort to share it with those who are also looking for spiritual understanding.

Stephen now works full time to help preserve, protect and promote a genuine understand of Vedic culture and Sanatana-dharma. To find out more about Stephen's books, articles, and projects, along with numerous resources, you can see his website at: http://www.stephen-knapp.com, or his blog at: http://stephenknapp.wordpress.com.

If you have enjoyed this book, or if you are serious about finding higher levels of real spiritual Truth, and learning more about the mysteries of India's Vedic culture, then you will also want to get other books written by Stephen Knapp, which include:

The Secret Teachings of the Vedas

This book presents the essence of the ancient Eastern philosophy and summarizes some of the most elevated and important of all spiritual knowledge. This enlightening information is explained in a clear and concise way and is essential for all who want to increase their spiritual understanding, regardless of what their religious background may be. If you are looking for a book to give you an in-depth introduction to the Vedic spiritual knowledge, and to get you started in real spiritual understanding, this is the book!

The topics include: What is your real spiritual identity; the Vedic explanation of the soul; scientific evidence that consciousness is separate from but interacts with the body; the real unity between us all; how to attain the highest happiness and freedom from the cause of suffering; the law of karma and reincarnation; the karma of a nation; where you are really going in life; the real process of progressive evolution; life after death—heaven, hell, or beyond; a description of the spiritual realm; the nature of the Absolute Truth—personal God or impersonal force; recognizing the existence of the Supreme; the reason why we exist at all; and much more. This book provides the answers to questions not found in other religions or philosophies, and condenses information from a wide variety of sources that would take a person years to assemble. It also contains many quotations from the Vedic texts to let the texts speak for themselves, and to show the knowledge the Vedas have held for thousands of years. It also explains the history and origins of the Vedic literature. This book has been called one of the best reviews of Eastern philosophy available.

The Vedic Prophecies:
A New Look into the Future

The Vedic prophecies take you to the end of time! This is the first book ever to present the unique predictions found in the ancient Vedic texts of India. These prophecies are like no others and will provide you with a very different view of the future and how things fit together in the plan for the universe.

Now you can discover the amazing secrets that are hidden in the oldest spiritual writings on the planet. Find out what they say about the distant future, and what the seers of long ago saw in their visions of the destiny of the world.

This book will reveal predictions of deteriorating social changes and how to avoid them; future droughts and famines; low-class rulers and evil governments; whether there will be another appearance (second coming) of God; and predictions of a new spiritual awareness and how it will spread around the world. You will also learn the answers to such questions as:

- Does the future get worse or better?
- Will there be future world wars or global disasters?
- What lies beyond the predictions of Nostradamus, the Mayan prophecies, or the Biblical apocalypse?
- Are we in the end times? How to recognize them if we are.
- Does the world come to an end? If so, when and how?

Now you can find out what the future holds. The Vedic Prophecies carry an important message and warning for all humanity, which needs to be understood now!

Proof of Vedic Culture's Global Existence

This book provides evidence which makes it clear that the ancient Vedic culture was once a global society. Even today we can see its influence in any part of the world. Thus, it becomes obvious that before the world became full of distinct and separate cultures, religions and countries, it was once united in a common brotherhood of Vedic culture, with common standards, principles, and representations of God.

No matter what we may consider our present religion, society or country, we are all descendants of this ancient global civilization. Thus, the Vedic culture is the parent of all humanity and the original ancestor of all religions. In this way, we all share a common heritage.

This book is an attempt to allow humanity to see more clearly its universal roots. This book provides a look into:

- How Vedic knowledge was given to humanity by the Supreme.
- The history and traditional source of the Vedas and Vedic Aryan society.
- Who were the original Vedic Aryans. How Vedic society was a global influence and what shattered this world-wide society. How Sanskrit faded from being a global language.
- Many scientific discoveries over the past several centuries are only rediscoveries of what the Vedic literature already knew.
- How the origins of world literature are found in India and Sanskrit.
- The links between the Vedic and other ancient cultures, such as the Sumerians, Persians, Egyptians, Romans, Greeks, and others.
- Links between the Vedic tradition and Judaism, Christianity, Islam, and Buddhism.
- How many of the western holy sites, churches, and mosques were once the sites of Vedic holy places and sacred shrines.
- The Vedic influence presently found in such countries as Britain, France, Russia, Greece, Israel, Arabia, China, Japan, and in areas of Scandinavia, the Middle East, Africa, the South Pacific, and the Americas.
- Uncovering the truth of India's history: Powerful evidence that shows how many mosques and Muslim buildings were once opulent Vedic temples, including the Taj Mahal, Delhi's Jama Masjid, Kutab Minar, as well as buildings in many other cities, such as Agra, Ahmedabad, Bijapur, etc.
- How there is presently a need to plan for the survival of Vedic culture.

This book is sure to provide some amazing facts and evidence about the truth of world history and the ancient, global Vedic Culture. This book has enough startling information and historical evidence to cause a major shift in the way we view religious history and the basis of world traditions.

Published through Booksurge.com, $20.99, 431 pages, ISBN: 978-1-4392-4648-1.

Toward World Peace: Seeing the Unity Between Us All

This book points out the essential reasons why peace in the world and cooperation amongst people, communities, and nations have been so difficult to establish. It also advises the only way real peace and harmony amongst humanity can be achieved.

In order for peace and unity to exist we must first realize what barriers and divisions keep us apart. Only then can we break through those barriers to see the unity that naturally exists between us all. Then, rather than focus on our differences, it is easier to recognize our similarities and common goals. With a common goal established, all of humanity can work together to help each other reach that destiny.

This book is short and to the point. It is a thought provoking book and will provide inspiration for anyone. It is especially useful for those working in politics, religion, interfaith, race relations, the media, the United Nations, teaching, or who have a position of leadership in any capacity. It is also for those of us who simply want to spread the insights needed for bringing greater levels of peace, acceptance, unity, and equality between friends, neighbours, and communities. Such insights include:

- The factors that keep us apart.
- Breaking down cultural distinctions.
- Breaking down the religious differences.
- Seeing through bodily distinctions.
- We are all working to attain the same things.
- Our real identity: The basis for common ground.
- Seeing the Divinity within each of us.
- What we can do to bring unity between everyone we meet.

This book carries an important message and plan of action that we must incorporate into our lives and plans for the future if we intend to ever bring peace and unity between us.

$6.95, 84 pages, ISBN: 1452813744

Facing Death
Welcoming the Afterlife

Many people are afraid of death, or do not know how to prepare for it nor what to expect. So this book is provided to relieve anyone of the fear that often accompanies the thought of death, and to supply a means to more clearly understand the purpose of it and how we can use it to our advantage. It will also help the survivors of the departed souls to better understand what has happened and how to cope with it. Furthermore, it shows that death is not a tragedy, but a natural course of events meant to help us reach our destiny.

This book is easy to read, with soothing and comforting wisdom, along with stories of people who have been with departing souls and what they have experienced. It is written especially for those who have given death little thought beforehand, but now would like to have some preparedness for what may need to be done regarding the many levels of the experience and what might take place during this transition.

To assist you in preparing for your own death, or that of a loved one, you will find guidelines for making one's final days as peaceful and as smooth as possible, both physically and spiritually. Preparing for deathcan transform your whole outlook in a positive way, if understood properly. Some of the topics in the book include:

- The fear of death and learning to let go.
- The opportunity of death: The portal into the next life.
- This earth and this body are no one's real home, so death is natural.
- Being practical and dealing with the final responsibilities.
- Forgiving yourself and others before you go.
- Being the assistant of one leaving this life.
- Connecting with the person inside the disease.
- Surviving the death of a loved one.
- Stories of being with dying, and an amazing near-death-experience.
- Connecting to the spiritual side of death.
- What happens while leaving the body.
- What difference the consciousness makes during death, and how to attain the best level of awareness to carry you through it.

Published by iUniverse.com, $13.95, 135 pages, ISBN: 978-1-4401-1344-4

Destined for Infinity

Deep within the mystical and spiritual practices of India are doors that lead to various levels of both higher and lower planes of existence. Few people from the outside are ever able to enter into the depths of these practices to experience such levels of reality.

This is the story of the mystical adventure of a man, Roman West, who entered deep into the secrets of India where few other Westerners have been able to penetrate. While living with a master in the Himalayan foothills and traveling the mystical path that leads to the Infinite, he witnesses the amazing powers the mystics can achieve and undergoes some of the most unusual experiences of his life. Under the guidance of a master that he meets in the mountains, he gradually develops mystic abilities of his own and attains the sacred vision of the enlightened sages and enters the unfathomable realm of Infinity. However, his peaceful life in the hills comes to an abrupt end when he is unexpectedly forced to confront the powerful forces of darkness that have been unleashed by an evil Tantric priest to kill both Roman and his master. His only chance to defeat the intense forces of darkness depends on whatever spiritual strength he has been able to develop.

This story includes traditions and legends that have existed for hundreds and thousands of years. All of the philosophy, rituals, mystic powers, forms of meditation, and descriptions of the Absolute are authentic and taken from narrations found in many of the sacred books of the East, or gathered by the author from his own experiences in India and information from various sages themselves.

This book will will prepare you to perceive the multi-dimensional realities that exist all around us, outside our sense perception. This is a book that will give you many insights into the broad possibilities of our life and purpose in this world.

Published by iUniverse.com, 255 pages, $16.95.

Reincarnation and Karma: How They Really Affect Us

Everyone may know a little about reincarnation, but few understand the complexities and how it actually works. Now you can find out how reincarnation and karma really affect us. Herein all of the details are provided on how a person is implicated for better or worse by their own actions. You will understand why particular situations in life happen, and how to make improvements for one's future. You will see why it appears that bad things happen to good people, or even why good things happen to bad people, and what can be done about it.

Other topics include:
- Reincarnation recognized throughout the world
- The most ancient teachings on reincarnation
- Reincarnation in Christianity
- How we transmigrate from one body to another
- Life between lives
- Going to heaven or hell
- The reason for reincarnation
- Free will and choice
- Karma of the nation
- How we determine our own destiny
- What our next life may be like
- Becoming free from all karma and how to prepare to make our next life the best possible.

Combine this with modern research into past life memories and experiences and you will have a complete view of how reincarnation and karma really operate.

Published by iUniverse.com, 135 pages, $13.95.

Vedic Culture
The Difference It Can Make In Your Life

The Vedic culture of India is rooted in Sanatana-dharma, the eternal and universal truths that are beneficial to everyone. It includes many avenues of self-development that an increasing number of people from the West are starting to investigate and use, including:

- Yoga
- Meditation and spiritual practice
- Vedic astrology
- Ayurveda
- Vedic gemology
- Vastu or home arrangement
- Environmental awareness
- Vegetarianism
- Social cooperation and arrangement
- The means for global peace
- And much more

Vedic Culture: The Difference It Can Make In Your Life shows the advantages of the Vedic paths of improvement and self-discovery that you can use in your life to attain higher personal awareness, happiness, and fulfillment. It also provides a new view of what these avenues have to offer from some of the most prominent writers on Vedic culture in the West, who discovered how it has affected and benefited their own lives. They write about what it has done for them and then explain how their particular area of interest can assist others. The noted authors include, David Frawley, Subhash Kak, Chakrapani Ullal, Michael Cremo, Jeffrey Armstrong, Robert Talyor, Howard Beckman, Andy Fraenkel, George Vutetakis, Pratichi Mathur, Dhan Rousse, Arun Naik, Parama Karuna Devi, and Stephen Knapp, all of whom have numerous authored books or articles of their own.

For the benefit of individuals and social progress, the Vedic system is as relevant today as it was in ancient times. Discover why there is a growing renaissance in what the Vedic tradition has to offer in *Vedic Culture*.

Published by iUniverse.com, 300 pages, $22.95.

The Heart of Hinduism:
The Eastern Path to Freedom, Empowerment and Illumination

This is a definitive and easy to understand guide to the essential as well as devotional heart of the Vedic/Hindu philosophy. You will see the depths of wisdom and insights that are contained within this profound spiritual knowledge. It is especially good for anyone who lacks the time to research the many topics that are contained within the numerous Vedic manuscripts and to see the advantages of knowing them. This also provides you with a complete process for progressing on the spiritual path, making way for individual empowerment, freedom, and spiritual illumination. All the information is now at your fingertips. Topics:

- A complete review of all the Vedic texts and the wide range of topics they contain. This also presents the traditional origins of the Vedic philosophy and how it was developed, and their philosophical conclusion.
- The uniqueness and freedom of the Vedic system.
- A description of the main yoga processes and their effectiveness.
- A review of the Vedic Gods, such as Krishna, Shiva, Durga, Ganesh, and others. You will learn the identity and purpose of each.
- You will have the essential teachings of Lord Krishna who has given some of the most direct and insightful of all spiritual messages known to humanity, and the key to direct spiritual perception.
- The real purpose of yoga and the religious systems.
- What is the most effective spiritual path for this modern age and what it can do for you, with practical instructions for deep realizations.
- The universal path of devotion, the one world religion.
- How Vedic culture is the last bastion of deep spiritual truth.
- Plus many more topics and information for your enlightenment.

So to dive deep into what is Hinduism and the Vedic path to freedom and spiritual perception, this book will give you a jump start. Knowledge is the process of personal empowerment, and no knowledge will give you more power than deep spiritual understanding. And those realizations described in the Vedic culture are the oldest and some of the most profound that humanity has ever known.

Published by iUniverse.com, 650 pages, $35.95.

The Power of the Dharma
An Introduction to Hinduism and Vedic Culture

The Power of the Dharma offers you a concise and easy-to-understand overview of the essential principles and customs of Hinduism and the reasons for them. It provides many insights into the depth and value of the timeless wisdom of Vedic spirituality and why the Dharmic path has survived for so many hundreds of years. It reveals why the Dharma is presently enjoying a renaissance of an increasing number of interested people who are exploring its teachings and seeing what its many techniques of Self-discovery have to offer.

Herein you will find:
- Quotes by noteworthy people on the unique qualities of Hinduism
- Essential principles of the Vedic spiritual path
- Particular traits and customs of Hindu worship and explanations of them
- Descriptions of the main Yoga systems
- The significance and legends of the colorful Hindu festivals
- Benefits of Ayurveda, Vastu, Vedic astrology and gemology,
- Important insights of Dharmic life and how to begin.

The Dharmic path can provide you the means for attaining your own spiritual realizations and experiences. In this way it is as relevant today as it was thousands of years ago. This is the power of the Dharma since its universal teachings have something to offer anyone.

Published by iUniverse.com, 170 pages, $16.95.

Seeing Spiritual India
A Guide to Temples, Holy Sites, Festivals and Traditions

This book is for anyone who wants to know of the many holy sites that you can visit while traveling within India, how to reach them, and what is the history and significance of these most spiritual of sacred sites, temples, and festivals. It also provides a deeper understanding of the mysteries and spiritual traditions of India.

This book includes:
- Descriptions of the temples and their architecture, and what you will see at each place.
- Explanations of holy places of Hindus, Buddhists, Sikhs, Jains, Parsis, and Muslims.
- The spiritual benefits a person acquires by visiting them.
- Convenient itineraries to take to see the most of each area of India, which is divided into East, Central, South, North, West, the Far Northeast, and Nepal.
- Packing list suggestions and how to prepare for your trip, and problems to avoid.
- How to get the best experience you can from your visit to India.
- How the spiritual side of India can positively change you forever.

This book goes beyond the usual descriptions of the typical tourist attractions and opens up the spiritual venue waiting to be revealed for a far deeper experience on every level.

Published by iUniverse.com, 592 pages, $33.95, ISBN: 978-0-595-50291-2.

Crimes Against India:
And the Need to Protect its Ancient Vedic Traditions

1000 Years of Attacks Against Hinduism and What to Do about It

India has one of the oldest and most dynamic cultures of the world. Yet, many people do not know of the many attacks, wars, atrocities and sacrifices that Indian people have had to undergo to protect and preserve their country and spiritual tradition over the centuries. Many people also do not know of the many ways in which this profound heritage is being attacked and threatened today, and what we can do about it.

Therefore, some of the topics included are:
- How there is a war against Hinduism and its yoga culture.
- The weaknesses of India that allowed invaders to conquer her.
- Lessons from India's real history that should not be forgotten.
- The atrocities committed by the Muslim invaders, and how they tried to destroy Vedic culture and its many temples, and slaughtered thousands of Indian Hindus.
- How the British viciously exploited India and its people for its resources.
- How the cruelest of all Christian Inquisitions in Goa tortured and killed thousands of Hindus.
- Action plans for preserving and strengthening Vedic India.
- How all Hindus must stand up and be strong for Sanatana-dharma, and promote the cooperation and unity for a Global Vedic Community.

Few people seem to understand the many trials and difficulties that India has faced, or the present problems India is still forced to deal with in preserving the culture of the majority Hindus who live in the country. This is described in the real history of the country, which a decreasing number of people seem to recall.

Therefore, this book is to honor the efforts that have been shown by those in the past who fought and worked to protect India and its culture, and to help preserve India as the homeland of a living and dynamic Vedic tradition of Sanatana-dharma (the eternal path of duty and wisdom).

Available from iUniverse.com. 370 pages, $24.95, ISBN: 978-1-4401-1158-7.

Yoga and Meditation
Their Real Purpose and How to Get Started

Yoga is a nonsectarian spiritual science that has been practiced and developed over thousands of years. The benefits of yoga are numerous. On the mental level it strengthens concentration, determination, and builds a stronger character that can more easily sustain various tensions in our lives for peace of mind. The assortment of *asanas* or postures also provide stronger health and keeps various diseases in check. They improve physical strength, endurance and flexibility. These are some of the goals of yoga.

Its ultimate purpose is to raise our consciousness to directly perceive the spiritual dimension. Then we can have our own spiritual experiences. The point is that the more spiritual we become, the more we can perceive that which is spiritual. As we develop and grow in this way through yoga, the questions about spiritual life are no longer a mystery to solve, but become a reality to experience. It becomes a practical part of our lives. This book will show you how to do that. Some of the topics include:

- Benefits of yoga
- The real purpose of yoga
- The types of yoga, such as Hatha yoga, Karma yoga, Raja and Astanga yogas, Kundalini yoga, Bhakti yoga, Mudra yoga, Mantra yoga, and others.
- The Chakras and Koshas
- Asanas and postures, and the Surya Namaskar
- Pranayama and breathing techniques for inner changes
- Deep meditation and how to proceed
- The methods for using mantras
- Attaining spiritual enlightenment, and much more

$17.95, 240 pages, 32 illustration, ISBN: 1451553269

www.Stephen-Knapp.com

Be sure to visit Stephen's web site. It provides lots of information on many spiritual aspects of Vedic and spiritual philosophy, and Indian culture for both beginners and the scholarly. You will find:

- All the descriptions and contents of Stephen's books, how to order them, and keep up with any new books or articles that he has written.
- Reviews and unsolicited letters from readers who have expressed their appreciation for his books, as well as his website.
- Free online booklets are also available for your use or distribution on meditation, why be a Hindu, how to start yoga, meditation, etc.
- Helpful prayers, mantras, gayatris, and devotional songs.
- Over a hundred enlightening articles that can help answer many questions about life, the process of spiritual development, the basics of the Vedic path, or how to broaden our spiritual awareness. Many of these are emailed among friends or posted on other web sites.
- Over 150 color photos taken by Stephen during his travels through India. There are also descriptions and 40 photos of the huge and amazing Kumbha Mela festival.
- Directories of many Krishna and Hindu temples around the world to help you locate one near you, where you can continue your experience along the Eastern path.
- Postings of the recent archeological discoveries that confirm the Vedic version of history.
- Photographic exhibit of the Vedic influence in the Taj Mahal, questioning whether it was built by Shah Jahan or a pre-existing Vedic building.
- A large list of links to additional websites to help you continue your exploration of Eastern philosophy, or provide more information and news about India, Hinduism, ancient Vedic culture, Vaishnavism, Hare Krishna sites, travel, visas, catalogs for books and paraphernalia, holy places, etc.
- A large resource for vegetarian recipes, information on its benefits, how to get started, ethnic stores, or non-meat ingredients and supplies.
- A large "Krishna Darshan Art Gallery" of photos and prints of Krishna and Vedic divinities. You can also find a large collection of previously unpublished photos of His Divine Grace A. C. Bhaktivedanta Swami.

This site is made as a practical resource for your use and is continually being updated and expanded with more articles, resources, and information. Be sure to check it out.

Made in the USA
Charleston, SC
30 November 2012